DATE DUE

The Mind Race

The
Mind

VILLARD BOOKS : NEW YORK : 1984

Race

UNDERSTANDING AND USING PSYCHIC ABILITIES

Russell Targ &
Keith Harary

FOREWORD BY WILLIS HARMAN

EPILOGUE BY LARISSA VILENSKAYA

Library of Congress Cataloging in Publication Data

Targ, Russell.
The Mind race.

Bibliography: p.
Includes index.
1. Psychical research. I. Harary, Keith.
II. Title.
BF1031.T285   1984   133.8   83-50860
ISBN 0-394-53356-9

Manufactured in the United States of America
9 8 7 6 5 4 3 2

Grateful acknowledgment is given to Robert Bly for permission
to reprint a selection from his translation of NOVALIS/1800.

Grateful acknowledgment is made to Colgems-EMI Music, Inc.,
for permission to reprint an excerpt from the lyrics to "Peace in
the Valley" by Carole King and Toni Stern. Copyright © 1972
by Blue Guitar Music Co. and Colgems-EMI Music, Inc. All
rights administered by Colgems-EMI Music, Inc., 6920 Sunset
Boulevard, Hollywood, California 90028. Used by permission.
All rights reserved.

For Judy Skutch and Hella Hammid,
whose inspiration and intuition
have broadened our understanding
of what is possible.

There is no place for dogma in science. The scientist is free to ask any question, to doubt any assertion, to seek for any evidence, to correct any error. Where science has been used in the past to erect a new dogmatism, that dogmatism has found itself incompatible with the progress of science; and in the end, the dogma has yielded, or science and freedom have perished together.

—J. ROBERT OPPENHEIMER
The Open Mind, 1955

CONTENTS

ACKNOWLEDGMENTS _____

The Institute of Noetic Sciences has made so many contributions to the publication of this manuscript that we cannot fully express our appreciation here. First of all, we want to thank Judy Skutch, Bill Whitson, Willis Harman, and Henry Dakin for their encouragement and steadfast commitment to this project from start to finish. We also want to thank the institute board members, Dorothy Lyddon, Henry Rolfs, and Paul and Diane Temple, for their belief in and generous support of our work, and Brendan O'Regan, Director of Research, for his thoughtful contributions.

We are very grateful for the insights, generosity, and untiring dedication to this project of our friend and partner Anthony R. White. We also sincerely appreciate the courage and open-mindedness of our editor and publisher, Marc Jaffe.

We wish to thank Larissa Vilenskaya for her patience and understanding in working with us on the difficult task of combining our different perspectives on Soviet and American psi research into a coherent picture.

We also want to express our appreciation to our other friends who made important suggestions and contributions for this manuscript, including George Kokoris, Filippo Liverziani, Marilyn Schlitz, Elisabeth Targ, Gene Roddenberry, Stephen Schwartz, Margaret Singer, George Hansen, Charles Tart, Zev Pressman, Joan Halifax, David Frederickson, Stephen McNabb, and D. Scott Rogo.

Our very special thanks to Dr. Hal Puthoff, our colleague of many years at SRI, and to Michael Murphy, founder of Esalen Institute, for his kindness and generosity in making it possible for us to compose our thoughts and plan future research with our colleagues in the unique and congenial atmosphere of Esalen.

FOREWORD

The fact that both the U.S. and Soviet governments have taken a serious interest in developing psychic abilities—"remote viewing," telepathy, precognition, and psychokinesis—may come as a surprise to some readers. Even a couple of decades ago, educated opinion tended to hold that such phenomena had been discredited. Since then, however, attitudes have changed. For example, it appears from survey data that highly educated people now are *more* inclined than others to see psychic abilities as a puzzle well worth investigating and potentially significant to understanding the human condition.

Psychic functioning has been found to be so dependable that police departments all over the world have often employed sensitives to aid them in solving difficult crimes and locating missing persons; and archaeologists have used clairvoyant remote viewing to locate buried ruins and artifacts. Within the scientific community there is also increasing willingness to see psychic research as part of a larger field of inquiry, namely research on human consciousness, which contains within it many puzzles no less mysterious than psychic abilities.

Ten years ago the Institute for Noetic Sciences, of which I am president, became one of the major initial funders of a fledgling project at SRI International (formerly Stanford Research Institute). The goal of this research was to examine an ability called *remote viewing* (RV). This term refers to the capacity of people to describe remote locations and events accurately through channels of perception whose very existence was being denied by the scientific community at large when the SRI project began.

Since that time in 1972, technical papers about remote viewing have been published in journals such as *Nature* in Britain and the *Proceedings of the Institute of Electrical and Electronics Engineers* (IEEE) in the United States. Books have been written. Symposia organized by both the IEEE and the American Association for the Advancement of Science have been devoted to this subject. Of course, there have also been howls of protest from dyed-in-the-wool, "don't-confuse-me-with-facts" skeptics and professional magicians, some of whom have built lucrative careers from delicately woven specious scenarios of "how it must have been done." Throughout it all, there has been continuing and increasing support for the remote-viewing program at SRI, from both military and nonmilitary sources. A number of independent teams at other laboratories have joined the scene, replicating the results claimed by the SRI researchers.

Those who have followed the published SRI reports will long ago have noted not only that the researchers have continued to receive closely monitored government support, but that they have also shown that the remote-viewing technology does not seem to be limited by distance, by the size of the target, or by whether or not the viewer is describing events that lie in the future. A more interesting claim throughout the years has been that the program as a whole does not depend completely on people with special talents, but that it may be possible to stimulate the latent psychic talents of most of us, given the proper conditions.

Accordingly, Russell Targ and Keith Harary, who have both been conducting pioneering psi research for more than a decade, have written the first comprehensive and popular book on this subject. They feel that the portion of their work that can be made public at this time should be made available to a large and popular audience in a practical "how-to" fashion. Here they make available techniques to a wide public, which will do more than a whole host of scientific papers to remove the cloak of mystery that has often surrounded psychic abilities. The effect of this may ultimately help achieve what William Blake suggested we do many years ago: "cleanse, once and for all, those doors of perception that have been clouded for too long."

Nobel Prize winner Roger Sperry noted the emergence of this field in his invited lead paper in the 1981 *Annual Review of Neurosciences.* From his groundbreaking work in the differential functioning of the right and left halves of the brain, he concluded:

Current concepts of the mind-brain relation involve a direct break with the long-established materialist and behaviorist doctrine that has dominated neuroscience for many decades. Instead of renouncing or ignoring consciousness, the new interpretation gives full recognition to the primacy of inner conscious awareness as a causal reality. . . . Once science modifies its traditional materialist-behaviorist stance and begins to accept in theory and to encompass in practice within its causal domain the whole world of inner, conscious, subjective experience (the world of the humanities), then the very nature of science itself is changed. . . . Recent conceptual developments in the mind-brain sciences rejecting reductionism and mechanistic determinism on the one side, and dualisms on the other, clear the way for a rational approach to the theory and prescription of values and a natural fusion of science and religion.

Recognizing this intimate relationship between consciousness research and social values invites the question: Why throughout the development of science has there not been more emphasis on research in human consciousness? How could this field have been so neglected, even maligned? The neglect has surely not been because this field is unimportant. Methodological, historical, and psychological reasons have no doubt contributed to this selective inattention. The methodological reasons include the puzzle of how to deal with reports of subjective experiences as data; the difficulty of replicating consciousness-related phenomena; the problem of observer influences; the problem of data reliability with sentient subjects capable of both conscious and unconscious choice; the issue of individual uniqueness; and the question of an appropriate basis for public validation of knowledge.

Another important factor has been the prevailing interests of the industrialized society in which Western science developed. Predominant cultural values included utilitarian ends and the ability to manipulate the physical environment to achieve comfort, physical well-being, and "control" over natural causes. Thus the kind of knowledge leading to technological mastery—that is, knowledge enabling one to predict and control —has been emphasized. Similarly, emphasis has come to be placed on measurable information, quantified descriptions, deterministic models, and reductionistic explanations.

However, there is another kind of knowledge that is applicable where the goal is not so much the ability to control as to understand—in particular, to understand human growth and development, and the search for meaning. This knowledge is much more concerned with such nonquantifiable factors as purpose, volition, and values. Models and metaphors used tend to involve holistic concepts (e.g., health, values, states of consciousness). Teleological explanations involving a sense of meaning and purpose seem appropriate; purely deterministic models do not fit with human experience. Above all, this kind of knowledge centers on human subjective experience—especially the deep intuitive insights underlying the central value commitments of both individuals and societies. This kind of knowledge also exists in Western society, but it is less systematized than conventional science, the degree of consensus is lower, and the knowledge has less prestige—it is not considered "hard science."

This second kind of knowledge, in some sense complementary to positivistic science, differs from it in several essential particulars. We should not find it surprising that there are many other phenomena, such as the effects of attitudes on illness and healing (e.g., psychosomatic illness, the placebo effect), which appear to be well-evidenced phenomena in this kind of knowledge, yet seem somehow anomalous in positivistic science.

To build a science that is useful for guiding the individual in his development, it is essential to explore thoroughly the occurrence of exceptional human capacities. The very fact that some individuals choose (consciously or unconsciously) to develop these abilities while others do not indicates that this is an area where the concept of reliability is not easily applied. It should not be surprising if these exceptional capacities (e.g., clairvoyant remote viewing) occur sporadically and in other ways seem to conflict with models of reality constructed from rigid prediction and control models. *There is no reason to expect them to fit these models.*

A few decades ago it was commonplace to encounter discussions and writings on the question "Does mind exist?" Is there in human experience something that is "real" in the sense of direct experience by the individual, yet not discernible by the probing methods of quantitative science? We are probably approaching a time when this question is as thoroughly settled as the question "Does the earth really revolve around the sun?"

With the expansion of science into the realm of human subjective experience we have a development rivaling the insights of Copernicus and Galileo in its revolutionary implications. The work described in this book is seen in its fullest significance by placing it within the context of this broader vision.

WILLIS W. HARMAN
Stanford, California

Senior Social Scientist,
SRI International
Member, Board of Regents,
University of California

"All I can say is that if the results were faked, our security system doesn't work. What these persons 'saw' was confirmed by aerial photography. There's no way it could have been faked. . . . Some of the intelligence people I've talked to know that remote viewing works, although they still block further research on it, since they claim it is not yet as good as satellite photography. But it seems to me that it would be a hell of a cheap radar system. And if the Russians have it and we don't, we are in serious trouble."

—CONGRESSMAN CHARLES ROSE

Chairman, House Sub-Committee on Intelligence Evaluation and Oversight; interviewed on the subject of the SRI long-distance remote-viewing experiments.

Omni, July 1979

PART I

U.S. and Soviet Psi Research

1

Introduction:
What's Going On?

Psychic abilities are being developed in government-sponsored research programs in both the United States and the Soviet Union. Yet, despite decades of research that has produced better and better results, most people have been led to believe that psychic abilities and experiences simply do not exist, or at least are beyond their understanding.

The public at large has been greatly misinformed about psychic functioning, or psi—films, television, and the news media have presented much distorted and misleading information about this area. Materialists have criticized reports of psi as fraudulent, impossible, or ridiculous. Cultists and other undiscriminating enthusiasts have given psi the undeserved reputation of their own irrationality and superstition.

Meanwhile, the governments of the United States and the U.S.S.R. have quietly spent millions in a long-term, careful, and successful effort to develop ever more proficient and potentially useful psychic abilities. The following is an excerpt from the report of a Congressional committee in 1981:

SURVEY OF SCIENCE AND TECHNOLOGY ISSUES
PRESENT AND FUTURE

COMMITTEE ON SCIENCE AND TECHNOLOGY
U.S. HOUSE OF REPRESENTATIVES

NINETY-SEVENTH CONGRESS
JUNE 1981

Recent experiments in remote viewing and other studies in para-psychology suggest that there is an "interconnectedness" of the human mind with other minds and with matter. . . . Experiments on mind-mind interconnectedness have yielded some encouraging results. . . . The implication of these experiments is that the human mind may be able to obtain information independent of geography and time. . . . Given the potentially powerful and far-reaching implications of knowledge in this field, and given that the Soviet Union is widely acknowledged to be supporting such research at a far higher and more official level, Congress may wish to under-take a serious assessment of research in this country.[1]

We have written this book for everyone who has wondered about what is really happening in psi research here and in the Soviet Union, and about what this research might mean for them. Information about the findings of this research should be easily available to everyone. But reliable information has often been hard to find, or to separate from the exaggerated claims of cultists, the confusing allegations of critics, and the distortions of the mass media.

Psi research has suffered as much from it's "true believers" as it has from critics who have suggested that accepting any of the scientific data of this field would be inherently irrational. Yet psychic functioning is neither a product of uncritical belief nor a matter of self-deception. Rather it is a real process that can easily be explored through direct personal experience and objective scientific research.

The Mind Race provides you with the compelling evidence of the existence of high-quality psychic functioning. We describe how psychic abilities might be useful to you in your everyday life, and in the later chapters, we describe techniques that you can use to begin developing your own psychic abilities.

This information is important for all of us. The best scientific research suggests that the capacity for developing genuine psychic abilities lies latent in many, or perhaps most, people. These conclusions are based on the results of hundreds of experimental sessions, many of which were conducted with research participants who did not have previous experience with psi.

We are certain that psychic abilities are a totally normal aspect of human awareness, and that you can learn to develop this potential sanely and rationally. You do not have to alter your relationship with reality or adopt a new set of values to learn about psi. However, you may well rethink your world view after you have had direct experience with high-quality psychic functioning.

The U.S. government has been supporting a psi research program at SRI International (formerly Stanford Research Institute) in Menlo Park, California, for more than ten years. This multimillion-dollar program has been exploring techniques to increase the accuracy and reliability of a human perceptual ability known as *remote viewing*. In remote viewing, individuals are able to experience and describe locations, events, and objects that cannot be perceived by the known senses, usually because of distance.

Both authors have been active in laboratory psi research since the early 1970s, at SRI and elsewhere. We are able to critically evaluate the speculation about U.S. government-sponsored psi research and discuss the progress in this field at home and abroad from an informed perspective. We do this in Part I.

The principal finding of remote-viewing research is that most participants in these experiments learn to accurately describe buildings, geography, objects, and activities from which they are separated by both space and time. They have often correctly described places thousands of miles away. Many have also correctly described events that would happen hours or days in the future. Again, this ability has been developed by previously inexperienced people, whose psychic functioning appears to improve with practice.

In laboratories across this country, and in many other nations as well, forty-six experimental series have investigated remote viewing. Twenty-three of these investigations have reported successful results and produced statistically significant data, where three would be expected.

This research suggests that the popular view of our relationship to space and time is inadequate. This idea is compatible with recent observations in physics, in which carefully conducted experiments were influenced by events that were supposedly far outside the experiment's apparent spatial and temporal sphere. One possible conclusion is that there *is something incomplete about our understanding of the space-time continuum in which we exist.*

The seriousness of these new observations was pointed out in a recent article in *Science:*

> The success of quantum theory in describing physical phenomena at the molecular level and below is unquestioned. But since 1965 it has been known that quantum mechanics makes certain predictions that are contrary to what is allowed by any member of the class of realistic, local theories. *Realism,* which to the modern mind might be called common sense, argues that there is an objective reality that exists independent of whether someone observes it or not. *Locality* stems from the special theory of relativity, and its premise that forces or information can only travel between bodies at velocities less than the velocity of light. *In short, quantum mechanics, special relativity, and realism cannot all be true.* [Emphasis added.][2]

We believe that psi research findings and the discoveries of modern physics will soon come together. We expect that the resulting conceptual changes in all fields of science will strongly complement one another, in ways that may greatly clarify our understanding of ourselves and our relationship with the rest of the universe.

While American laboratories have struggled for acceptance of their data and tried to reconcile the implications of this work for modern physics, scientists in the U.S.S.R. have been very busy. The Soviet Union has officially sponsored psi research since the early 1920s. Unfortunately, reports about Soviet psi research have come mostly from journalists without the scientific experience necessary to evaluate developments in this field. Their accounts have done little to inform the public accurately about what the Soviets are doing in their psi research program, although they have alerted us to the magnitude and direction of the Soviet efforts.

As Vilenskaya describes in the epilogue, many Soviet researchers have been conducting potentially aggressive experiments in which their main goal is the modification of the behavior and feelings of remote humans and animals by psychic means. This focus represents a continuation of nineteenth-century Soviet interests in developing a means for hypnotic control of behavior at a distance.

There is a great deal of interest in psychic healing among the Soviet people themselves, but much official psychic research in the U.S.S.R. appears to be directed toward developing psychic abilities as a means of control and manipulation. At the same time, many Soviet scientists are struggling, as we are, to understand the human potential implications of psi research.

Larissa Vilenskaya was personally involved in Soviet psi research for more than a decade. Vilenskaya is a Soviet-trained engineer, and has also been a successful participant in numerous psi experiments. She understands not only the methods and priorities of this research, but also the context of the Soviet political system in which this work is being conducted. Vilenskaya also knows many Eastern Bloc psi researchers and experimental participants personally. She has translated dozens of Soviet research papers and reports into English—reports which most Westerners did not even know existed.

The information that follows represents an interdisciplinary effort to inform the public about the real findings of psi research. Russell Targ is an experimental physicist with broad experience in lasers, microwaves, and plasma research. He, with Dr. Harold Puthoff, founded the psi research program at SRI. Keith Harary is a clinical counselor and experimental psychologist who specializes in psi research, and in the psychology of cults, crisis intervention, and stress. He is also one of the most extensively and successfully tested psychics in the world.

We believe that a well-informed public is the first line of defense against deliberate misrepresentations of psychic functioning, or attempts to manipulate those who have had psychic experiences or simply want to learn more about this subject. In our years of work in psi research, we have found that many people have had numerous apparently psychic experiences; more will have at least one during their lifetimes. These range from relatively common sensations of thinking about some coming event, such as an otherwise unexpected phone call from a long-lost friend just before it happens, to less frequent impressions of some distant occurrence, such as awareness of an airplane disaster while it is taking place, beyond the reach of the known senses.

As we discuss in Part II, people who have what they believe are psychic experiences are often drawn into cults that claim to offer explanations of psychic functioning, but at great personal, emotional, and financial expense to their followers. We think that giving away your mind is too high a price to pay for psychic development. People who might enjoy learning about their psychic potential often feel uncomfortable about it because of mass-media portrayals of psychic abilities as abnormal, supernatural, or the product of self-deception. We would like to help bring an end to this unnecessary confusion.

Despite claims to the contrary by numerous factions, there is no evidence of an exclusive relationship between psychic functioning and any particular leader, doctrine, or way of life. Scientific evidence does, however, strongly suggest that the ability to function psychically is a genuine human capacity which, for many people, seems to improve with practice.

The remote-viewing exercises that we describe in Part III are designed to offer a safe and entertaining introduction to the development of psychic capabilities. We think of these exercises as "psychic sit-ups." We believe that success in remote viewing can help you to "tone up" your awareness, so that you may become more familiar with the kinds of sensations that accompany psychic impressions.

Many people who have responded accurately in remote-viewing exercises, and in other types of psi experiments, soon notice that useful psychic information is also available in their everyday lives. Learning to distinguish between genuine psychic information and other types of mental images will help you to respond more reliably to spontaneous psychic impressions.

Although we think that psychic awareness is a completely natural human capacity, it is still a rather new experience for many people. We therefore also suggest ways you can comfortably integrate psychic functioning into your present way of life.

We hope this book makes psi research more understandable and less mysterious to you, while giving you the means to make psychic functioning a useful and enjoyable part of your awareness. This seems a better alternative than allowing psychic abilities to be monopolized by cults or co-opted by competing governments.

Psi is too important to become the exclusive property of governments, either at home or abroad, who might become interested in exploiting these abilities for their own purposes.

The United States and the Soviet Union are currently locked in a massive arms race. Without a shot being fired, this arms race is bleeding both nations emotionally, spiritually, and economically. Although we totally support and encourage individual freedom and the protection of traditional American ideals, we do not want psychic functioning to become caught up in the current military and ideological struggles between Eastern and Western societies. The importance of psi as a possible weapon of war is tiny and trivial compared with its potential for increasing our understanding of ourselves and the world around us. It is through openness and cooperation that the genius of science makes its greatest and most empowering discoveries and contributions.

Reliable, publicly available information about psi research can help protect us all from the damaging effects of misinformation. Learning to discriminate our own psychic impressions from externally induced suggestions by others may also ultimately protect us from the possibility of remote psychic manipulation. There are, of course, many more positive potential benefits of learning about psychic functioning and psi research, which we also discuss.

The Mind Race should not be seen as a psychic competition between nations. Rather, it is a race to develop our own innate potential for extended awareness. Our most sincere hope is that each of us will win his own mind race, thereby contributing to the betterment of life on this planet.

2

Psi in the United States: An Inside View

WASHINGTON-The CIA financed a project in 1975 to develop a new kind of agent who could truly be called a "spook," CIA Director Stanfield Turner has disclosed.

The CIA chief said that the agency found a man who could "see" what was going on anywhere in the world through his psychic powers.

Turner said CIA scientists and officials would show the man a picture of a place and he would then describe any activity going on there at that time.

The tight-lipped CIA chief wouldn't reveal how accurate the spook was, but said the agency dropped the project in 1975.

"He died," Turner said, "and we haven't heard from him since."

Chicago Tribune
Saturday, August 13, 1977

Based upon our past ten years of research, and upon hundreds of experimental trials, we can confidently report that some aspects of the psychic puzzle are becoming clear. We know, for example, that through remote viewing, many individuals can sit quietly, with their eyes closed, and use their psychic abilities to describe accurately activities, events, and geographical locations all over the planet, and possibly beyond.

People who have learned to use this ability in the laboratory are called *viewers* (not *subjects,* the term used for the people in most psychological experiments). We know that the distance that separates viewers from the places they decide to "visit" psychically does not affect the accuracy of their descriptions or make them harder to obtain.

We have also found, in fact, that distant sites are sometimes easier to perceive psychically and to describe than nearby sites. This may be because the viewers find the distant places more interesting. They may also have less difficulty in separating their analytic thoughts or guesses from actual psychic impressions when they are describing locations with which they are totally unfamiliar.

We did not invent remote viewing. Remote viewing is a type of psi, or psychic functioning, that occurs naturally in the everyday experiences of many people. For hundreds of years psi has been described, rather imprecisely, as second sight, traveling clairvoyance, fortune-telling, extrasensory perception, the paranormal, and so forth. We have made a conscious effort to avoid using such terms in this book because they are misleading and portray psi as being outside the realm of normal human experience. For the same reason, we have chosen not to use the term *parapsychology* to refer to our field of study (except when quoting others). We prefer the more appropriately descriptive term *psi research* for our endeavors.

AN EARLY REMOTE-VIEWING EXPERIMENT

To the best of our knowledge, the first description of a well-controlled remote-viewing experiment was given to us by Herodotus. The experiment he describes was carried out by Croesus, King of Lydia, in 550 B.C. Croesus was interested in evaluating the accuracy of the half-dozen oracles that had sprung up, in and around Greece, as a result of the success of the oracle at Delphi. We have a detailed account from Herodotus of just what happened.

Croesus considered himself endangered by the Persians, who were daily becoming more powerful. Herodotus tells us: "With this in mind he resolved to make instant trial of the several oracles in Greece, and one in Lydia. . . . The messengers who were dispatched to make trial of the oracles were given the following instructions: They were to keep count of the days from the time of their leaving Sardis, and reckoning from that date, on the hundredth day, they were to consult the oracles, and to inquire of them what Croesus, king of Lydia, was doing that moment. The answers given to them were to be taken down in writing, and brought back to him."

At Delphi, the holy men would receive the questions whose answers were to be foretold. These questions would be put to the Pythian priestess, who would be in a stuporous condition from chewing the leaves of the sacred bay laurel, drinking the water from a spring inside the temple, and applying a generous dose of self-hypnosis. In this semi-trance condition, the priestess would give her impressions to the holy men of the temple. These utterances were interpreted by the holy men, reduced to verse, and returned to the questioner. Thus, we see that it was already known twenty-five hundred years ago that the analysis of psychically derived data is best done by someone other than the psychic. In modern remote-viewing studies, the viewer reports his or her intuitive impressions to an interviewer, who assists in the analytic interpretation of the information the viewer provides.

But, back to Croesus: As soon as the messengers entered the sanctuary at Delphi and put their questions to the priestess, they were answered in hexameter verse—

> I can count the sands, and I can measure the ocean;
> I have ears for the silent, and know what the dumb
>   man nameth;
> Lo! On my sense there striketh the smell of a
>   shell-covered tortoise,
> Boiling now on a fire, with the flesh of a lamb, in
>   a caldron—
> Brass is the vessel below, and brass is the cover above it.

The Lydians wrote down these words as she recited the description of her vision. They then set off on their return to Sardis.

Herodotus continues: "When all the messengers had come back with the answers which they had received, Croesus undid the rolls and read what was written in each. This he had no sooner done, than he declared that Delphi was the only true oracle. For on the departure of his messengers he had set himself to think what was most impossible for anyone to conceive of his doing, and then waiting until the day agreed on came, he acted as he had determined. He took a tortoise and a lamb, and cutting them in pieces with his own hands, boiled them both together in a brazen caldron, covered over with a lid that was also brass."

Croesus was enormously impressed with this result. He uttered a prayer, and set about to give thanks to the Delphic god with a magnificent sacrifice, which included three thousand of each kind of sacrificial beast. When the sacrifice was ended the king melted down a huge quantity of gold, causing it to flow into 117 large ingots, seen by Herodotus at Delphi. These bricks were made into a pile which was surmounted by a lion of pure gold, weighing 570 pounds. We estimate this gift, which included many other items, to be worth more than $100 million in 1983 dollars.

In his book, *The Delphic Oracle* (1953), Oxford historian H. W. Parke writes about this occurrence, "The extraordinary wealth of these offerings makes one pause. But, the truth and accuracy of the description of them by Herodotus is beyond serious doubt. . . . Modern scholars have been tempted at times to be skeptical. But the existence of these treasures at Delphi cannot seriously be questioned."

Since the time of Croesus many other people have been interested in evaluating and understanding remote viewing. Some of the most important work in this area was carried out in the early 1900s.

PIONEER PSI RESEARCHERS

Our work has been greatly influenced by two researchers from the early part of this century, the American writer Upton Sinclair and the French engineer René Warcollier. They left us an incredible legacy of data and insights pertaining to psychic functioning. In 1930, Sinclair published a book entitled *Mental Radio,* in which he presented more than a hundred psychic-communication experiments that he and others had carried out with his wife, Mary Craig.[1] Both his data and the descriptions that Mary Craig gave of her approach to visual imagery agree remarkably with our own experiences in the laboratory.

With regard to René Warcollier, one cannot say enough in praise of his remarkable understanding of psychic functioning. His 1948 book *Mind To Mind* details the skills that a person has to learn in order to develop reliable psychic abilities.[2] In his decades of research, Warcollier analyzed each of the sources of *mental noise* that a person might experience, sensations that could interfere with or degrade his interpretation of intuitive information. (More about mental noise in a few pages.)

To give a picture of Warcollier's important contribution, we summarize his detailed observations about the nature of psychic functioning at the end of this chapter. By then the reader will have seen enough recent data to appreciate the concise coherence that Warcollier was able to bring to psi research almost forty years ago.

In 1972 the SRI research team coined and began using the term *remote viewing.* The term seemed neutral and free of any prejudgment about how psychic functioning works, and described the data we had seen in the laboratory. (If we were to do it over again, we might want to call this ability *remote sensing,* because it involves much more than just a visual experience. But since that would mean calling the experimental participants *sensors,* we are happy with the original choice.)

In the book *Mind Reach,* Targ and Puthoff presented the results of more than fifty of these early experiments at SRI, in which a dozen remote viewers accurately described and drew distant buildings, parks, bridges, etc. in the San Francisco Bay area.[3] At the beginning of each remote-viewing session, a pair of researchers would meet with a prospective viewer. They would explain that one of them, the *outbound experimenter,* or *beacon,* was about to be sent off to a distant location, or *target site,* which had not yet been chosen.

After leaving the viewer, the beacon would randomly choose a target site from a pool of sixty possibilities. He would then go to this site, and remain there for fifteen minutes. During this time, a second experimenter, the *interviewer,* asked the viewer to focus his psychic attention on the target site and say what the site looked like and what the outbound experimenter was doing there. Needless to say, the interviewer was also unaware of where the beacon had gone.

These early experiments showed that a great many people were able to use their psychic abilities to describe remote sites accurately, under controlled laboratory conditions. People who had never before experienced any psychic functioning often did as well as people who had participated in many experiments. In fact, the main difference between experienced and inexperienced viewers was not so much in the quality of their remote-viewing descriptions but rather in their overall psychic reliability from session to session.

Since the publication of *Mind Reach*, many more remote-viewing experiments have been conducted at SRI and elsewhere. They have focused upon replicating the results of the original research, and also upon developing a better understanding of how remote viewing works and improving its general dependability.

One example of successful remote viewing of local target sites at SRI involved a technically trained man who visited the laboratory and took part in several remote-viewing sessions. Although unusual things had happened once or twice in his life, he by no means considered himself to be psychic. We spent a lot of time together, discussing earlier remote-viewing experiments; our goal was to get his agreement that it would be OK with him to get a good result in such an experiment. Finally we sat down in the lab to begin our first session together. He agreed that he felt comfortable with the idea of describing a target site, even though it might be miles away.

In this case, the outbound experimenter had gone to the Stanford University Art Museum, a few miles from SRI. As always, the site had been randomly chosen from the general target pool. As I (R.T.) interviewed the man, he described a great many fragmentary images, which he also sketched around the edge of a piece of paper. His description of the target condensed into a building made of two rectangular solids, a low one in the foreground and a higher one farther away. He then made a detailed pen-and-ink drawing of his impressions. His final drawing, together with a photograph of the target site, is shown on page 16.

The remote-viewing technique is still imperfect. Viewers do not always accurately describe target sites. Descriptions usually contain a mixture of correct and incorrect information. We have observed, however, that the psychic abilities of viewers with whom we have worked for several years appear to improve with practice. We have also found that, on occasion, remote viewing provides remarkably precise and accurate descriptions of distant locations and activities.

For example, an experimental series of remote-viewing trials might have six target sites, and six descriptions from a viewer. We would ask an evaluator, the *judge,* to visit each of the six sites, and at each site to choose the description best matching that site. A match would be said to be correct if the judge successfully paired up a given day's transcript with its corresponding target site. Roughly two-thirds of the remote-viewing trials that have been carried out at SRI have been successfully matched in this way by independent judges. This 66 percent reliability of remote viewing

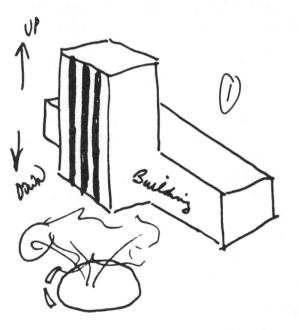

Stanford Art Museum Target (above) and response (below) in beacon remote-viewing experiment.

is statistically highly significant. In order to be statistically significant an individual experiment's outcome must depart from the results expected by chance by odds of at least twenty to one—in this case, the odds are approximately one hundred to one against chance.

A similar ratio of success has been found in several laboratories across the country that have attempted to replicate the SRI remote-viewing experiments. Princeton University, Mundelein College in Chicago, and the Institute for Parapsychology in Durham, North Carolina, have all carried out and published successful remote-viewing studies. In an examination of the twenty-eight formal published reports of attempted replications of remote viewing, Hansen, Schlitz, and Tart at the Institute for Parapsychology found that more than half of the papers reported successful outcomes. These experiments are listed in the bibliography.

Remote viewing is primarily an ability to process pictorial, nonanalytic information. For example, if an experienced viewer were working with the police, looking for a kidnap victim, he might be able to describe the location or house where the kidnap victim was being held, but would be much less likely to provide a correct street address. Names, numbers, letters, and other analytic material are among the most difficult information for viewers to describe.

We believe this problem is not caused by difficulties in obtaining psychic information. Instead, we think it is the result of *mental noise* that interferes with the viewer's ability to *process* this information. A better understanding of mental noise is one of the principal factors that is helping us to make progress toward harnessing psychic functioning and making it a more accurate and reliable tool.

Memory and *imagination* are the main sources of mental noise. For example, if we ask you to guess a number from 0 to 9, you have an opportunity to imagine and remember all the numbers you have ever seen. The same is true of letters, and other very familiar potential targets for psi experiments. Psychic information does not identify itself as such; there is no television announcer in your head who says, "The impressions you are now having are brought to you by psychic functioning." Psychic impressions are usually much more subtle.

On the other hand, if we ask you to describe a place that we know quite well, but that you have never seen, the situation is quite different from the known-symbol guessing game. In this case, you will start with a blank mental screen, not one buzzing with remembered letters and numbers. If you begin to have impressions of your own living room, you will know it could not be the place we have in mind, because we agreed you have not seen the target site before.

In radio communications, engineers talk of the signal-to-noise ratio, which is the proportion of desired information to incorrect data in a given broadcast. Similarly, we believe that the reliability of psychic functioning can be improved either by increasing the psychic signal or by reducing the mental noise caused by memory and imagination. So far, we have devoted most of our research efforts to finding ways of doing the latter.

A group of researchers who hoped to replicate the early SRI remote-viewing research carried out an experiment in which they chose a half-dozen target sites near their laboratory and made photographs of them. They then showed their viewers all six photographs and asked them to guess which site the outbound experimenter was hiding at during a partic-ular session.

Needless to say, this experiment did not succeed.[4] By giving the viewers a fixed set of known targets from which to choose, the experiment-ers merely reduced the remote viewing of natural targets to an old-fashioned psychic card-guessing type of experiment. The viewers were faced with the monumental task of separating their psychic impressions from their memories of the six photographs they had just seen.

One problem that often comes up in traditional psi experiments is that a viewer may accurately describe a picture that is in the pool of possible targets, but not the specific picture that has been designated as the target for that session. In psi research, this all-too-common phenomenon is called *displacement.* We consider displacement to be a type of psychic noise.

This is our reasoning: When an experimenter brings a group of pic-tures together as potential targets in a psi experiment, he effectively places the pictures in a "psychic bubble." The pictures may be very different from one another, but they become psychically associated by all being put in the same target pool. So a viewer who tries to describe the designated target picture may have difficulty distinguishing that picture from the others in the pool. He may describe details of more than one picture, or give an excellent description of one that was not chosen as that session's target.

In contrast, geographical remote-viewing sessions rarely produce displacement, perhaps because geographical targets cannot be collected in one place—they stay put. Instead, the target site is randomly chosen from a list of various geographical locations. Possibly because written material makes a poor target for psychic perception, the list itself does not generate psychic noise, the way a collection of actual possible targets would.

This leads to another important factor that seems to influence the success of remote viewing. The task the viewer is asked to perform must be felt to be intrinsically worthwhile. For viewers to feel comfortable and motivated to participate in remote-viewing studies, these experiments must not trivialize psychic functioning. Ideally, each experiment should teach us something useful, while providing the viewer with an opportunity to learn about and improve his own psychic abilities.

Obviously it is simply more interesting for a viewer to try to describe an unknown target site than to guess a number, or to choose again and again from a group of pictures or symbols already seen. This was one shortcoming of the card-guessing experiments that were common in psi research for several decades. Such experiments, aimed at measuring a viewer's ability to name hidden cards, were part of J. B. Rhine's successful attempt to bring quantitative statistical measures to psi research. This pioneering work is well summarized in *Extrasensory Perception After Sixty Years* by J. G. Pratt, J. G. Rhine, et al.[5]

Although some people were able to achieve highly significant scores in the traditional card-guessing experiments, their results were generally much less successful and reliable than those of participants in "free-response" experiments, such as remote viewing, or picture-drawing experiments like those of, for example, Sinclair or Warcollier. We have come to expect a statistically significant result from an experimental series consisting of only eight or ten trials, whereas card-guessing experiments often required hundreds or even thousands of trials to reach significance.

To put it another way: It is easier for viewers to give a detailed description of a distant location, chosen from an infinite number of possibilities, than it is for them to guess numbers from 0 to 9. Even in remote-viewing experiments in which the outbound experimenter randomly chooses from a limited number of potential target sites, if the viewers do not know what those target possibilities are, they are effectively infinite to the viewer.

One of the most often replicated findings in card-guessing experiments is that people invariably get worse at the task after repeated trials. This so-called "decline effect" is exactly the opposite of what we would expect to see if the subjects were learning. Charles Tart, a frequent writer and researcher on psychic functioning, has said that the participants in these experiments were "bored into a decline."[6] It is as though card guessing were a highly refined technique for *unlearning* or extinguishing psi in the laboratory!

On the other hand, at SRI we conducted a NASA-sponsored study in which 147 viewers were each asked to repeatedly choose which one of four possible pictures had been selected as the target by a four-state random target generator. This study was very successful, with a significant number of the participants learning to improve their psi scores. We think the reason they were able to do this is that the machine gave them immediate feedback as to the correct answer after each trial. They also had the option of intuitively sensing the color and position associated with each correct choice. This task was intrinsically more interesting for the viewers than guessing cards. An important way in which such a psi teaching machine could be improved would be through the use of a microcomputer that could offer viewers an entirely different set of target possibilities, presented in varying colors and positions, for each trial. In cooperation with Atari we have designed just such a device in the form of a home video game.

In remote-viewing research, we have found that people do well when they are excited about the psychic task, but are not under stress. Medical studies suggest that adrenaline increases brain functioning as measured by performance on mental tasks. Perhaps as the necessity for obtaining more complex psychic information increases, the viewers' brain functioning and psychic abilities increase to meet the demand. In card-guessing research, however, the task is so repetitive and uninteresting that viewers might actually find their ability to process psychic information decreasing as the experiment continues.

Ideally a viewer should be relaxed, attentive, and meditative, but still focused. We believe it is also most important that a viewer's ego should not be at stake in an experiment. A person who feels that he is "nothing if not psychic" will probably not do well in any psychic task. Psychic functioning should be viewed as an adventure, not as a test of one's worth as a human being.

In fact, we have seen that the attitudes of all the participants in an experiment seem to matter a great deal in achieving successful results. However, distance and electromagnetic shielding from the target site do not seem to matter at all. The size of a target also seems not to affect the accuracy of remote viewing. We have carried out trials in which the target site was as big as Hoover Tower at Stanford University and as small as a pin. In both cases the target descriptions were excellent.

Before we describe some of the latest remote-viewing experiments at SRI and other laboratories, we will explain the approach to remote viewing that the SRI team has used successfully for the past decade. Using this approach, even many first-time viewers have had good remote-viewing experiences. The description that follows is drawn from our experience, and is also based upon a remote-viewing recipe that has been sent to many psi researchers who were interested in replicating the original remote-viewing experiments.[7]

An important feature of the SRI remote-viewing experiments is that the viewer and interviewer work as a single information-gathering team. The remote viewer acts as the psychic-information gatherer, while the interviewer acts as the analytic navigator.

This division of labor parallels the two main modes of brain functioning. One is the nonanalytic style, which relates to spatial-pattern recognition, and which we think to be associated with psychic functioning. The other type of mental activity is reflected in a more verbal and analytical cognitive style. Only very experienced remote viewers seem able to handle both tasks at once, and even for them, it is often difficult.

The potential target sites for SRI remote-viewing experiments are selected by lab personnel who are not otherwise involved with the viewers or interviewers during these experiments. The pool of potential targets is constructed to contain several examples of each target type—several churches, several fountains, several boathouses, and so forth. This is done specifically to avoid the chance that, for example, a viewer might think that because the target site was a fountain yesterday, it will not also be a fountain today.

We believe this redundancy in the target pool prevents viewers from feeling tempted to form analytical strategies for figuring out what kinds of targets have not yet appeared in their experimental sessions. This way, any given target site is independent of the previous targets a viewer has experienced. In the vocabulary of card guessing, this would be called an "open deck" design. As we mentioned earlier, being ignorant of the possible target sites seems to make it easier for viewers to describe their intended targets accurately, not harder.

While the beacon is on his way to the randomly chosen target site, the interviewer and viewer relax and discuss the session that is about to begin. The interviewer during this period tries to help the viewer feel it is "safe" to experience psychic functioning. Typically he will discuss how remote viewing appears to be a natural rather than abnormal capability and will mention the fact that many others have already done remote viewing successfully under similar conditions.

The viewer is told explicitly that memory and imagination constitute noise in the psychic information channel. Therefore, the closer the viewer can come to describing his raw uninterpreted imagery, without free-associating about it, the more accurate his description is likely to be. The viewer is strongly encouraged to report his images directly rather than to analyze them, since initial impressions are more often correct than analyses.

Remote viewing is a demanding task, requiring the full attention and concentration of the viewer. Therefore, the environment and procedures used in remote-viewing experiments are designed to be as natural and comfortable as possible.

Anything that might divert a viewer's attention away from the task at hand is minimized. No hypnosis, strobe lights, or sensory deprivation is used. In our view, these novel techniques would probably divert a viewer's much-needed attention and make it more difficult for him to distinguish mental noise from any psychic impressions.

Nonetheless, many successful free-response-type experiments have been carried out in what is called the *Ganzfeld*. In this sensory-deprivation approach to psychic functioning, a viewer (or subject in this case) has halves of Ping-Pong balls glued over his eyes. They are bathed in red light, while earphones over his ears play continuous static or white noise. Home was never like this.

Although the Ganzfeld approach, developed by William Brand and Charles Honorton, has been shown in their laboratories, and many others, to lead to statistically significant results,[8] it in no way convinces anyone that psychic functioning is an ordinary or normal ability. Instead, the Ganzfeld conveys a picture in which psi functioning looks weird, is weird, and requires an altered state of consciousness. Our research and experience indicate that none of these assumptions about psi are valid. It is essential to realize that altered states are by no means prerequisites to excellent psychic functioning. Apparently, the way in which a person expresses psychic information is *influenced* by his state of mind, but this state does not *determine* the availability of psychic information to him. The Ganzfeld seems to lead a subject to free-associate more readily than a remote viewer might, thereby mixing his psychic impressions with potentially greater amounts of undiscriminated mental noise in an experimental session. We discuss the Ganzfeld approach in more detail in Chapter 8. Suffice it to say, for now, that such elaborate experimental preparations have not been shown to be necessary for successful psychic functioning, in our experiments.

When the time agreed upon for the start of a remote-viewing trial arrives, the beacon has presumably reached the target site. He should arrive exactly on time at the target site, so that he will come upon the location fresh, just as the viewer is beginning to describe it. The beacon is asked simply to pay attention to what he finds at the site. (He is not considered to be a "sender," because the viewer will often describe aspects of the target site that were not noticed by the beacon.)

At this point, the interviewer simply says to the viewer, "Close your eyes, and tell me about any mental pictures that you have, with respect to the place our outbound traveler has gone." The interviewer does not pressure the viewer to talk all the time. If he did, the viewer might embroider his descriptions in an attempt to please the interviewer.

If a viewer reports what appear to be analytical interpretations of his psychic impressions, such as "I see a building with bricks and arches. I think it's Macy's," the interviewer will gently try to guide the viewer away from such potential mental noise. He might say, "You don't have to tell me what it is; just tell me what you see. What are you experiencing as you look around at the target site?" Reports of sounds, smells, or tactile sensations are especially good indications that the viewer has psychically contacted the target site.

This *psychic navigation* is the most important and difficult task for the interviewer. It seems particularly helpful for inexperienced viewers. But it must be circumspect. In a remote-viewing transcript quoted later in this chapter, an experienced viewer quite properly tells the overzealous interviewer to be quiet, so that she can collect her thoughts.

It is often helpful for an interviewer to surprise a viewer with a request to change psychic viewpoints. "Why don't you drift up in the air above the site, and tell me what it looks like from above?" The viewer's perspective on the site appears to shift rapidly after a question like this, and he is usually able to expand a description from this new vantage point without difficulty.

The interviewer must pay close attention to what the viewer is saying, in order to elicit information that will later be useful in distinguishing actual target sites from other possible targets. The interviewer must be aware that some future judge reading the transcript of a session will not be able to decide among various possible target sites based upon a viewer's description of a particularly interesting marigold that catches his psychic attention. The interviewer's responsibility is to make sure that there is adequate information in a transcript. The viewer's responsibility is confined to exercising his remote-viewing capabilities and communicating his psi perceptions.

The viewer is encouraged to sketch what he is experiencing about the target site, even though he may claim not to be able to draw. The drawings that come out of a remote-viewing session often contain striking correspondences to the target site.

After the beacon returns to the lab at the end of the session, the viewer, interviewer, and beacon all go to the target site together. This allows the viewer to review what it felt like during those parts of his remote-viewing experience when he was most correctly describing the target. Besides providing this important learning function, this *feedback* brings the experimental trial to a definite close, so that the viewer will not wonder about what today's target site was during tomorrow's remote-viewing session.

How important is feedback? This is one of the most important questions to be explored in psi research. The answer to this question may eventually give the key to understanding the physical mechanisms that may underlie much of psychic functioning.

In any case, the viewers in most SRI remote-viewing experiments were provided with immediate feedback. So in principle, viewers could be getting their psychic information by looking slightly into the future and describing the feedback they will later receive.

Dr. Gerald Feinberg, a physics professor at Columbia University, has called this possible ability to describe one's own future experiences "remembrance of things future."[9] He has suggested that the presence of a beacon person at a target site may simply give psychological support to a viewer, which allows him to believe that he is telepathically in touch with someone at a distant location.

The idea that remote viewing is not necessarily telepathic is supported by the research of Brenda Dunne and John Bisaha of Mundelein College, Chicago. They conducted successful remote-viewing experiments in which the target was not chosen and the beacon did not visit the target site until *after* the interviewer had recorded a complete description from the viewer.[10] The viewer in these experiments had to look into the future to obtain her psychic information. This precognitive task was found to be no more difficult than the present-time experiment described earlier.

In another one of Dunne and Bisaha's precognition experiments, the viewer did not receive any direct feedback about the target sites until weeks after the remote-viewing sessions ended, since her beacon was traveling in the U.S.S.R.[11] The viewer had to wait for the beacon to return and tell everyone where he had been during each day of the experiment. Only then did she receive her feedback. This delay did not impede the success of the endeavor.

In research conducted by Marilyn Schlitz at the Institute for Parapsychology, the viewer did not receive feedback until months after the experimental sessions.[12] The viewer was in Detroit, Michigan, and her outbound experimenter was in Rome, Italy. She received feedback only after the judging was completed, through a German intermediary. This experiment was also highly successful.

From the above, it appears that several possible channels of psychic communication may be open simultaneously in remote viewing. If there is a beacon at the target sites during remote-viewing experiments, the viewer's psychic impressions may be aided by telepathic communication. Schlitz's results suggest that her experiments may have been supported either through telepathic contact with the beacon at the target sites five thousand miles away, by direct remote viewing of the target site itself, by precognition of the feedback she was to receive months later—or by all three.

In Dunne and Bisaha's research, however, there could not be any present-time remote viewing, because the target sites had not yet been selected when the remote-viewing sessions were carried out. Therefore, these experiments must have been precognitive. In the SRI experiments, all possible channels—telepathy, clairvoyance, and precognition—were open.

From the research conducted outside of SRI it appears that immediate feedback to viewers is not necessary for successful remote viewing. We nevertheless think that feedback helps, since experiments at SRI in which viewers did not receive feedback have not usually been successful.

Jule Eisenbud, a Denver psychiatrist and psi researcher, deals with the question of feedback in his book *Paranormal Foreknowledge.* [13] He suggests a kind of complementarity principle for psychic functioning, in which several different explanations of how this ability might work may all be correct. A similar situation occurs in physics—in some physics experiments light is observed to behave like a wave, in others like a particle. Similarly, Eisenbud argues, psychic functioning may also have a dual nature, which varies with the experimental context. Maybe it is too much to ask for psi research to develop a unified theory before one has also been formulated to describe the apparently contradictory phenomena of ordinary physics.

REMOTE-VIEWING OF LOCAL TARGETS: THE LAB WITH A BAY VIEW

One series of remote-viewing experiments at SRI was carried out in 1978 with Hella Hammid, a talented free-lance photographer and an early participant in the SRI remote-viewing research program. The SRI team had just concluded a study examining the importance of feedback to viewers. In six remote-viewing trials, this study found that Hella clearly described the first three target sites for sessions in which she was taken to the sites immediately after each session. However, she was unsuccessful in her later three attempts without feedback.

Although a series of controlled experiments always has a fixed and predetermined number of trials, Hella did not want to go back home to Los Angeles after having just missed three target sites in a row. In a sense she felt starved for feedback—for that good feeling of being taken to a

Photo of Hella
Hammid by Judy
Angelo Cowen.

site that closely corresponds to the remote-viewing experience a viewer has just had in the laboratory.

So although the feedback study was completed, and three of Hella's trials had been successful, the research team agreed to dip randomly once more into the collection of sixty San Francisco Bay area target sites and carry out an additional session with feedback just for her. Two beacons were sent off to a new hiding place where Hella could try to find them just for fun.

This extra session is included to illustrate the experimental protocol we use in the laboratory. The previous six experimental sessions had been carried out at the rate of two per day, for three days. The next day was Thursday, and Hella's final session was carried out that morning, just before she started her drive back to Los Angeles.

Hella and I (R.T.) sat in the comfortable but windowless experimental room on the third floor of the Radio Physics building at SRI, shown on page 28. While we drank our morning coffee and discussed what we would

Remote-Viewing Interview Room.

do next, the two beacon experimenters went to the second floor of the building and used an electronic random-number generator (RNG) to get the number that would determine their destination for the experiment.

The beacons brought the number to our secretary, who opened her safe and took out a metal box holding the cards that listed possible target sites for the remote-viewing experiments. She looked through the sixty envelopes and pulled out the one with the number called for by the RNG. The beacons took the envelope, went to the SRI parking lot, got in a car, started the engine, and only then opened the envelope. Since the target envelopes had been assigned numbers randomly, there was no possibility that anyone in the building could know where the beacons were going.

The card in the envelope said: "AIRPORT TOWER—Cross Bay-shore Freeway on Embarcadaro Road. On your left will be the Palo Alto Airport. Follow the Airport road to its end, which will take you to the tower. Notice the square concrete base, and pentagonal glass top. Walk around the tower, look up at it. Also notice the aircraft nearby, and the surrounding trees." The airport tower had never been used as a target site before. Neither Hella nor I, the interviewer, had ever seen it, so it was a complete surprise for both of us.

A person standing at the airport and looking up at the control tower might describe it as a square stone tower, about fifty feet tall, with a slightly larger pentagonal glass room sitting at the top. There are a number of antennas for radar and communications on the roof of the tower. Several Monterey pines flank the base of the tower near its entrance. A chain-link fence surrounds the entire area. The tower is just west of the edge of the airport's main runway, which in turn is a short distance from San Francisco Bay. A photograph of the tower is shown on page 30, along with Hella's final drawing of the target site, based upon her remote-viewing experience.

The following is the verbatim transcript of the tape recording of that Thursday's session:

AIRPORT TRANSCRIPT:

HELLA HAMMID AND RUSSELL TARG

HH: It looks like a kind of large cabbage shape, with intercon-nected petals, around the base of this towerlike building. The tower has sort of a thing on top. I am going to have to draw it.

RT: Tell me about it.

HH: No. I am going to have to think about it again. It's just an impression, I am not sure at all whether that's it.

RT: Can you tell me about the towerlike building?

HH: I don't want to push it. I just want to see whether it comes up again. It may have been the wrong flash. But I won't forget about it. [long pause] There is definitely this tower which seems to be rising out of a large organic petal-shaped area, which could be bushes around the base of it, or flower beds with ornamental designs. And the tower seems to be facing a gully, or a river, or a stream, on one side, on the right, which I would guess is east.

RT: Can you tell me anything about the shape of the tower?

HH: It seems to be quite square, it is not a round tower, it is a square tower, with slightly curved surfaces. But definite cor-ners, four corners, and it does seem to have a sort of enlarged tip at the top.

RT: Will you be able to draw that for me later?

HH: I have begun to draw that right here. It is almost as if the tower was standing in a slight depression, with either mounds

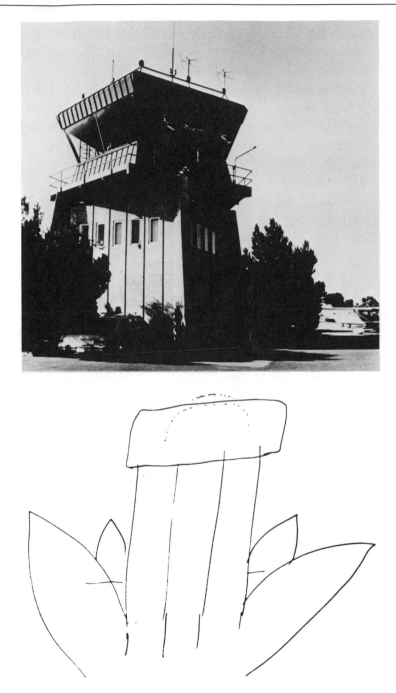

Palo Alto Airport tower target (above) and drawing made by viewer Hella Hammid during local remote-viewing experiment (below). Viewer describes site as a "square tower . . . some technical installation."

of earth piled up around it, slightly higher than the earth's surface, or with these leaflike protrusions growing up around it, or as if it grew organically out of the center of a plant. And it doesn't seem like a huge tower. It seems like a rather small structure.

RT: Why don't you go up above it then, and see what kind of place it is in? See if there is anything around it.

HH: Well from the top it looks like it has winglike projections on either side of it, what look like petal leaves don't go all the way around it, but just on either side, projecting.

RT: That's at the base?

HH: Yes. In a V-shape. This would be the bird's-eye view. It does seem to have something round at the top.

RT: You said that it is enlarged at the top, compared with the base?

HH: Slightly, yes. There seems to be an extra piece around it. There is some kind of a cross grid. I get a sense that it is something mechanical that needs to be visible from the sky, and that's directional. Definitely a kind of marker.

RT: Where is the cross grid you describe? Is it on the tower, or on the ground?

HH: It is emanating from the tower. And the tower may have more than four sides, but it is definitely not round. It has flat surfaces, vertical ones, and definite ridges. It could be multifaceted. It is made of stone. But those things on the ground are not made of stone. They seem to be metal? Something quite metallic about these things here. And there is something that is moving. Something mechanical that is moving in a circular motion, like a weathervane.

RT: Where is that moving thing? How is that associated with your tower?

HH: It seems to be an integral part of the tower, I can't see anything. . . .

RT: What are our friends doing?

HH: I see them not too close to the tower. I have the feeling that they can't get to it, too close. It is not an inhabited building. It is not something that you live in. I get more and more the feeling that it is an installation, some technical installation. Like a weather station, or an airport tower, or a radar installa-

tion or radio. . . . No, it's not radio. It is not that high, and
it is not metal. It is a mixture of stone and metal. There is
a lot of metal around, a lot. And there is a definite indentation
in the earth. It is not sitting on top of the earth, it is sitting
slightly below and protruding out over the surface.

RT: Do you have a feeling for the kind of place it is standing in?

HH: Yes. It stands in a fairly isolated empty place with chain-
link fence around the area. Which makes me think of
some technical out-of-bounds place. It is definitely out of
doors, of course. It seems to be rather on a height, than in a
valley. It is out in the open. It is not a protected or cozy
place.

RT: It is about time for them. Would you like me to turn on the
lights and let you make a more detailed drawing?

HH: OK.

END OF TRANSCRIPT

This is an excellent example of what is right and wrong with remote
viewing. Hella eventually identifies the target as an airport tower, which
we consider remarkable. However, she does not resolve her vagueness
about the things at the base of the tower with "winglike projections." She
never realizes that there are both trees and airplanes at the base of the
tower, and that the projections do not belong to the trees. This transcript
shows the nonanalytical—"It looks like a kind of large cabbage shape"—
but also leads to an unusually good analysis at the end, where Hella says
the target site could not be a radio tower, because it is not metal, and is
not tall enough.

We have seen transcripts of this quality many times. Sometimes
viewers have experienced this high level of remote viewing after only one
or two initial trials. Hella Hammid excels, however, not only in her
accuracy, but also in her reliability. In the past ten years, Hella has almost
always shown enough psychic functioning in experiments to help her
fellow researchers find their way through the maze of uncertainties in the
design of experiments to end up with something that works, and that adds
another piece of evidence to the psychic jigsaw puzzle.

The feedback issue is still far from settled. When you learn to do
remote viewing, you will have to decide for yourself whether it is important for you to know immediately how well you did on a particular psychic
task. For example, if you correctly tell a friend where to find a bracelet

that she has lost, because you are able to visualize it in its hiding place, you may not need any more feedback than to know that she found it. The need for feedback will probably be different for different people, depending upon their personal preferences.

REMOTE VIEWING OF DISTANT TARGETS:
ON A CLEAR DAY YOU CAN SEE
TWO THOUSAND MILES

After having carried out more than fifty remote-viewing trials in which viewers were asked to describe local targets, the SRI team began trying to learn whether remote viewing was more difficult for more distant target sites. The Soviets had published several papers which proposed that psychic information was carried by extremely low-frequency (ELF) radio waves. Some Western researchers also hold this view.[14] But if electromagnetic radiation is responsible for psychic functioning, we would expect to find some decrease in the accuracy of remote-viewing descriptions when viewers are thousands of miles away from target sites. We have not yet found, however, any such decrease in the accuracy of remote viewing over long distances.

The SRI team has carried out many long-distance experiments from the earliest days of laboratory remote viewing. Viewers have psychically looked at New York City from California; at California from New Orleans; at San Andreas, Colombia, from Menlo Park, California; and so forth. Most of these exciting long-distance experiments have been successful. Five long-distance experiments were conducted together as a series in the summer of 1976. All five gave quite satisfactory results.[15] We will describe two of these here.

The viewer for these experiments, Dr. Susan Harris, was a medical student at Tulane University in New Orleans at the time. She is now completing her residency in psychiatry at Harvard. Susan became involved in the SRI remote-viewing experiments when I (R.T.) overheard her telling another person, at a party, that she had read an interesting German poem in a dream the previous night! Always on the lookout for potential remote viewers of unusual ability, I asked Susan if she would be interested in spending part of her summer vacation in California, where she might have an opportunity to see the world. I felt that a person who was able to read

Photo of Susan Harris
by Hella Hammid.

in a dream and remember what she had read must be remarkably in touch
with her internal mental processes. Reading in dreams is a highly unusual
occurrence.

In an early experiment with Susan, while she was still in New Orleans,
she described the activities of two outbound experimenters at a randomly
chosen target site two thousand miles away in California. This experiment
is one of very few instances in which a viewer definitely described motion
occurring at a target site, in a way that allows us to be sure that her psychic
perception was simultaneous with the remote events. Susan provided a
good description of the building where our beacons were standing, but the
most interesting aspect of this remote-viewing experience for Susan was
that the beacons seemed to be throwing something back and forth between them.

Susan then drew a picture of a little stick-figure person throwing a
Frisbee. During that time, the two beacons at the target site were feeling
bored standing next to a fairly uninteresting bank building. They had
picked up a piece of paper from a recent political rally. They folded it into
a paper airplane, and amused themselves by throwing it back and forth.
They too considered this activity to be a significant part of their target-site

experience, and took a photograph of the paper airplane in the air between them.

The two long-distance experiments that we next describe were conducted with Susan acting as a viewer at SRI, while I (R.T.) was in New York City. During these trials, Susan typed her impressions directly into a computer terminal, so that her impressions would be automatically recorded with time and date as soon as she began entering them into the machine. The computer was part of the ARPA (Advanced Research Projects Agency) network.

Even though Susan typed her own mental impressions, she still worked with an interviewer. The interviewer was electrical engineer and longtime psi researcher David Hurt, who asked her questions from time to time. As always, the interviewer had no idea where in New York I would be for the experiment—and nor did I, until half an hour before each experimental session.

These experiments were carried out in New York because I had taken my son Nicholas there to see the tall ships from a boat in the harbor, on the Bicentennial weekend of July Fourth, 1976. The first transcript reflected the fact that Susan knew Nicholas was with me.

Both target locations were selected in the same way: I made a list of six interesting New York City locations that could be reached in half an hour from midtown Manhattan. Then, with a witness present, I threw a die on the sidewalk, and went to the location thus chosen.

The first target was Grant's Tomb, in Riverside Park, on the Upper West Side of New York City. It is a white domed building that looks rather like a Greek temple. It stands in a plaza of paving blocks, on high ground, where it overlooks the Hudson River. It is the final resting place of General Ulysses S. Grant and his wife, Julia. The building also holds much Civil War memorabilia, including books and postcards for sale.

The following is what Susan typed into the computer in California, while I stood in front of Grant's Tomb in New York City:

Date: 2 July 1976 1126-PDT
Subject: Susan's report
To: Targ

Russell—I thought of a high place with a view. I saw a tree on your left in a brick plaza. It seemed to be in front of a building you were entering. [All correct.] You waited as if for an elevator, and read something on the wall. You came out (off the elevator) and there was a room on the left with a view. I could not clearly identify the activity. A restaurant. A museum. A bookstore. You looked at something, a carving, a menu, directions on a post, before entering. From the room, I thought there was a view of the harbor or some water. At one time I thought you were looking at coins in the palm of your hand, maybe giving some to Nicky [Yes; he used them to buy the postcard which appears on page 37], which were then put into a slot—jukebox? Pinball? [This was followed by several unsuccessful attempts to read words and letters seen at the site.]

While Susan was doing her remote viewing, a second viewer was also working at SRI, without an interviewer, in an attempt to describe the same target site. He is a physicist and at that time was an SRI systems analyst. He reported the following in his tape-recorded opening paragraphs:

Outdoors, large open area, standing on, and then off asphalt (rough material) dark for a path. A white building, like a ticket booth. Wooden structure, white in color, and has an arched look about it. There is a large shade tree close to Russ.

He then made the drawing shown on page 37.

The second target site, which was chosen randomly two days later, was the central fountain in Washington Square Park. This outdoor fountain is large and circular. It has a curved rim that runs all the way around it, and concrete steps that lead into the fountain itself. The concrete bottom of the fountain has a post in its center, from which water can be sprayed.

Susan again worked with an interviewer at SRI, while typing into a computer terminal.

Date: 6 July 1976 1354-PDT
Subject: Susan's report, part 2
For: Targ

The first image I got, at about the first minute, was of a cement depression—as if a dry fountain—with a cement post in the

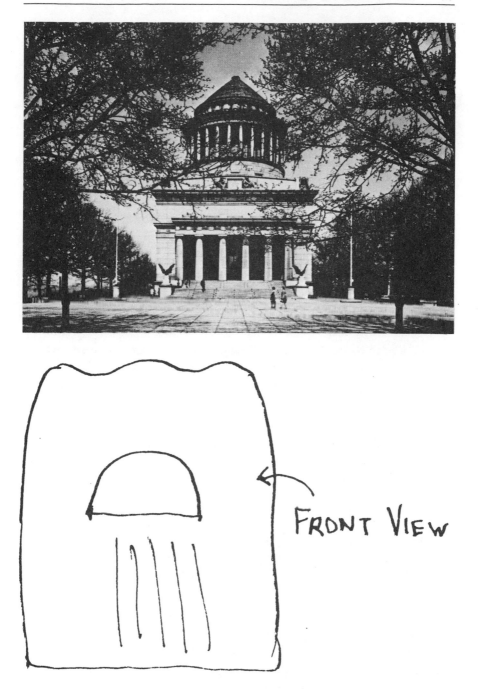

FRONT VIEW

Grant's Tomb target (above) and drawing (below) made by viewer in coast-to-coast remote-viewing experiment. Viewer describes site as being "outdoors, large open area . . . white building . . . arched look about it . . ."

middle or inside. There seemed to be pigeons off to the right flying around the surface out of the depression. [All correct.] Then I saw as if in the distance a real stadium, with grass in the center and perhaps stadium lights.

Other images were of houses/picket fences—some vertical units with jagged tops. Then a fluted, grooved vertical column. But, I couldn't sense what it was related to. Again, you were in the depressed area with cement sides looking out at the surface outside. The cement sides are not straight, but sloping. Almost S-shaped.

Also a clear feeling of the heavy worn metal bar on top of a typical NYC fence. There didn't seem to be anything really special inside. Just a separation between two similar areas. At one point I thought you were opening a cellophane bag. [Yes, it was ninety-five degrees, and I bought some ice cream.] And later I sensed you were feeding popcorn to the pigeons.

There was also a rectangular wooden frame, a window frame. But I wasn't sure if it was on a building or a similar structure with a different purpose. All in all, I thought that you were at Riverside Park near a track and play area. [Then some additional park scenes.]

Susan's sketch of the side of her depressed fountain area with the post in the center is shown on page 39, along with a photograph of the target site in Washington Square Park.

In the formal judging of most remote-viewing experiments, the judge goes to the site, rather than being given photographs such as the ones we show here. These have been taken after the completion of the experiments and are used only for illustrative purposes.

There are obviously many accurate correspondences in both of Susan's transcripts, along with many errors. We wanted to make a quantitative assessment of her accuracy. A statistical analysis of the correct and incorrect statements was carried out to determine if these transcripts really do contain more correct statements than incorrect.

For example, in the Washington Square transcript, Susan correctly describes a concrete fountain. She then goes on to say that perhaps there was a stadium in the distance, which there was not. Once having psycho-

Washington Square target (above) and drawing (below) made by viewer Susan Harris in coast-to-coast remote-viewing experiment. Viewer describes site as "cement depression—as if a dry fountain—cement post in the middle or inside." Photo © 1984 Rose Wallach.

logically created a stadium out of the fountain, Susan was then able to imagine lights on the stadium. Without good psi functioning, there is no limit on how far such elaborations of memory and imagination may go. A good interviewer can be of great help in quenching this mental noise before it gets totally out of hand.

To assess Susan's transcripts, two evaluators made lists which contained every concept that Susan described in her text. Concepts are phrases that pertain to a single idea in the transcript. Examples of such concepts would be: "A high place with a view, a brick plaza, a building you were entering, a cement depression," and "a dry fountain." On a scale of 0 to 10 for correspondence with the target site, all of these concepts would rate 10.

Statements such as "coins put in a slot" would receive a rating of 0, because that did not occur at the site. Other examples of concepts with 0 ratings would be the "stadium" with its "lights" and the "elevator" at Grant's Tomb. "Heavy worn metal" would receive a 7, because there are several large copper posts in the fountain.

The transcript evaluators found twenty-one such concepts in the Grant's Tomb transcript, and their average accuracy rating was 6.4. The Washington Square transcript had sixteen concepts, with an average rating of 6.8. One way of describing this result would be to say that about two-thirds of the transcript concepts were found to pertain to their intended target sites.

To see if these concepts would pertain to any other sites equally well, the Grant's Tomb concept list was rated against the Washington Square site, and the Washington Square concepts were similarly cross-matched against the Grant's Tomb target. The concepts did not match the wrong targets very well at all. The Grant's Tomb concepts got a score of 3.1 as applied to Washington Square, and the Washington Square concepts received an average score of 3.8 as applied to Grant's Tomb. From this we might say that about one-third of the concepts apply to the cross-matched target, and must therefore be considered to have general applicability. This result has held up in similar analyses of many other remote-viewing transcripts.

To check the validity of these results, the thirty-seven concepts were numerically compared with their intended and their cross-matched sites in two standard statistical tests—the t-test and the Mann-Whitney U-test. These tests were used to determine whether the scores given to the properly matched ratings differed from those of the cross-ratings by an amount that was significantly more than the difference to be expected by chance.

These statistical tests showed that the odds are more than a hundred to one against obtaining the split of two-thirds to one-third for thirty-seven concepts. That is, the data from these sessions offer statistically significant evidence that Susan actually described the intended target sites.

A final trial in this series was carried out with a viewer in Menlo Park, California. It was agreed that at noon the outbound experimenter (R.T.) would be at a randomly chosen site in the city of New Orleans. The viewer was the same SRI physicist who made the drawing of Grant's Tomb shown earlier. In this trial he was interviewed by Dr. Elizabeth Rauscher, a physicist from the University of California at Berkeley.

The target site for this experiment was chosen by slipping a card arbitrarily between the pages of a New Orleans guidebook. The target turned out to be the Louisiana Superdome. As a beacon, I stood looking at the building and made the following tape-recorded comments: "It is a bright sunshiny day. In front of me is a huge, silvery building with a white dome gleaming in the sun. It is a circular building with metal sides. It looks like nothing so much as a flying saucer. The target is in fact the eighty-thousand-seat Louisiana Superdome stadium."

The viewer in Menlo Park described the target as "a large circular building with a white dome." The viewer also expressed feelings of wanting to reject what he saw because the dome looked to him "like a flying saucer in the middle of a city." Page 42, showing his drawings, together with guidebook photographs of the target, seems to make it clear why he had this impression.

INTERCONTINENTAL REMOTE VIEWING

In 1979, Marilyn Schlitz and Elmar Gruber carried out the series of remote-viewing experiments referred to earlier. They not only spanned intercontinental distances with their remote viewing, but also achieved the greatest statistical significance of any remote-viewing experiment that has so far been conducted.

In their experiments, Marilyn was the remote viewer. She remained in Detroit, her home at the time. Marilyn has a degree in philosophy and

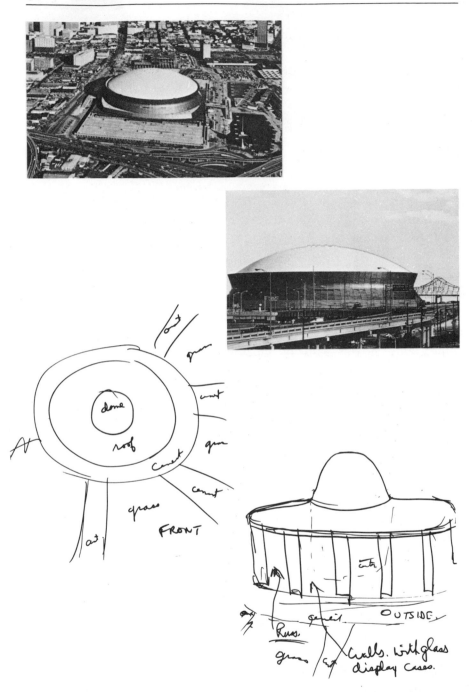

Louisiana Superdome Target (above) and drawing made by viewer (below) in long-distance remote-viewing experiment. Viewer described site as "a large circular building with a white dome." Photo courtesy Grant L. Robertson.

Photo of Marilyn Schlitz.

is a graduate student studying anthropology and cross-cultural approaches to psi research. Her current research at the Mind Science Foundation in San Antonio, Texas, is concerned with various aspects of psychic healing and with rituals that may be used to elicit psi, both in the laboratory and in the field. Elmar Gruber is a researcher at the Institut für Grenzgebiete der Psychologie und Psychohygiene, in Freiburg, West Germany. During the experimental sessions, Elmar, the beacon, was in Rome, Italy.

The researchers' purpose in this study was to investigate the methods a viewer uses to make contact with a distant beacon. Besides looking for evidence of psychic functioning, the researchers wanted to gain firsthand insight into what a viewer experiences during remote-viewing sessions.

In six of her ten trials, Marilyn gave descriptions that were sufficiently accurate to allow five independent judges to give the correct transcript the highest rating. The judges in this experiment were asked not only to choose the transcript that best matched each day's target site, but also to find the second-best, third-best, and so on, to the tenth-best match for each. (Besides the six first-place matches, several other transcripts were in second place.) The odds against the overall scores for this experiment being achieved by chance are better than a hundred thousand to one.

Before the experiment began, Elmar and an Italian colleague selected forty target sites of various types, while walking through the streets of Rome. As they describe in their paper in the *Journal of Parapsychology*, [16] the target pool was carefully constructed to contain several targets of each type, just as in the SRI remote-viewing studies.

For each remote-viewing session, Elmar would arrive at his randomly selected target site at 5:00 P.M. Rome time, corresponding to 11:00 A.M. in Detroit, and stay for fifteen minutes. Elmar was free to walk around the site, sit down, or generally observe and experience the site in any way that seemed appropriate. He would remain at the target site for fifteen minutes. During that time he would tape-record his impressions.

Back in Detroit, on each of the ten consecutive days, Marilyn sat in a dimly lit room and tried to describe Elmar's whereabouts. Marilyn was in a calm state of mind, and she did not use any formal relaxation procedure during the remote viewings. She simply made an effort to think constantly about the target site and the beacon, trying not to let other thoughts intrude. She recorded her thoughts and impressions, and also made sketches of her mental pictures.

One of Marilyn and Elmar's principal interests in this remote-viewing series was to study the types of psychological responses a viewer uses in remote viewings, as compared with other free-response experiments, or with forced-choice procedures like card guessing. In their paper, Marilyn tells us of her mental processes in trying to describe and experience the activities of her distant friend:

> It should be noted that 11:00 was not usually a good time for E_1 [Marilyn], and she would often sit down for a session at the very last minute taking no time to induce any type of relaxation. She used a picture of Elmar as a starting point with which to focus her attention. She would then use a game-type of strategy, asking over and over again in her mind: "Where is he?" Impressions developed in several ways. Often it was . . . the appearance of faint lines, frequently followed by a more complete picture. On several occasions, impressions triggered a distinct memory, which was then recounted as the response. It was tempting in such cases to avoid an analytical response to the impressions, as the impressions appeared to be too complete. This was in line with Targ & Puthoff's . . . warning to avoid an analysis of information. As an example we

have included the verbal description from November 8, 1979, which reads as follows:

> Flight path? Red lights. Strong depth of field. Elmar seems detached, cold. A hole in the ground, a candle-shaped thing. Flower—maybe not real. Maybe painted. Outdoors. See sky dark. Windy, cold. Something shooting upward.

After the fifteen-minute viewing period Marilyn expanded further on her impressions:

> For some reason a boat comes to mind. The impressions that I had were outdoors, and Elmar was at some type of—I don't know if institution is the right word—but some *place*. Not a private home or anything like that—something—a public facility. He was standing away from the main structure, although he could see it. He might have been in a parking lot, or a field connected to the structure that identifies the place. I want to say an airport, but that just seems too specific. There was activity and people, but no one real close to Elmar.

In this session the target site was Rome International Airport, where the outbound experimenter had been standing on a little hill away from the main structure. Near the hill were holes in the ground where clandestine diggers had been looking for Roman coins. This transcript shows a striking correspondence between Marilyn's impressions and Elmar's location. Many other transcripts in this series had similarly strong matches, as indicated by the judges' ability to form them into corresponding pairs with great statistical significance.

One of the important things to notice from this example is that Marilyn's ability to describe the target site did not end when Elmar left it. He was primarily a beacon, who demarcated the target site for her. Once the viewer had found the site, she was able to continue describing it, even after the outbound experimenter had left. She might also have been able to psychically experience the target site again at a later time.

The outcome of this experiment with its hundred-thousand-to-one statistics showed conclusively that the distance involved did not inhibit psychic functioning. As we mentioned earlier, Marilyn received no feedback on this experiment until months after it had been evaluated, so we have additional evidence that immediate feedback cannot be considered essential for good remote viewing.

Recently, the Schlitz-Gruber experiment was reevaluated; this time, Elmar's notes from the target site were not included in the judging materials. The thought was that these notes might have been contaminated with world news of each day. If Marilyn's notes also contained any comments about the day's news, the judges might (even unintentionally) match Marilyn's transcripts with Elmar's notes based upon this nonpsychic information (a possibility we consider farfetched). New judges also found that the transcripts significantly corresponded to the appropriate target sites.

The long-distance experiments we have discussed, which cover ever-increasing distances between viewer and beacon, suggest that distance does not affect the quality of remote-viewing results. In experiments in which a tower is described as a tower, a fountain is identified as a fountain, and an airport is called by name, the argument that transcript judges reached their successful matches by some artifact of the experimental protocol seems unsupported by the data. The results that we have described are typical of hundreds of remote-viewing trials that have been carried out in laboratories across the United States. These include two series of nine each, carried out at SRI, with Hella Hammid and Pat Price. Both of these series—described in detail in *Mind Reach*—achieved highly significant results. Price's series had seven first-place matches.

LONG-DISTANCE REMOTE VIEWING
FROM A SUBMARINE

As we will discuss in Chapter 4, Vasiliev in the U.S.S.R. was very interested in the effects of electromagnetic shielding on psychic functioning. In *Experiments in Mental Suggestion* [17] he describes his delight in reading that the American government carried out telepathy experiments in the summer of 1959 on the submarine *Nautilus*. Vasiliev says:

> This experiment showed—and herein resides its principal value—
> that telepathic information can be transmitted without loss
> through a thickness of seawater and through the sealed metal

covering of a submarine—that is, through substances that greatly interfere with radio communication.

The only problem with Vasiliev's observation, which has been widely repeated, is that it is based upon a pair of French newspaper stories that we believe to be entirely fictional.[18] In our many years of working intensively in psi research, in and out of the U.S. government, we have been unable to find any evidence for a real event behind this story.

Stephen Schwartz, concerned with the same questions, decided to actually carry out the experiment that had been reported, instead of merely wondering about it.[19] In early 1973, Schwartz, then Special Assistant to the Chief of Naval Operations, unsuccessfully tried to get the Navy to carry out a submarine experiment. The SRI team had also failed to interest the Navy in a similar experiment. The missing ingredient— a submarine—was finally made available, thanks to Don Keach and Don Walsh, friends of Schwartz's, who had retired from the Navy and now headed the Institute for Marine and Coastal Studies of the University of Southern California.

Schwartz arranged for the use of a submarine through his Möbius Group in Los Angeles, which also investigates psychic functioning. His experiment, called Deep Quest, used the *Taurus*, a five-person submersible made by the International Hydrodynamics Company (HYCO) of Canada.

In July 1977, two preliminary tests of remote viewing from a submerged submarine were carried out. This experiment was conducted in the Pacific Ocean near Santa Catalina, in cooperation with the SRI researchers. The viewers were under several hundred feet of seawater, five hundred miles away from the outbound experimenters whose activities were to be described.

The goal was to determine if great depths of seawater blocked psychic signals. Psi experiments have been successfully carried out at SRI and other laboratories for years using a variety of electrically shielded rooms. Although these rooms very effectively shield radio waves whose frequency is above several kHz (thousand cycles per second), they are almost transparent to extremely low-frequency (ELF) radio waves.

Since psychic functioning is seen to occur over great distances, it has been hypothesized by many researchers (notably Kogan in the U.S.S.R. and Persinger in Canada[20]) that if psychic information is carried by electromagnetic radiation, it must have a very low frequency and long wavelength. Seawater is known to be an excellent shield for both ELF and higher-frequency signals, which explains why governments are trying to develop other ways to communicate with their submerged submarines.

Schwartz has written to the authors about the Navy's efforts to construct a

> giant ELF submarine communications facility. In the course of planning [this system] SANGUINE the Navy had amassed considerable knowledge about seawater's shielding effect on ELF and, more importantly, on exactly how much data could be transmitted in a given amount of time. This research demonstrated that while ELF could penetrate seawater far deeper than any other form of radio wave, it took enormous power and, because of the very low frequency, only a very few bits of information could be transmitted in any reasonable time period.
>
> Because of this restriction the Navy, even with a uniquely powerful broadcasting facility, was planning to settle for getting across a few numbers, which would key to an existing orders book aboard the submarine—'Number 37 means FIRE' sort of thing. Thanks to the Navy's research, it was possible to make a direct transference of this scheme to Deep Quest, while at the same time studying the validity of an ELF-Psychic link.

The Navy scheme applied to psychic functioning worked beautifully. Since it is known to be extremely difficult to send words and numbers psychically, six messages to be sent to the viewers were encoded by arbitrarily linking each message to a geographical target site, of the type that both viewers had been successfully describing in remote-viewing experiments for the previous five years. For example, message 1 might have been associated with Hoover Tower, message 2 could have been linked with a big oak tree, and so on. Thus, if the viewers chose the correct target site in their remote viewing, this would result in their receiving the correct message.

The viewers in this experiment were Hella Hammid and Ingo Swann. On each of two days, they were towed miles out to sea in the submarine before it submerged. This resulted in their having the unusual experience of trying to be psychic underwater—while seasick.

The experiment was carried out at a prearranged time each day. The viewers knew that their beacons would be at some San Francisco Bay area target site at that time, for fifteen minutes. During that time, the viewer was to describe into a tape recorder his or her mental pictures and impressions of where the outbound experimenters were.

After completing each of their remote-viewing descriptions, the viewers were given a sealed packet that contained six cards. Each card had the name and description of one of that day's six possible target sites on one side, and one of the possible messages on the other side. These cards, of course, were not shown to the viewers or anyone else on the submarine until after the remote viewings had been carried out. The viewers then tried to decide which of the cards had a description of a site that best matched the target descriptions given during their remote-viewing sessions.

In both sessions, the viewers were able to choose their correct cards, and thus received the correct message. This procedure for obtaining analytical data through psychic functioning is referred to as *associative remote viewing* (ARV).

The remote-viewing descriptions in the submarine experiment were of better-than-average quality—which again suggests that when the necessity level is up, an experienced viewer may produce the best data. In Hella's session, the randomly chosen target was a huge oak tree on the edge of a cliff, which overlooks Stanford University and San Francisco Bay. The beacon experimenters climbed up into the tree during the experimental period. Hella's first words were:

A very tall looming object. A very, very huge, tall tree, and a lot of space behind them. There almost feels like there is a drop-off or a palisade or a cliff behind them.

Hella also said the beacons were behaving in a very "unscientific fashion" at the site.

Swann's target site was a large indoor shopping plaza with an ornamental pool. He made a drawing of the place and labeled it as showing "flat stone flooring, walls, small pool, reddish stone walk, large doors, enclosed area, walking around." All of these impressions were correct, allowing him to choose the correct site and message from a new set of six randomized targets. Swann also commented that the site "could be City Hall," which was not correct. But his experience told him that analyses of that sort are rarely on target.

The results of these two successful ARV sessions in the submarine, each with a probability of one in six, lead us to the conclusion that deep seawater, which diminishes even ELF radio waves a hundredfold, does not diminish psychic functioning. This offers further evidence that psychic information is not transmitted by ELF waves. The hundredfold decrease in radio transmission is calculated for radio waves of 10 cycles per second (which corresponds to brain-wave frequencies), among the lowest of the ELF waves that theorists have considered. Ordinary radio waves, at much higher frequencies, are blocked even more than ELF signals by seawater.

These research results indicate that remote viewing is not adversely affected by distance, electromagnetic shielding—or seasickness.

The images that viewers come up with seem to have a highly personal character. The tone of voice of a viewer at the time of his or her best contact with the site also seems to have a special quality, which apparently differs for each viewer.

This is an important point, because an experienced interviewer can ask additional questions about an aspect of the remote-viewing description that he associates with the viewer's special mode of psychic functioning. Although the interviewer is ignorant of the target site—possibly even of the target pool—he can still help a viewer separate the psychic signal from other impressions that confuse his psi perceptions of a target.

In the following section, Warcollier gives some additional insights on the nature of both the psi signal and the mental noise in remote viewing.

RENÉ WARCOLLIER:
FIRST TO SEE THE PATTERN

In what follows, the questions are our own version of those that constantly come up, and the answers are taken from Warcollier's 1948 book, *Mind to Mind*, though not in the order in which they appear in his book.

Q: What is the nature of the mental noise that interferes with accurate and reliable psychic functioning?

RW: *"Secondary elaboration* takes place, which frequently gives rise to a large number of associations that attach themselves to the impression. The impression of the latent image excites the imagination and the memories of the percipient. Conscious imagination is a negative force in telepathic communication."

We tell our viewers again and again, "Don't try to analyze your impressions. Don't try to imagine *what* the target is. Just tell us what you are feeling and experiencing."

Q: What is the nature of the psychic impression?
RW: "I believe that the primitive, direct, and intuitive perception is the telepathic reception of a total and undifferentiated impression of the target. There seems to be an analogy between the paranormal perception of drawings and the normal perception of drawings exposed for very short periods of time by means of a tachistoscope."

He points out that one often has only the "global form," the Gestalt of what is perceived.

A: What sort of detail can we expect to find in psychically derived data?
RW: "Distance never seemed to affect the results. The image is scrambled, broken up into component bits. Movement is injected into what would otherwise be a static image. One often has the reduction or fusion [of target material] into a few simple forms or shapes repeated in the target."

This latter process often makes it hard to count objects at a target site or in a picture.

Q: What are the psychological forces governing psychic functioning?
RW: "There is very little doubt that the use of language can cause difficulty in receiving a telepathic [or remote-viewing] impression, because the medium of expression in telepathy is not language [but images]. If what is perceived seems illogical and

irrational, the chances are greater that it is a hit, than when the percepient restricts himself to certain persons, places, and things. [To be successful] he must draw upon his organized patterns of feeling and thinking, to give meaning to what arrives from his subconscious [primary process perception].

The above explains why a viewer's drawings may sometimes be more accurate than his verbal descriptions of target sites.

From the time of Croesus to the days of Sinclair and Warcollier, through the early days at SRI and other modern laboratories, remote viewing was shown to be capable of transcending spatial limits. What remained to be discovered was the extent to which remote viewing could transcend the apparent limits of time as well.

3

Precognition at Home and Abroad: It's About Time

For us believing physicists the distinction between past,
present, and future is only an illusion, even if a stubborn one.
—Albert Einstein
March 21, 1955

In psi research it has often been useful to divide psychic perception into three general classes. These are *telepathy*, which is mind-to-mind communication; *clairvoyance*, the perception of current events, objects or people that are hidden from the known five senses; and *precognition*, the knowledge of future events that cannot be perceived by any known means.

Psi researchers recognize that there may be important overlaps and combinations of these divisions, but over the years these designations have been useful. Many people find precognition the least believable of all psychic abilities. This view is often the result of limited assumptions about the nature of cause and effect.

Many hold that for one event to be the cause of another, it must occur before the event it causes. If you dream about an event, you might reasonably argue that it is necessary for you (or someone, at least) to have experienced the event before you dreamed about it, not after.

The findings of psi research seem not to, however, support this view. Neither do many modern philosophical theories about causality. Events are closely tied to their causes, so that you cannot have the one without the other. Events can also be acausally related. That is, the occurrences A and B are always associated with each other, but both are caused by some third factor C, which may or may not be apparent. Synchronistic events are probably examples of acausally related happenings. Still, the causes do not necessarily have to come first. We will explain the variety of evidence that supports this seemingly odd statement.

A favorite question of people who think about precognition is: What happens if you "see" the future, and do not like what you see? Do you have to experience that future anyway? Apparently not. An article about train wrecks published by W. E. Cox suggests that if you are attuned to psychic information, it may be usefully incorporated into your life.[1]

Cox's survey of twenty-eight documented train wrecks between 1950 and 1955 shows that significantly fewer people rode certain trains when they crashed than rode them on the same day of the week in earlier weeks or months. This can be interpreted as showing that impending train crashes appear to have caused regular riders to refrain from getting on those trains at their usual times, prior to the crashes.

We do not think that bad weather can be responsible, since more commuters probably ride trains in bad weather than in fair. It appears from Cox's data that hundreds of people got up in the morning and, for reasons they might have found hard to explain, decided not to take trains that were going to have wrecks later in the day.

A related study was conducted by Dr. Stanley Krippner and others at the dream laboratory of Maimonides Medical Center in Brooklyn.[2] In this highly successful experiment, Malcolm Bessent, a famous English psychic, was asked to dream about an event that would be prepared for him the following morning. A total of sixteen such precognition trials were carried out in this study.

On each night of the study, Bessent would be awakened whenever his brain waves indicated that he was having a dream. The researchers would record his description of his dream, then let him go back to sleep. By morning, the researchers would have recorded several related dreams.

In the morning, another experimenter would arrive at the Maimonides laboratory. He would have no contact with the researchers who recorded Bessent's dreams. This experimenter's task was to randomly open a book of dream symbols, and then construct an awakening experience for Malcolm around one symbol that he found on the chosen page. In a typical case, this resulted in Bessent's having ice cubes dropped down his back upon awakening, a short time after he had dreamed about ice cubes. In his dream he also experienced being cold and chilled, and in a white room—much of which closely mirrored his chilly morning activities. One possible description of this sequence of events would be that Bessent's earlier dream of ice cubes was caused by the experience he would have the following morning.

This view does not run counter to scientific views of causality. Although future events may *affect* the past, such events cannot *change* the past. One cannot make something that *has* already happened into a nonevent that has *not* happened. These two studies (Cox and Krippner) are typical of many experiments in which information from the future appears to have been available in the past.

Another treasure trove of data pertaining to precognition is *An Experiment with Time,* by the English engineer J. W. Dunne.[3] This book, first published in 1927, describes the years of efforts by the author to organize and understand the precognitive content of his dreams. He also shares with the reader his various techniques for increasing the frequency and vividness of such dreams.

One of Dunne's most interesting findings was that in many cases, it was the newspaper story reporting an event that showed up in his dream, rather than the event itself. He reports one instance in which he dreamed that four thousand people had been killed in a volcanic eruption, which is exactly what he misread in the next day's newspaper. It was not until years later when he copied out the article for his book that he learned that the actual story said that the loss of life had been forty thousand. In fact, he had learned, within a few weeks after the disaster, that the actual number was different from both numbers:

> Now, when the next batch of papers arrived, these gave more exact estimates of what the actual loss of life had been, and I discovered that the true figure had nothing in common with the arrangement of fours and naughts I had both dreamed of, and gathered from the first report. So my wonderful "clairvoyant" vision had been

wrong in its most insistent particular! But, it was clear that its wrongness was likely to prove a matter just as important as its rightness. For *whence* in the dream did I get the idea of 4000? Clearly, it must have come into my mind *because of the newspaper paragraph.*

EXPERIMENTS IN PRECOGNITIVE REMOTE VIEWING

Psi researchers did not seek out the possibility of precognition. Instead, precognition stood up and demanded their attention. In 1974 the SRI team was in the midst of its first formal series of remote-viewing sessions.[4] The viewer for these early sessions was Pat Price, a former police commissioner from Burbank, California.

Pat had come to SRI as a volunteer, because he felt that he had been using something like remote viewing all his life. He explained that he used psychic functioning to catch criminals in his police work. Pat's claim is convincing, because his was the series of nine remote-viewing sessions that led to seven first-place matches of the target sites. The probability of this occurring by chance is less than one in one hundred thousand. The early sessions with Pat Price were of the present-time clairvoyant variety which were discussed in the preceding chapter.

In the fourth trial of that early series, Pat demonstrated that remote viewing was capable of even more than was being asked of it. In the first three trials, Price had provided good descriptions of the target sites, even to the extent of identifying one site by name. Since this was a brand-new activity for SRI, the experiments were still under special scrutiny of the institute's management. They viewed the entire project with a mixture of scientific curiosity and healthy skepticism.

On trial four, Pat Price and I (R.T.) were in an electrically shielded room on the second floor of the Engineering Sciences building. With us was Dr. Hugh Crane, a staff scientist at SRI. The outbound team consisted of Harold Puthoff and the laboratory director, Bonnar Cox. Dr. Cox had decided that he wanted personal experience with the remote-viewing experiments so that he could describe this research to others with as much accuracy and confidence as possible.

Cox's plan, after leaving SRI with Puthoff, was to select a target site not by using a random-number generator and target cards, but rather by following a random drive, in which each left and right turn for half an hour would be determined by arbitrary factors in the flow of traffic, e.g., the unexpected arrival of a freight train at a grade crossing, which caused them to change direction. When Cox and Puthoff got into the car to go to their target site, no one in the world knew where they were going. (Or so they thought.)

The outbound team left SRI at 3:00 P.M. At 3:05 I started the tape recorder in the shielded room, and put a little preamble on the tape in which I described who we were and what we were doing, and said that the outbound team would arrive at their target site at 3:30. At that point, Pat chimed in and announced on the tape, "We don't have to wait till then. I can tell you right now where they will be." After that, Pat's first words on the tape were as follows:

> What I'm looking at is a little boat jetty or a little boat dock along the bay. In a direction about like that from here [he pointed in the correct direction]. Yeah, I see the little boats, some motor launches, some little sailing ships, sails all furled, some with their masts stepped, others are up. Little jetty or little dock there. [He went on to say]: Funny thing—this just flashed in—kinda looks like a Chinese or Japanese pagoda effect. It's a definite feeling of Oriental architecture that seems to be fairly adjacent to where they are.

Photo of Pat Price by Hella Hammid.

He also correctly described decomposed granite slabs leading down to the water. So, by 3:10 on the afternoon of the fourth session, Pat had provided a quite complete remote-viewing description of some site. At 3:30 the travelers arrived at their target site, where they stayed for fifteen minutes. At a little after 4:00 P.M. they returned to SRI to learn what Pat had to say. It turned out that we all had plenty to say, because the randomly selected target site happened to be the Redwood City Marina.

The marina is a harbor and boat dock about four miles northeast of SRI. It is full of small and medium-sized sailing and motor boats, and is also the home of the Stanford University rowing club. It has a modern, Oriental-looking glass-and-redwood restaurant right on the dock, just to the left of where the outbound experimenters were standing.

Pat Price, who died in 1975, had psychic functioning totally integrated into his daily life. He would tell us each day about the course of world events—the day and hour of the Israeli-Arab cease-fire in the Yom Kippur war, the eventual outcome of a celebrated kidnapping, the breakup of an OPEC conference by terrorists. Nearly every day it seemed that Pat would have some new piece of precognitive news for us to think about over lunch, days in advance of the event's actual occurrence.

In the year following that early remote-viewing series with Pat, the SRI team carried out a series of four deliberately precognitive sessions with Hella Hammid. In these sessions, Hella was asked to describe a target location that would be randomly chosen and visited by an outbound experimenter half an hour after she had given her description.[5]

For Hella and me, these trials had a peculiar science-fiction quality. At 10:00 A.M. each day, I recorded her impressions of the location where the beacon would randomly be sent at 10:30. The remarkable part of this experience came at around noon each day, when we would all go to the target site for feedback. We would then play the tape of Hella's earlier description of the site and what she thought we would be doing there.

In one session, a Stanford Hospital courtyard was the target. As Hella's tape described our walking through a double colonnade, we were doing just that. The tape then said we would walk from the shade into bright sunlight, and into a "formal garden with manicured trees and shrubs." That is just what we were experiencing. It was like having an experience of prerecorded déjà vu. We knew that Hella had no ordinary way to figure out in advance where the beacon's random-number generator would send us, especially since that decision was made in a distant car, *after* she had finished her remote-viewing description.

All four of Hella's precognitive descriptions were correctly matched to their corresponding target sites by three independent judges.

Apart from the statistical significance of this particular series of experiments, encounters such as these with Pat and Hella suggest that there is something seriously inadequate about our current model of the space and time in which we live.

We are given a metaphor of flowing time, in which we are all said to creep along a timeline at the rate of one second per second from birth to death. This model provides no way to obtain information on what is waiting for us in the future. Since there is strong laboratory evidence that appears to contradict this point of view, it is clear that more must be going on than meets the eye in our mysterious relationship with what we call time.

Many laboratories have carried out experiments in which viewers were asked to describe the contents of 35mm slides that were projected on the wall of a distant room. Experiments of this type were the basis for much of the successful research originated by Dr. Montague Ullman in the Maimonides Hospital Dream Laboratory.[6] The SRI team wanted to know what a viewer would describe if his target was a *slide* of a San Francisco Bay area site, rather than the site itself with an outbound experimenter standing there.

In this series of experiments, an experienced viewer was asked to describe slides that were being viewed by another researcher at the time. The quality of the viewer's description of the target slides turned out to be just as good as his previous descriptions of actual target locations. It was still difficult to tell, however, whether he was "seeing" the slide or the original site.

A later experiment was able to approach this question more completely. The viewer in these trials had not been very successful in ordinary remote-viewing experiments, for he seemed to be describing target sites he would see the next day, rather than the current day's target location. But that was not his task, and his earlier results were not statistically significant. However, we thought an experiment might be designed for this viewer in which the target sites would exist only in his future. This approach was successful.

The protocol for this series had the viewer in our laboratory all by himself with a sketchpad and a tape recorder. Charles Tart, a psychology professor at the University of California, Davis, and I (R.T.) were downstairs behind the building in an office trailer. The idea was for the viewer to describe the slide that we would randomly select after his description was completed.

In one trial, the viewer described a building with a pointed roof that had something to do with a big star. He carefully counted the points on the star he was seeing: "There are one, two, three, four, five points, like on a sheriff's badge," he said.

After his description was over, the viewer buzzed us on an intercom to signal that he was finished. I pressed the button on a random-number generator; the output number was 27. Charley and I turned on the slide projector and rotated the carousel to show slide number 27. We then went to get our viewer and show him what we had.

The target turned out to be a picture of an automobile showroom; page 61 shows the photograph and the sketch the viewer made during his remote viewing. We were all struck at once by the large five-pointed stars in the windows of the building. No other target in our collection would have matched his description as well as this.

It occurred to us that this might be just the opportunity we were looking for, to determine whether a viewer psychically perceives the slide or the target of which the photograph was taken. Since the stars in the windows were only an advertising gimmick, it was possible that they might not be in the showroom window anymore, because the photo had been taken several months earlier.

We quickly drove to the showroom and found, to our delight, that no stars hung in the windows. This was strong evidence that a viewer looking into his future can describe a picture that he is actually going to be shown at the end of an experiment, rather than the target site itself.

This led us to consider that precognitive remote viewing might be harnessed to give us information about the future— information on which we might be able to act. For example, the outcome of a horserace could provide the "random" number to select a target slide that a viewer will be shown after an experiment. If we have only seven slides (corresponding to seven horses), and the viewer gives us a good description of one of these

Ely Chevrolet showroom target slide (below), and viewer response (above) given fifteen minutes before random selection of target.

slides, we might be able to know which horse will win the race, before the race is run. This happy marriage of precognition and associative remote viewing will be described in detail in our discussion of possible applications of psychic functioning.

PRECOGNITION IN CHICAGO

In 1975 Harold Puthoff and I (R.T.) presented a paper at the Parapsychological Association conference in Santa Barbara, Calif., describing all our remote-viewing studies, including the precognition experiments.[7] John Bisaha, a psychology professor at Mundelein College in Chicago, attended the meeting.

John was teaching a methodology course in experimental psychology at Mundelein. He thought the formal protocol of the precognitive remote-viewing experiments would interest his students. He was apparently as interested in seeing if the protocol could be followed by his students as in possibly observing precognition in the laboratory.

John and his associate, Brenda Dunne, then a graduate psychology student at the University of Chicago, designed an eight-session precognition experiment using various Chicago sites as remote-viewing targets. Their viewers were two female volunteers who were inexperienced with using psi in the laboratory.

Following the SRI precognition protocol, Brenda, the outbound experimenter, left Mundelein College before the viewer began giving her precognitive description of each day's target site. After the viewer's alloted fifteen minutes of description time had passed, the beacon would randomly choose one of ten numbered slips of paper from an envelope, then open the traveling instructions that corresponded to the number on the selected piece of paper. The two students in the psychology laboratory had to reach forward half an hour in time to describe the site where Brenda would be at that time. (One of these successful precognitive remote-viewing sessions was filmed live, by CBS television, in 1977.)

Much to everyone's amazement, the volunteer viewers were very successful. The experiments were also successful, at odds of better than one hundred to one against chance. Four of the trials resulted in first-place matches with striking correspondences between the viewer's impressions and the target sites.

We will excerpt two of the viewer's transcripts from Dunne and Bisaha's 1976 paper in *Research in Parapsychology.* [8] The two are interesting because they pertain to target sites that had many things in common. Each, however, was matched to their correct locations.

Trial 5, ranked as a first-place match:
The target was Lincoln Park Conservatory. This is a large open space, a park with a circular fountain, several large trees, a stone bridge which extends to a stone wall on either side, and at the time of the trial, large bare flower beds on the lawn. This is the percipient's description: "A small pond. . . . In the middle of grass. . . . Something like a sand trap or something in a golf course. . . . A lot of grass around, very green. Trees too. . . . A sense of openness. A big wide expanse. . . . There may be a stone wall. . . . Could be some sort of park."

Trial 8, also ranked as first-place:
The final target was a florist shop, the Angel Guardian Orphanage Florist. The shop was a square-shaped building, with a pointed

roof, distinguished by four blue mosaic tile-covered columns before an almost solid glass front. Behind the glass was a large display of colorful flowers and plants. This description was probably the most accurate in terms of detail of the eight. The participant saw: "A lot of colors, small groups of colors. Lots of reds, and yellows, greens, pinks. Probably flowers. They look like they are all bunched together. . . . On display. . . . There's some kind of building. . . . Windows, poles, glass. . . . Concrete around that she is walking on. A couple of raised round things. . . . A sensation of blue."

The greatest favor that one scientist can do for another is to replicate his or her work. Dunne and Bisaha's paper was the first replication of the SRI remote-viewing research. It showed that high-quality remote viewing could be found somewhere other than our laboratories in California. A replication of this kind tends to make research results seem more real. It also answers other researchers' questions about whether reported results are simply an indication of strange happenings in some distant laboratory.

The Chicago researchers were also pleased with their results. The following year they carried out fourteen additional precognitive remote-viewing sessions. These experiments made use of several new viewers, and like the first series, they proved to be significantly successful.[9]

PRECOGNITIVE REMOTE VIEWING
OF EASTERN EUROPE

In the summer of 1976, Bisaha was traveling in the U.S.S.R. and Czecho-slovakia. He thought it would be an excellent chance to carry out a long-distance remote-viewing study. Because John and Brenda had previously had such success with their precognition study, they elected to continue with this same type of experimental protocol. They decided to carry out three remote viewings of Moscow and two of Bratislava, incorporating target distances of up to fifty-two hundred miles. The five sessions were carried out on five consecutive days.

Because of the great time difference between Russia and America, the sessions required the viewer to describe a scene and activities that would be taking place twenty-four and a half hours in the future. The viewer in the Midwest would begin a description at 8:30 in the morning, Chicago time, with the intention of describing the scene that Bisaha would be photographing at 3:00 in the afternoon of the following day, Moscow time.

These long-distance experiments, too, were judged highly successful by three independent judges. We will quote the description of the first session. Bisaha was on the Danube River in Bratislava, Czechoslovakia, and the viewer was in Wisconsin.

> The target was a "flying saucer" restaurant, a circular building raised high in the air on heavy pillars, above a bridge near the bank of the Danube River. The percipient described the experimenter as being "near water . . . a very large expanse of water . . . boats. Vertical lines like poles. . . . A circular shape like a merry-go-round or gazebo. . . . It seems to have height, maybe with poles. . . . A dark fence along a walk . . . at the top of the steps, like a walkway. . . . A boardwalk, and there is a fence along it."[10]

Bisaha and Dunne conclude their description of these experiments in their chapter in the book *Mind at Large* as follows:

> The results of these two experiments provide further evidence of the apparently widespread availability of a perceptual/communication channel in which time and distance appear to pose no barriers, and which seems to become accessible when ordinary modes of perception and communication become inoperable. It further appears that this channel can be "tuned into" by individuals with no extraordinary psychic ability.

DEFLECTING TIME'S ARROW: TIME DOES NOT "FLOW"

We agree with Olivier Costa de Beauregard of the Poincaré Institute in Paris, who has said that the apparent irreversibility of time is more "fact-like" than "law-like." That is, our view of time is the result of certain types of personal observations of events, rather than the result of time's implacable arrow.[11]

Space and time are measuring units that become real only in relation to what they measure—namely, the properties of matter and events. It is not possible to describe space without paying attention to mass, or to describe time without specifying certain events.

It is important to note that we are not arguing against the existence of irreversible processes such as chemical reactions, heat conduction, or diffusion, all of which clearly illustrate the apparent irreversibility of certain events. But there are also reversible physical processes, such as electromagnetic propagation, and the dynamic equations governing bodies that behave in accordance with Newton's laws.

Whether or not an event seems irreversible depends upon the type of event that is being observed. Therefore we resist ascribing irreversibility to time itself, rather than to the probabilistic nature of certain events. As Prigogine points out, "The structure of motion with 'randomness' on the microscopic level emerges as irreversibility on the macroscopic level."[12]

Although the evidence for the existence of precognition is excellent, we do not believe that this evidence necessarily supports the fatalistic argument that our future lives are already cast in concrete, with no opportunity for change. Precognition does not mean that there is no free will. Instead, we would like to suggest that precognition is a *forecast* rather than a prophecy. That is, it may be falsified.

If, for example, a doctor tells you, "Your appendix is about to burst, and you will die shortly," that *could* be a correct statement. However, if you want to avoid this future, you might make use of this forecast and check into a hospital. We believe that this so-called "intervention" paradox is one of the "vicious circle fallacies" described by Whitehead and Russell in the *Principia Mathematica*. [13]

The state of affairs predicted by a precognitive forecast can be true for all objects and events, excluding the forecast itself. The forecast might be said to belong to a higher logical type than the events it describes. The inclusion of a forecast into the class of things about which it is commenting can generate a paradox, in addition to falsifying the forecast. We might, therefore, distinguish between a predictive statement's being *true*, and its being *necessarily true* (at some later time).

Suppose you forecast that a person is going to do something at a later time, when even he does not know what he will do for certain. Such precognition can be accurate and successful in making a forecast, judging from the many studies of Bisaha and Dunne. However, if you take your forecast to a person who is about to carry out the actions called for by your precognition (or his own decision) and show him your forecast, he may deliberately falsify your forecast by declining to become the "effect of your fantasy." We must, therefore, conclude that there can be no such thing as a perfect forecaster, unless he is also omnipotent and has godlike psychokinetic (PK) abilities.

A true-to-life example of the possibility of retro-causal behavior is provided by philosopher Bob Brier. His story goes as follows:

> Imagine that you are at a party on Saturday night and someone who works with your good friend Smith, mentions that yesterday, Friday, he saw someone place a bomb in Smith's desk drawer. The bomb was set to go off in one hour. He also tells you that urgent business called him out of the office and he forgot to warn Smith. As a matter of fact he had forgotten about the incident until now, and doesn't know what happened to Smith. Is there anything that you can do to save your friend? Seemingly not. Either he was blown up by the bomb in which case he is dead, or he or someone else discovered the bomb and safely removed it (or the bomb did not go off, etc.), and he is now alive. In any case, there is nothing that you can do about it. *But,* if backward causality is possible, there may be something you can do to save your friend. While at the party, you could call out, "Smith, this is me warning you from the future. There is a bomb in your desk drawer. Get rid of it!" So far there is nothing impossible in the situation I have described; it is merely somewhat bizarre. But now let us imagine that you meet Smith on the street, the day after the party. He tells you of his strange experience on Friday. He was sitting at his desk and he had a vision of you at a party saying, "Smith, this is me, warning you from the future. There is a bomb in your desk drawer. Get rid of it!" He found the bomb and safely disposed of it.[14]

What would we say about such a situation, were it to actually happen? We might consider it as an example of backward causation. Something you did on Saturday (the warning called out at the party) would have caused something to happen the previous day (Smith's precognitive experience, which in turn caused him to be saved). Note, we do not suggest that you would have *changed* the past. Had Smith been blown up, then you still could have tried to save him, but it simply would not have worked.

There are at least three possible sources for precognitive information.

First, data may "come from the future," and be an example of actual precognition as we have been describing it. In this case a future event may cause you to have some sort of appropriate perception of the future, or approximate future, in advance of the event itself.

Second, precognition may be accomplished by using ordinary present-time psychic functioning to assess the world of present-time events, and then reach correct conclusions about the future using logical inference based upon the psychic information. The perceptions would appear to be precognitive, because the predictor would have access to psychic information that no one else thought was available.

Predicting natural disasters may be an example of this. In the Aberfan disaster in Wales, where a slag heap fell on a school and killed more than a hundred children, there were many reported premonitions of the event the preceding night.[15] We can assume that the avalanche was already initially underway and therefore may have been accessible by psychic functioning applied to the micro-events of the day before the disaster.

The third description of precognition data, especially from psi research, involves alleged psychokinetic (PK) control of the random-number generators (RNGs) that are used to choose the targets for experiments. Instead of forecasting the future, it is often suggested that you might psychically control the RNG that is supposed to choose your target.

Stephen Braude, a philosophy professor at the University of Maryland, deals explicitly with this problem in his book *ESP and Psychokinesis*.[16] He points out that one striking feature of the definition of precognition is that it does not distinguish precognition from possible PK—i.e., control of the RNG in the future.

With regard to explaining away precognition, our examination of the evidence for RNG PK offers little evidence to indicate that laboratory PK achieves a success rate comparable to that which has been achieved in free-response research such as the Maimonides dream studies or the remote-viewing experiments. This makes PK a poor but theoretically possible explanation.

In the precognitive studies of Bisaha and Dunne, viewers often had 50 or 60 percent of their descriptions matched in first place in groups of six trials. This would be roughly equivalent to a participant in a PK experiment with dice averaging 50 percent in his attempts to cause a given die face to come up. In actual dice experiments, and other experiments in which people attempt to use PK on RNGs, the deviation from chance expectation is rarely greater than a few percent.[17] We consider it unlikely that such a demonstrably small effect could account for the statistical significance of the precognition studies we have discussed, especially in an experimental series of only six trials.

Therefore, there appear to be few supporting data to indicate that a successful precognitive remote viewer obtains his correct matches by psychokinetically influencing the random-number generator. We feel more comfortable with a description of psi forecasting that is based upon a combination of the first two potential explanations for precognition.

Professor Robert Jahn, Dean of the School of Engineering, Brenda Dunne, and R. D. Nelson of Princeton University have just published *Precognitive Remote Perception*, a 178-page evaluation of 227 formal precognition trials. They find their data significant at "less than 10^{-11} (one in a hundred billion) by any method of scoring employed." They say, ". . . it is our conclusion that precognitive remote perception techniques can acquire statistically significant amounts of compounded information about spatially and temporally remote target locations, by means currently inexplicable by known physical mechanisms."

We can conclude from all this that there is good evidence to suggest that the future may in some cases "cause" the past, and may therefore sometimes also be felt before it occurs. This present-time experience of the future may be rare, but it strongly suggests that our customary view of linear time, in which information is only carried forward along the time line, may not be a correct picture of our world.

4

Lunch with the Soviets: From Mesmer to Salyut

His card reads:

Vitali Sevastyanov
Twice Hero of the Soviet Union
Pilot-Cosmonaut of the U.S.S.R.
Candidate of Science (Technology)
Moscow, Stellar-Town

How wonderful to have one's accomplishments so forthrightly recognized by the government!

On October 18, 1976, Vitali came to SRI to discuss some apparently psychic experiences that occurred both while he was flying his spacecraft and during his cosmonaut training. Accompanying him on his visit were Professor Lev Lupichev, a director at the Institute of Control Problems, Moscow, and Oleg Sidorenko, the Soviet vice-consul from San Francisco. We met for a lengthy lunch at SRI's beautifully appointed International Dining Room.

Six months earlier, the SRI team had published a major scientific paper in the *Proceedings of the Electrical and Electronics Engineers* (IEEE).[1] The twenty-five-page paper describing the previous six years of remote-viewing research at SRI had been immediately translated into Russian by Larissa Vilenskaya (then still living in the Soviet Union). Our report had been reprinted in the Soviet IEEE journal only a few days before our meeting with the Soviet scientists, but they had already read it thoroughly and were full of questions.

While we all enjoyed ice-cream sundaes dripping with chocolate sauce, three American psi researchers nonchalantly discussed the human, social, and political implications of psi with three Soviet scientists. The possibility of psychic espionage was never explicitly mentioned, but much of our conversation centered upon potential applications of psychic functioning, on the question of whether any information could be shielded from psychic access, and on the levels of perceptual detail (resolution) that had been achieved in psi experiments. Everyone present tried not to appear too obvious in his motivation, but each group of researchers was really trying to find out what the other was up to.

We listened as Sevastyanov described his experience of seeming to enter into telepathic communication with his fellow cosmonaut while they orbited the earth together in a Salyut spacecraft. Sevastyanov told us that while floating in his capsule, he had discovered that he apparently had only to think of a tool he needed for his comrade to hand it to him. This startling experience seemed to extend to the details of complicated plans that existed only in his mind, and that could not otherwise be known to his partner.

Another type of experience that Sevastyanov described amazed him even more. When he was training other Soviet pilots to become members of the cosmonaut corps, they rode in high-velocity centrifuges, similar to those used by American astronauts preparing for space flight. In the Soviet training exercises, Sevastyanov would "fly" in a centrifuge with each trainee, as they were subjected to various kinds of randomly programmed equipment failure during a simulated spacecraft lift-off. Sevastyanov told us he found that during these exercises he would often activate the appropriate backup systems even *before* particular equipment failures happened.

Of the three Soviet visitors, Lev Lupichev, the scientist from the Soviet Institute of Control Problems, was most familiar with SRI's past work in psi research. He asked us how we found research participants who were able to function so well psychically. We explained that we did not need to select people who were famous for being gifted psychics for our work. Rather, our hundreds of experimental trials had convinced us that psychic functioning is a normal ability, although it is generally repressed in our society; we considered psychic abilities to be latent to some degree in most people, and we had found many people who, with practice, had been able to develop these abilities to a surprisingly high level.

Lupichev wanted to know if we used drugs, hypnosis, or some other "equipment" to cause our research volunteers to develop psychic abilities. I (R.T.) tried politely to explain that it probably was easier for people to function psychically in California than in his laboratory in the Institute of Control Problems, in the Soviet Union. Lupichev's question clearly suggested that the Soviets had used all three approaches to improving psychic functioning on their own subjects.

Our visitors seemed most excited by the published finding that so many people could learn to develop psychic abilities, including even in-experienced visitors to our laboratory. Lupichev wanted to know if he could take part in such a demonstration right then and there. We ex-plained that a crowded dining room would not be the best place for an initial remote-viewing session, even with such a highly motivated research participant as himself.

The SRI researchers proposed, instead, that they do some long-distance trials between the Soviet Union and the United States. We could carry out trials in which each research team would take turns using the remote-viewing protocols to look psychically into the other's institute. Lupichev seemed to think that was a very promising suggestion, but we have not heard anything further from him.

It seemed obvious that the Soviet scientists' interest in our remote-viewing research was not casual or frivolous. Nor was there any trace of doubt in their questions about their acceptance of the existence of psi. To the contrary, they seemed to consider it important to get answers to their detailed questions about our work.

Our visitors' line of inquiry, however, reminded us of a question that several Soviet scientists had asked a member of our research team sev-eral years earlier, at the 1973 International Conference on Psychotronic Research in Prague, Czechoslovakia. The Soviet scientists had wanted to know, "What do you do to keep your subjects from cracking up or going crazy during the experiments?" Questions like these made us wonder about what the Soviets were doing to their psi research participants.

Of course, our answer to such questions is that we do not *do* anything to our remote viewers, and they do not go crazy. In fact, people who have worked with us usually consider their laboratory psychic experiences to have given them a gift of enhanced awareness that they continue to use in their everyday lives.

To understand the rationale behind the Soviet questions, it helps to know something about psychic research in the Soviet Union, and how the Soviet approach has come to differ from that of scientists in other parts of the world.

All of our remote-viewing research, and certainly most other psi research in the United States for the past several decades, has focused upon the development of mental techniques for psychically *perceiving* and *experiencing* information about things and events that are blocked from ordinary perception. An exception would be the few experiments directed at trying to affect the output of computers or random-number generators.

Psi research in the U.S.S.R., which is, of course, controlled by the Soviet government, is not primarily concerned with remote information gathering. The Soviets are already able to obtain much useful information from the American press, by talking with American scientists, and through more covert methods about which we could only speculate.

Of course, information gathering has not been ignored entirely. One year after our luncheon, *The Chicago Tribune* of August 13, 1977 describes a breakfast meeting with reporters in which then CIA Director Stanfield Turner "confirmed reports that the Russians are studying persons who claim to be able to read minds and 'teleport' themselves into secret meetings and into the future. Turner confirmed that U.S. intelligence operatives have discovered that the Soviet Union is spending money and time researching whether occult and psychic methods could be used for spying on other nations."

The Soviet psychic research effort is primarily aimed at learning to use psychic functioning to *influence human behavior*. While there is much interest in psychic *healing* among the Soviet people themselves, much of the psychic research in the U.S.S.R. has been directed toward developing psychic abilities as a means of remote behavior influence.

MESMER IN MOTHER RUSSIA

The Soviets have a long and continuing history of experiments with telepathy and hypnosis at a distance. In these studies, hypnotists have attempted to influence or control the feelings or behavior of distant persons, most of whom did not know they were being used as subjects in the experiments.

As long ago as 1778, Viennese physician Franz Mesmer found that he could apparently cure many of his patients' ills by merely pointing his forefinger at them. His medical treatments involved "magnetized" water, seemingly magical gestures in which he moved his hands up and down in the air over the patient's body, and trance techniques that were the forerunners of modern hypnotherapy.

Many of Mesmer's discoveries had been for centuries the common property of shamans and medicine men throughout the world. To Europeans of the Enlightenment, however, the idea that one person could put another into a trance was electrifying.

Mesmer's findings were looked upon as both horrifying and fascinating. They were horrifying because Europe was just then in the process of separating itself from the last vestiges of superstition and witchcraft. The last known witch-burning in an English-speaking country had occurred not very many years earlier, in 1730.[2] The reappearance of what seemed to be magical practices threatened to undo the good works of the Encyclopedists, who had predicted that belief in the occult would fall before the demonstrable successes of the Industrial Revolution. Even in the nineteenth century, the well-respected English physicist John Tyndall had made materialism into a religion. He denounced even the investigation of Spiritualism as "intellectual whoredom."[3]

Hypnosis and animal magnetism were abominations in the eyes of the Rationalists. Yet, medical doctors found these phenomena to be incomparably compelling. The reason for this is easy to understand. Medicine in the late 1700s was generally not very successful. That is, a good doctor could at best tell a patient the name of his disease and describe the probable outcome. Yet, Dr. Mesmer repeatedly demonstrated that he could appear to "miraculously" cure a wide variety of very sick people without using leeches or bloodletting, which were commonly prescribed by other medical practitioners. Such success, however unorthodox, generated considerable envy—and further experimentation.

The history of Mesmer and animal magnetism is well recorded in many volumes, especially in Brian Inglis's fascinating book *Natural and Supernatural.* [4] What interests us here is that as a result of Mesmer's work, physicians all over Eastern and Western Europe began to experiment with medical applications of hypnosis. This research led directly to the discovery that not only could one person cause another to fall into a trance, but that this effect could also apparently be induced from a distance!

In 1818, D. Velinski, a Russian physician, surgeon, and professor of physiology at the Imperial Academy of St. Petersburg, wrote extensively about this subject in his book, *Shivotniy Magnetizm (Animal Magnetism).* He stated that of all of the physical discoveries of the past centuries, animal magnetism was the most important.

Velinski was one of the earliest writers to discuss the remote induction of hypnotic trances. He described the many methods of trance induction that were then in use, and pointed out that "mental action alone could also produce magnetic sleep, since it has been shown experimentally that a magnetizer could act on his patient at a distance by simply concentrating his thought."[5] Velinski, however, considered this to be a dangerous practice, and urged that "it should not be used for any other reason than healing the sick." This makes us wonder what other possible uses for mental influence at a distance Velinski had in mind.

During the years immediately following the 1779 publication of Mesmer's original *Animal Magnetism,* there continued to be much medical interest in the hypnotic treatment of patients throughout Europe. Russian research in this area was carried out almost entirely by physicians, since the practice of "magnetism" by anyone outside the medical profession was forbidden by law.

In his *Abnormal Hypnotic Phenomena,* Eric Dingwall (ed.) describes the case of an experienced nineteenth-century Russian magnetizer Andrey Ivanovitch Pashkov, who spent much of his life in prison because of his interest in these activities. The book describes Pashkov's 1845 treatment of an aristocratic Russian woman, the sister of Count Korsikov. The woman had an advanced rheumatic-arthritic condition which had increasingly threatened her health for over a decade. Even the initial magnetic sleep induced by Pashkov seemed to greatly improve the woman's condition, according to her brothers, who were present at the meeting. The woman is reported to have recovered, after which she is said to have remained in magnetic rapport with Pashkov. "Although he lived some 300 miles away, at his command she would fall into a somnambulistic state," it is related.[6]

By 1898, experimental hypnosis research was being carried out in several Russian laboratories. One experiment of this period that is still being done in Eastern Bloc countries today was described by Dingwall. Experiments carried out by Dr. M. B. Pogorelski examined hypnosis at a distance: "One of his subjects, a student, Mr. L.F., was told, while in the hypnotic state, that his sensitivity would be localized in a glass of water which he could not see, but nevertheless every time that the surface of the water was touched with a knife he reacted as though he felt a sharp pain."[7]

One of the easiest techniques that the nineteenth-century magnetizers were able to demonstrate involved putting good hypnotic subjects into trances with almost no visible signal from the hypnotizer. This led researchers to become interested in finding out just how little suggestion was needed to effect a change from waking to sleep in a research subject. This question was pursued not only in Russia but also in France and England. The formation of the Society for Psychical Research in England, in 1882, was largely the result of interest in the various apparently psychic occurrences that were associated with hypnosis, in addition to a widespread interest in séances during that period.

During the nineteenth century, Western European scientists began to use hypnosis for medical purposes and also to examine apparent psychic functioning in the laboratory as a separate issue from hypnosis. Russian researchers, however, viewed these two areas as intrinsically related. This may explain why a Soviet scientist visiting an American psi research laboratory today would want to know how the researchers manipulate experimental participants in order to make them function psychically. Perhaps those researchers have not yet realized that psychic abilities do not have to be the result of hypnotic manipulation.

Experiments that feature induced pain or behavioral manipulation at a distance have been the distinguishing characteristic of almost all official Soviet psi research since the early 1920s. At that time Dr. L. L. Vasiliev joined the Leningrad Institute for Brain Research, under the guidance of the eminent Soviet researcher V. M. Bechterev. Vasiliev's work during the ensuing forty years is summarized in his important and comprehensive book *Experiments in Mental Suggestion.* [8]

Vasiliev tells us that the first public demonstration of "Mental Induction to Sleep and Awakening" ever held in the U.S.S.R. took place in 1924 at the All-Russian Congress of Psychoneurologists, Psychologists, and

Teachers. This Leningrad demonstration was carried out in a lecture auditorium by Professor K. I. Platonov, who also worked with Bechterev at the Institute for Brain Research. Professor Platonov described his demonstration in a 1962 letter to Vasiliev:

> The subject M. sat at the presidential table, talking with Professor A. V. Gerver. She sat sideways, while Professor G. faced the audience. Behind her back, at a distance of about twenty feet there was a blackboard, edge-on in relation to the spectators. I stood behind the blackboard, in full view of the audience, but outside the range of sight of the subject. It had been arranged with the audience, prior to the arrival of M., that when I silently covered my face with my hands, this would mean that I had begun the experiments of mentally sending her to sleep. Having covered my face, I formed a mental image of the subject M. falling asleep while talking to Professor G. I strenuously concentrated my attention on this for about one minute. The result was perfect: M. fell asleep within a few seconds. Awakening was effected in the same way. This was repeated several times.

Platonov's experiment could in principle have been compromised by inadvertent signaling to the subject from the audience. His demonstration does show, however, that the Russians seriously considered the possibility of mental influence over behavior at a distance as long as sixty years ago.

In a similar letter from the same period, Dr. K. D. Kotkov also reminisced about the 1924 Russian experiments in mental influence. Like most subjects in the Soviet experiments, the participants described here were not told the nature of the tests in which they were taking part. In many cases these subjects were hospital patients. As Kotkov explained, in this experimental series the subject was a perfectly healthy but predominantly depressed student, "a perfect somnambulist." He repeated that she used to fall asleep instantly under the influence of mental suggestions transmitted to her and that "she remembered nothing." The hypnotist used to sit in a comfortable armchair in complete silence and mentally murmur the words of suggestion, "sleep, sleep, sleep." The subject used to be invited to the experiments under pretexts which could not suggest to her the real reason she had been asked. At the actual times of the experiment the girl's attention was kept occupied, as much as possible, by anything that might interest her. She was given no opportunity to concentrate on anything of her own choosing. The first experiments were carried out in the same building. They were separated by only a few rooms but then passed on to experiments in which they were at different ends of town. According to Kotkov the success was the same.

In his laboratory at the Institute for Brain Research, Vasiliev conducted hundreds of similar experiments. These eventually culminated in a lengthy series in which he was closeted in an electrically shielded enclosure while the subject to be put to sleep was several rooms away. Vasiliev was concerned, as the Soviets still are today, with the possibility that psychic communication may be transmitted by ordinary electromagnetic radiation. As we explained earlier, this is conceivable but we think it very unlikely, based upon the research evidence.

In the 1930s, in order to examine the electromagnetic hypothesis, Vasiliev constructed a cage made of steel sheets welded together. The upper half of the cage could be lifted off by means of a pulley in the ceiling. The experimenter climbed into the open box formed by the bottom, and the top was then lowered onto it. The top fitted onto a trough that was filled with mercury, to assure perfect electrical contact. The box was light-tight and pressure-tight and had no electrical input or output. (Under these conditions, it is surprising that Vasiliev did not suffocate, or die of mercury poisoning.)

In the next room, the subject to be put to sleep was told to squeeze a rubber balloon rhythmically, which would pneumatically put a mark on a moving chart that was recording the experiment. At a prearranged time the experimenter in the box would press on the side of the box to close a switch that would also mark the chart, and indicate the start of his efforts to put the subject to sleep.

The experiment's success would be indicated by the subject's no longer squeezing the balloon. After this the experimenter would wait a randomly determined period of time and attempt to mentally awaken the subject, who would then resume squeezing the balloon as though nothing had happened, according to Vasiliev. The subjects in these experiments were apparently never aware that they had been put to sleep. From his published data, it usually took from two to three minutes of concentration to put a subject to sleep (or to wake the subject up).

Vasiliev's most famous experiment of this series was conducted between Leningrad and Sevastopol, a distance of seventeen hundred kilometers. Two experiments were planned. However, in the first case, the distant hypnotist was ill and did not send any message to the subject. The subject showed no signs of falling asleep. Two days later, Vasiliev reports, the experiment was carried out on schedule, and the subject fell asleep and awakened at the times that the distant experimenter had noted for his mental suggestions.

Vasiliev's experiments provided early evidence which strongly suggests that neither electromagnetic shielding nor distance diminishes the accuracy or reliability of psychic functioning. This evidence is still being accumulated in studies such as the submarine experiment with the two submerged viewers, described earlier.

As Larissa Vilenskaya discusses later, another Soviet experimental *modus operandi* has often been to shock a sender electrically or to have a sender imagine that he is choking or bludgeoning a receiving person, who is usually a friend of the sender. The receiver is then monitored for the presence of potentially adverse physiological effects of this attempted psychic manipulation. Experiments have also repeatedly been carried out to raise burns psychically on the arms of volunteer observers.

At the 1979 Conference of Psychotronic Research in São Paulo, Brazil, Zdenek Rejdak described a recent knife-in-the-water experiment that he had conducted. Rejdak is the best-known Czech psi researcher, and is the organizer of the International Psychotronic Conferences. In Rejdak's experiment a hypnotized subject was asked to try to have an out-of-body experience and focus his attention upon a jar of water in the next room.

In this modern version of the nineteenth-century experiments, the subject was connected to an electromyograph (EMG) that showed the level of muscular activity occurring throughout his body. When the subject said through the intercom that he was experiencing the jar of water, the experimenters stabbed an icepick into the water. They noted with interest that the subject's entire body was seen to twitch when the icepick entered into his remote focus of attention.

A similar experiment was conducted by hypnotist Vladimir Raikov in Moscow in the late 1960s. Dr. Raikov hypnotized a subject and gave her a suggestion that her sensitivity was transferred into a glass of water located in another room. At a randomly selected moment, Raikov's assistant stuck a needle into the water. When he did this, the subject reportedly screamed in severe pain. When the subject's actual hand was stuck with the needle, she apparently showed no reaction.

We do not believe that Rejdak and Raikov intended any harm to their subjects by conducting this experiment. Nor do we believe that Soviet psi researchers are malevolent in shocking their volunteer subjects to study the effects of this upon distant psychically receptive people. These experiments are simply a result of the Soviets' behavioristic and Pavlovian view of human activity, as consisting entirely of stimuli and responses.

A well-documented example of this type of approach in the United States involves a reported psychic healer named Dean Kraft. In 1975 Kraft was taking part in experiments at a San Francisco medical research institute. He was to try, psychically, to lower the blood pressure and heart rate of a laboratory rat in a Plexiglas cage. Kraft was unfortunately not given any feedback about his progress during this experiment. The observers, however, had an opportunity to watch for twenty minutes, and record the steady decrease of the rat's heart rate, all the way to zero. At that point the researchers told Kraft that he had killed the rat. Even though Kraft readily admits his loathing for rats, he feels that if he had been given any kind of feedback during the experiment, he would have ended the session with the rat still alive.[9]

THINKING CAN MAKE IT SO

Since psychic functioning has definitely been shown to exist, only a small stretch of imagination is required to understand that an individual who is competent in telepathy might possibly introduce his thoughts into your awareness. We think it is possible that if you have not learned to recognize the difference between your own thought processes and psychically generated information, you might respond to outside telepathic inputs as if they had originated within your own mind.

Such responses could potentially have a measurable impact upon your feelings and behavior. In Chapter 10 we will, therefore, discuss ways in which you might separate your own feelings, thoughts, memory and imagination from actual psychic impressions. This ability is as vital for successful remote viewing as it may be for psychic self-defense.

Professor Yuri Gulyaev is a director of the Soviet Institute of Radio-Engineering and Electronics. He is also one of the best-informed people in the world on the state of the art in psi research. He is a charming and cheery Russian gentleman, and we were delighted to spend an afternoon with him in November 1978.

Professor Gulyaev came to SRI to discuss his latest thoughts about psi research, or psychotronics, as the Soviets call it. We had a very good meeting with this highly regarded physicist, who discussed with us theories of psychic functioning with a full understanding of the latest ideas in modern physics, in addition to the latest results of experimental psi research.

Although the SRI team had just published the successful experiment in which messages were psychically sent to a submerged submarine, Gulyaev was uninterested in seeing the film of this exciting experiment. He said that he was completely familiar with our research, and had come to SRI principally "to see what kind of men" we were, rather than to hear about specific experiments.

Although Gulyaev is mainly known in technical circles for his research in acoustics and crystallography, he and his institute co-director, Yuri Kobserev, a member of the Soviet Academy of Sciences, have carried out many different kinds of experiments with Nina Kulagina, the celebrated Soviet PK subject. In one of Gulyaev's more interesting experiments, he had Kulagina try to affect the passage of a surface acoustic wave as it traveled along an acoustic-delay line.

In this experiment, a sound signal would enter the array of crystals at one end, pass along their surface, and emerge at the other end. The passage of the sound wave was monitored by an oscilloscope, with the whole delay line under a glass jar. Gulyaev was pleased to tell us that Kulagina was regularly able to shift the phase of the signal as viewed on the oscilloscope screen, by focusing her attention on the crystals under the jar.

Gulyaev described these experiments with great exactness and care, just as he did when discussing experiments in which he said Kulagina raised burns on the arms and backs of skeptical visiting scientists. In these latter experiments, Kulagina used the same type of mental concentration that she used to apparently perturb the acoustic beam. Gulyaev also described several other types of psychokinetic experiments in which, he said, individuals were able to move or even levitate objects without touching them. He showed us photographs of apparently floating rulers and balls that he said he had personally seen acted upon by the two Soviet psychics, Elvira Schevchik and the well-known Boris Ermolaev.

.   .   .

Shortly after his visit to us, Professor Gulyaev became an associate member of the Soviet Academy of Sciences and director of his institute. In keeping with his great interest in psychokinesis, it appears that there is a new official Soviet approval for the investigation of psychokinetic effects on living systems.

The Soviet Union has many people who are well respected as psychic healers. We hope that the new Soviet acceptance of this important field will give their psi research in it a turn toward more humanitarian directions and away from stopping frog's hearts, starving mice, raising burns on visitors' skin, and the other seemingly aggressive applications described in the epilogue.

Before he left, Gulyaev wanted to take pictures of the SRI psi researchers in front of the laboratory building, especially including our very attractive secretary.

In the Authors' Note at the end of this book we present an update on this material based on our recent trip to the Soviet Union.

PSYCHOTRONIC CONFERENCE IN BRATISLAVA

In June 1983, I [R.T.] attended the Fifth International Conference on Psychotronic Research, in Bratislava, Czechoslovakia, which gave me another opportunity to talk with Eastern researchers about their latest ideas and experiments.

The International Association for Psychotronic Research (IAPR) has broad interests, covering many borderline areas of science. These include, principally, psychotronic interactions with physics (the physics of consciousness and mechanisms of psychic functioning), medicine (psychic healing and dermo-optic perception or "skin" vision), and geology (dowsing for water, natural resources, and favorable places to build houses or barns).

The organization is now ten years old and has held five conferences attracting international participation. These were in Prague (1973), Monaco (1975), Tokyo (1977), São Paulo (1979), and this most recent one in Bratislava in 1983. The president and founder of the IAPR is Dr. Zdenek Rejdak, from Czechoslovakia. The two vice-presidents are Dr. Heinrich Huber, from Austria, and myself. The three scientific directors are Dr. Shiuji Inomata from Japan, Dr. Erik Ingenbergs from the GDR, and Prof. Fedor Romachov from the USSR.

At the June 1983 conference, there were approximately three hundred attendees at three simultaneous sessions for three of the five days of the meeting. These sessions were divided as follows: I—Psychotronics and Medicine; II—Psychotronics, Psychology, Pedagogy, and Creativity; and III—Psychotronics, Physics, and Methodology. There were approximately seventy-five papers presented on these topics.

During the conference I was able to visit a striking remote-viewing target site that was used in an experiment conducted by Mr. John Bisaha and Brenda Dunne in 1976. For their series of long-distance remote-viewing experiments, Bisaha traveled in the USSR and in Czechoslovakia. As we discussed earlier, one of his targets was a circular restaurant on a bridge tower high above the Danube River in Bratislava, the 1983 conference city. It was thrilling for me to visit this exotic target, the Café Bystrica, and observe for myself that the distance separating the viewer and the target didn't interfere with the accuracy of her perception. The viewer in this experiment was six thousand miles away in Wisconsin. As you will recall, she described the target's location as ". . . near . . . a very large expanse of water . . . boats. . . . vertical lines like poles . . . a circular shape like a merry-go-round or gazebo. . . . it seems to have height."

At the conference, two Soviet researchers, Dr. André Berezin, a biochemist, and Dr. Konstantine Goubarev, a theoretical physicist, told me about a variety of interesting projects. The one I found most striking was an experiment in apparent rat telepathy, in which two groups of caged rats were housed a mile apart. Each group had been conditioned to move to the left side of their cage when a red light was turned on, to avoid an electric shock to their feet. After both groups were reliably conditioned to this response, a computer-controlled experiment was carried out using individual rats from each group. The researchers found that when one rat was randomly signaled and shocked, his brother rat (litter mate) in the distant cage would also move to the left side of his cage. The timing signals and selection of which rats were to be shocked were controlled by a central computer and sent to the cage controllers via phone lines. A similarly successful experiment had been carried out several years before by Leutin in the Soviet Union, with human subjects also conditioned by electric shocks (described by Vilenskaya later). This appears to be a serious, well-thought-out, and well-controlled experiment.

A second experimental investigation was carried out in a hospital in which continued research is being done on the effects of electromagnetic radiation on consciousness. In this work, an 18 KHz oscillator was modulated with different types of stochastic (random) noise. The output of the generator was brought near the patients' heads, apparently causing them to have "mystical or religious types of experiences." In other experiments with electromagnetic generators, it was found that heart attacks could be induced in susceptible rats, and relief from hypoxia obtained in rats suffering from oxygen deprivation.

We also learned from Guy Playfair, an English researcher at the conference, about a Soviet invention called Lida-4, which is a signal generator producing 100 Hz modulation in a 40 MHz carrier. According to a report from Dr. Ross Adey, this device put an entire hall full of people to sleep in fifteen minutes.

Dr. Zdenek Rejdak spoke to the initial session about the desirability of finding physiological correlates to dowsing. He decribed several approaches to this task. Dowsing and prospecting for oil and minerals with psi was a recurring theme at the conference. It seems clear that dowsing on the site of interest with a dowsing rod in hand, map dowsing, and purely mental dowsing for the answer to specific questions are all aspects of the same psi process, and can all be equally successful. A finding described by Dr. Edith Jurka, an American psychiatrist, was the persistent, stable, and symmetric low-frequency (delta) EEG output of successful dowsers. Rejdak says that anyone can learn to do dowsing, but that one should beware of occultists and secret societies who claim to have all the answers. There was also a discussion of dowsing for thought forms. In this experiment, a researcher formed a mental image of a wall someplace in his office. A dowser with whom he was working then called him on the telephone and correctly told him the location of the wall, as he dowsed over a drawing of the experimenter's office.

It was evident that the 1982 paper "The Persistent Paradox of Psychic Phenomena: An Engineering Perspective" had a great effect on both researchers and policy makers. This paper on remote viewing and psychokinesis was published in the March 1982 *Proceedings of the IEEE* by Dean Robert Jahn of Princeton University.

Several speakers stressed the position of IAPR in favor of understanding nature rather than humbling it, and studying the boundary between inner and outer self. Also, a clear desire for openness and cooperation—rather than for developing military uses of psi—was expressed by many speakers at the conference. We certainly agree with this position.

5

Viewing Little Objects: A Step Toward Harnessing Psi

HOW DOES A VIEWER FIND THE TARGET?

A lot of progress has been made since the SRI psi research group last met with visitors from the Soviet Union. We have learned quite a bit about the kind of information that viewers need in order to focus psychically upon distant targets. We have found that people can use their psychic abilities to describe not only remote locations, but hidden objects. And that may be the key to harnessing psychic functioning for many kinds of real-world applications.

At first, in the remote-viewing experiments described earlier, viewers were asked to describe distant locations in the San Francisco Bay area and in various parts of the world. We did this primarily in an effort to understand the nature and capabilities of psychic functioning.

In some cases, viewers were psychically "pointed" to target sites by sending experimenters to the sites to act as beacons for the viewers to home in on. In other cases, viewers were given the geographical coordinates (latitude and longitude) of sites anywhere on the planet, to be described during experimental sessions. In numerous experiments, these two targeting approaches proved equally accurate.

Then researchers began to wonder if the use of geographical coordinates might not be a kind of superstitious—that is, unnecessary—behavior on the part of experimenters. These coordinates are a completely arbitrary grid laid out on our globe by geographers, so if a viewer can give an accurate description of a location demarcated only by coordinates, it might reflect a more general ability to provide psychic information about targets that are identified in any arbitrary way. It would also be meaningless to conduct trials in which the interviewer reading the coordinates to the viewer had prior knowledge of what the target location was. In such a case, the interviewer might inadvertently cue the viewer by providing subtle reinforcement for descriptive elements he knew to be correct. Furthermore, a viewer who was very well versed in global geography could not help but use the geographical coordinates as a source of non-psychic information about the target site. So it was essential to conduct remote viewing sessions in which both the viewer and the interviewer were equally blind about the identity of the target site for each session.

Several experimental series were carried out at SRI to examine the effects of an arbitrary designation of remote-viewing targets having no relation to any existing coordinate system that could have been known to the viewer. The results of these experiments were first presented to the 1979 Annual Convention of the Parapsychological Association, and the International Psychotronics Conference, in São Paulo, Brazil.[1]

REMOTE VIEWING OF TARGETS
SMALLER THAN A BREADBOX

Hella Hammid was chosen to be the viewer in all three of the experiments in this series. The conditions in these experiments were very different from those of earlier remote-viewing studies. For the first time at SRI, not only were arbitrary coordinates used to designate target locations, but the targets themselves were small objects rather than geographical locations. It was, therefore, important to carry out this series with a viewer who had established a track record of accuracy and reliability in remote viewing.

As the target selector for the first experiment, I (R.T.) worked from a prepared target list assembled with the help of two other SRI researchers. Because I had known Hella for many years, since before the first experiments with her at SRI, I was the person most likely to be able to select specific objects that she would find aesthetically pleasing and interesting to describe.

For example, because Hella is a sensitive and artistic person whom I know to be opposed to guns and violence of any sort, it would not be a good idea to use a gun as a target object. Hella would probably not want to experience that kind of target either directly or psychically.

I visited several local toy and hardware stores and collected sixteen objects for the target pool. As in the geographical experiments, it was important for the target objects to be different from each other, but not too different. Hella could not assume that because the target might be a clock for one session, it would not also be a circular object during the next session. The objects are shown on page 87. I had no further involvement in the experiment as either interviewer or judge, once the target pool was assembled.

Even though we generally do not like to work with target pools (as we discussed earlier), the objects were housed in a wooden box divided into sixteen one-foot cubes in a four-by-four array as shown on page 87. The rows and columns were designated A, B, C, D; 1, 2, 3, 4. For each remote-viewing session, Hella was asked to describe the object in a randomly chosen cell, such as cell A3 or B4.

Before we ran this experiment, all the objects were turned over to a person who was not otherwise associated with the SRI psi research project. This woman kept the objects locked in her laboratory in a separate wing of the SRI Radio Physics building. She was also responsible for placing each object in its own randomly chosen cell of the matrix. At the start of the experiment, therefore, she was the only person who knew which objects had finally been assigned to each cell.

The interviewer, Hal Puthoff, who worked with Hella during each day's trial, was kept totally ignorant of the objects in the target pool and their assignments to the cells in the grid. At the beginning of each session, he would generate the two target coordinates, say B and 3, by means of an electronic random-number generator (RNG). He would then ask Hella to describe the contents of that particular target cell. Six sessions were carried out in this study. The six randomly generated targets were located in cells D2 (eyeglasses), A1 (compass), B3 (book), B2 (plant), D3 (doll), and D1 (trumpet).

As usual, Hella tape-recorded her remote-viewing descriptions, and was also encouraged to make drawings. At the end of a ten-minute viewing period, the interviewer would call the person who had the targets and ask her to bring the target object designated by that day's coordinates. The person in charge of the targets would then go to the matrix of objects, select the proper one, and carry it to the laboratory, where Hella and her interviewer would be waiting for feedback.

Each tape-recorded session was transcribed, and the six texts were given to an independent judge, who was asked to rank the unmarked transcripts from 1 to 6, corresponding to her opinion of whether the transcripts were a good or a poor match to each of the six objects. Using this evaluation method, the judge was able to rate four of the transcripts in a correct first-place match with their correct object. This is a significant

4 × 4 array of objects used in coordinate box experiment.

departure from what one would expect by a purely random matching of transcripts and objects, with odds of almost one hundred to one against chance.

As an example of the quality of Hella's successful descriptions of the objects in this experiment, we can report her comments in each of the four first-place transcripts. In the first trial, Hella described and drew what she summarized with the statement, "It's like eyeglasses. Two things that are round, that belong together." The target was indeed a pair of eyeglasses.

For the second correctly matched target, a book, Hella described "flat features, like sheets of metal connected somehow." She also made a drawing that resembles the pages of an open book.

When the target was a Raggedy Ann doll, Hella described something "velvety, feeling . . . spongy texture, soft, resilient, [having] mid-calf boots on . . . pliable and floppy, [with] knots of material. There are just layers on top of each other." She correctly drew the doll's boot, with the striped sock above it.

For the fourth correctly matched target, a brass trumpet, Hella described "a gold bell-shaped object, brass." The other two targets, which were not correctly matched by the judge, were a compass and a plant.

This experiment offers good evidence that a viewer can psychically describe target objects when provided only with a set of arbitrary coordinates to designate the objects' locations. However, we cannot exclude the possible effects of feedback at the end of each session. This might allow the viewer to "look" a few minutes into her future to determine which target she will soon be handed. In any event, this experiment does show that there is nothing magical about the earth's latitude and longitude coordinates. They are merely functional.

This experiment also suggests that *any* unambiguous designation of a target may elicit an appropriate remote-viewing description. In fact, in recent experimental sessions, interviewers have simply told viewers, "I have a target that needs a description." Even with such a cryptic instruction as this, many viewers are able to give excellent psychic descriptions of target sites and objects. We conducted our first formal series of geographical remote-viewing sessions of this type in 1980. The viewer (Keith Harary) accurately described and drew six sites in various parts of the planet, including two beaches—one with "coarse yellow sand" and the other with "fine white sand,"—both correctly, as well as a fishing village on a frozen fjord, a row of columns in Yemen, a desert, and Canyonlands

National Park, all excellently described without any information other than the above statement. Of course, as the interviewer, I did not know which target sites were in the pool.

In appears that our former almost slavish adherence to elaborate procedures of directing viewers to targets—using outbound experimenters, or providing coordinates of target sites in degrees, minutes, and seconds—was an unnecessary ritual. If so, it is not much different from using the Ganzfeld technique or elaborate progressive-relaxation procedures to elicit psychic functioning. In our case, the ritual may be as much for the benefit of the experimenter as for that of the viewer.

All of these strategies work, yet none of them is necessary, in our opinion. As our research progresses, we will continue to tease out any ritualistic elements from our procedures that we think can be done away with. We will also try to better identify and understand those elements which presently seem indispensable to good remote-viewing results.

REMOTE VIEWING OF SMALL OBJECTS IN FILM CANS

What color is a piece of unexposed color film? In order for film to have a color, some light must illuminate it, but then the film is exposed! Similarly, how can a remote viewer correctly describe the color of a small object that is sealed in a metal 35mm film container that admits no light? This question was dealt with in a second experiment with small target objects. The experiment also explored whether the size of target objects affects the quality of remote-viewing descriptions.

This time, the very small objects were placed in each of ten metal film cans. The objects were selected and sealed in the cans by a person who was not at all involved with the SRI remote-viewing experiments. The sealed cans were then delivered to the experimental team at SRI, and a number was placed on each one. Thus, at the outset of the experiment, no one anywhere knew the contents of a specific numbered can.

For each session, as in the procedure for local remote-viewing experiments with geographical targets, the outbound experimenter would use a random-number generator to obtain a target number. He would then take this number to the lab secretary, who would open a safe and give him the can marked with the right number. The beacon, without knowing what was in the can, would then put it in his pocket, go to the park an eighth of a mile away, and wait for ten minutes. Back in the laboratory,

Hella Hammid would attempt to describe the contents of the can.

Some of the ritualistic behavior in this experiment may be described as follows: If the metal film can for each session had simply been placed on a laboratory table in front of the viewer, she would have been immediately confronted with a seemingly impossible task—looking through a metal can. Hella would be forced into the Superman mode of trying to look through metal with X-ray vision. We believe that this would not be a state of mind conducive to good psychic functioning.

Instead, she was asked to do something she was used to doing well—to describe a remote site. This time, it just happened to be the interior of a 35mm film can.

Since I (R.T.) was ignorant of the contents of the target pool, I could ask Hella questions to facilitate her descriptions. They were tape-recorded, then transcribed and combined with her drawings for later evaluation. At the end of each viewing period, the beacon would return to the lab with his sealed film can. We would then open the can so Hella could see what the target object had been for that session.

We had decided to divide these sessions for judging into two series of five each, because ranking more than half a dozen items is more than almost any judge can humanly handle. In the film-can experiment, a judge was asked to rate each transcript from first to last place against each of the objects. Thus the judge would determine which transcript she felt best matched each object.

In the first series of five sessions, four of the transcripts received first-place matches to their target objects and one received a second-place match. This is a significant departure from chance, with odds of better than fifty to one against these matches occurring randomly. The second set was not quite significantly matched, but when taken together, the two sets of sessions still yielded a significant outcome, with odds of better than twenty to one against chance.

As an example of the quality of some of the descriptions obtained in this experiment we show the results of the first five trials on page 91. Each caption contains a quotation from the first paragraph of Hella's description. For a spool and pin, we have: "It's definitely something thin and long . . . with like a nailhead at the end . . . silver-colored." For a curled-up leaf: "A nautilus shape with a tail." For a leather-belt key-ring: "The strongest image I get is like a belt." For a can of sand: "Like a miniature tower . . . scalloped bottom . . . light beige." And for the gray-and-white quill: "Like a penguin . . . gray and black and white . . . it's organic and

 SPOOL AND PIN	 "IT'S DEFINITELY SOMETHING THIN AND LONG. . . WITH A NAIL HEAD AT THE END . . . SILVERED COLORED."
 CURLED UP LEAF	 "A NAUTILUS SHAPE WITH A TAIL."
 LEATHER BELT KEYRING	 "THE STRONGEST IMAGE I GET IS LIKE A BELT."
 CAN OF SAND	 "LIKE A MINIATURE TOWER . . . SCALLOPED BOTTOM . . . LIGHT BEIGE."
 GREY AND WHITE QUILL	 "LIKE A PENGUIN . . . GREY AND BLACK AND WHITE . . . POINTED OR SLIGHTLY ROUNDED OFF AT THE TOP . . . OPEN OR POINTED AT THE BOTTOM."

Target objects in metal containers (left). Captions under viewer drawings (right) are quotes from first paragraphs of transcripts.

has been alive . . . pointed or slightly rounded off at the top . . . open or pointed at the bottom."

The film-can results offer evidence that a viewer can psychically perceive and describe objects down to the size of a pin, inside a light-tight container viewed from an eighth of a mile away. She was also able to tell the color of certain objects.

When the results of this experiment were first published, it appeared as though the primary information channel for remote viewing might be precognition of the feedback. However, we have recently seen some excellent descriptions of small objects in experiments in which a viewer was never given any feedback, and the experimenter working with the viewer also had not seen the targets. Consequently, direct clairvoyance cannot be ruled out.

REMOTE VIEWING OF MICROSCOPIC OBJECTS

This third small-object experiment with Hella at SRI was conducted to explore further the extent to which the size of the target affects a viewer's psychic perceptions. The targets in this experiment make the pinhead in the previous experiment seem like a baseball.

The target materials used for this experiment started out as posters that were for sale by a local lithographer. Each of the twelve posters was photographed and reduced to a 1mm square dot on a photographic slide. Microdots such as these are mainly used by spies, who can glue a microdot to a period in a letter, and thereby send a great deal of information in a very hard-to-spot manner.

This experiment was designed to see if an experienced remote viewer could describe the pictorial information on a microdot inside an opaque, double-sealed envelope. A microdot cannot be read with the naked eye, and one can project a microdot on a screen with a slide projector and still see nothing but a black dot, so a microscope was needed to give the viewer feedback at the end of each session.

The procedure in this experiment was the same as in the film-can study just described. After the beacon returned from the park to the laboratory, the microdot target would be put under a microscope. The viewer, interviewer, and beacon would then see what the target picture had been.

After the six trials in this experiment were completed, the transcripts and drawings were given to a judge for evaluation. The judge used a scale of 0 to 100 to indicate how well he thought each transcript corresponded to each of the original full-sized target posters. As always, the judge did not know the correct target-transcript assignments.

The judge gave the highest ratings to four out of the six corresponding pairs of targets and transcripts, yielding another statistically significant result. Here are excerpts from two transcripts rated 100 percent: When the target was a Swiss alpine ski area, Hella said, "It is like a white large area . . . a mountain encircled with highways . . . or a snow-covered hillock. . . . White mountain with lines . . . natural . . . but it was used and adapted and fitted out with some machinery." A large photograph of an open hand she described this way: "A lot of earth colors, brown. A five-pointed base with a round thing fitting about it, it has five legs. . . . It has five points."[2]

It is interesting to note that Hella correctly described the hand poster as brown and earth-colored—even though the microdot on which she was supposedly targeting was a black-and-white transparency. It is not easy to make high-resolution microdots on color film.

We cannot say for sure what the actual source of psychic information was in this experiment—the microdot or the original poster. We also do not know whether Hella made contact with the target by means of remote viewing or precognition of her feedback.

Therefore it is not possible to conclude for certain that in remote viewing a person can decipher a submillimeter target. However, we can say that there is no evidence that reducing the size of the presumed target to millimeter dimensions greatly diminishes the quality of remote viewing.

A correction to the statistical assessment of this last experiment should perhaps be made because the interviewer (R.T.) was also the target selector. As a result, I knew the twelve pictures in the target pool, though I never knew which one was the target. However, after Hella had gone through five targets, my own chance of guessing the next day's target had increased from one in twelve to one in six. There is no evidence that this allowed me to help Hella, since her scores actually got worse rather than better as we went through the sessions.

HOW TO USE PSI:
ASSOCIATIVE REMOTE VIEWING

We described associative remote viewing (ARV) in Chapter 2, when viewers in a submerged submarine responded to encoded messages from beacons on land. In ARV, a viewer is not asked to directly provide information of interest, but instead to describe an object that has been *linked* with the desired information for a particular session. After the description is completed and the correct answer is known, the viewer is told about or shown the correct object.

In this approach, the viewer need never be concerned with ascertaining the actual information. For example, in an oil-drilling project, an investor might want to know which of six sites should be drilled first, which would be the most productive. By definition, there will be one "best" well, and that is the one that everyone would like to start with.

But if we asked a viewer to describe which well would be best, his response might well be "How should I know?" His psychic impressions would probably be affected by his own ideas about what a successful well site looks like, in addition to the hopes and judgments of everyone else concerned. He would potentially have to cope with a great deal of mental noise—from his own analysis of the situation. He might also experience psychic noise in the form of telepathic misinformation from the other people associated with the drilling project.

One way to overcome these problems may be to give the viewer a totally different kind of task, but one that still provides the information we want. We can tell the viewer that we have linked a small object with each of the six well sites, and that eventually all the sites will be explored. When that exploration is finished, we will know which is the best site, and can then show the viewer the object associated with it. Our request to the viewer now is for him to describe the object that we will show him. We have carried out many experimental tests of this technique, with very encouraging results.

Two experimental sessions using this approach were conducted at SRI in the fall of 1980. Marilyn Schlitz, then of the Institute for Parapsychology, was the viewer in both sessions. In the first session, a packet of ammunition was hidden by the SRI secretary in one of the five drawers of her locked safe.

Marilyn's remote-viewing task was to find out which drawer held the hidden ammunition. This would be a simulation of the type of problem in which we might, for example, be asked to discover psychically which of several buildings, suitcases, or persons has the bomb in a terrorist situation.

As we explained earlier, we believe that asking a viewer to tell us which drawer of a group numbered 1 to 5 has ammunition in it is like inviting her to guess a number. This has historically been a psychic task of very limited success. All numbers look more or less the same as the last time you saw any of them. We mention this analytical problem once again because it appears to be the principal, and almost only, factor limiting the success of an otherwise willing remote viewer.

In this experiment, five small wooden boxes were labeled 1 to 5 to correspond to the drawers of the safe. Five target objects were then selected to be as different from each other as possible—a red plastic die, a pipe, a pair of eyeglasses, a gold figurine of King Tut, and an apple.

The target pool was unknown to the viewer, and the correct drawer number was unknown to the experimenters. The viewer was simply asked to describe the object that would lead to the correct drawer. The entire experiment was carried out by telephone, with Marilyn in North Carolina and the ammunition and experimenters in California.

Marilyn described "an object like a metal padlock . . . an eagle medallion . . . a mushroom cap with a stalk coming out of it." A judge who did not know the correct answer decided that Marilyn's remote-viewing description most favored the King Tut figurine, which was wearing a hat that greatly resembled a mushroom. It was also the only metal object. King Tut was in box number 3. That was also the correct number for the drawer containing the ammunition.

In a second trial of this type, we asked a woman to hide herself in one of five laboratory rooms. The viewer's task was to find the hidden woman. In this kidnap simulation, the rooms were again labeled 1 to 5, and a new group of five different objects was assembled—a daisy, a wineglass, a pair of scissors, a *Star Wars* doll, and a wooden domino.

This scenario was described to Marilyn as the familiar "lady and tiger" problem. It is as though there were a lady behind one door and tigers behind the other four. The interviewer asked Marilyn to describe the object that would lead us to the lady.

Marilyn provided a telephoned remote-viewing description containing images of a "propeller . . . a ceiling fan . . . and silvery intersecting lines." The judge receiving Marilyn's impressions, along with her drawings, said that he would choose the scissors as the most appropriate target to fit her description. This again led to a successful outcome, with the target person being correctly located in her hiding place.

Experiments of this type have often given good results. From the unsuccessful trials, we have learned that it is very desirable for the interviewer to be ignorant of the target pool of objects. In some cases, we found that a viewer would give excellent descriptions of more than one object in the target pool.

A second source of confusion may have been created by allowing a viewer to be her own judge. In this case, we obtained an almost photographic description of one object in the judging pool which the viewer found especially attractive when she was later judging her own transcript. However, this was not the correct target object for that session!

In psi research it is a common practice to ask a viewer to describe a remote target object or picture, and later ask that viewer to choose the target he or she described from a group of possible candidates. Since neither the experimenter nor the viewer knows the correct answer at that time, this is a scientifically valid form of judging.

The problem that we find is that viewers will often psychically describe a target from the pool that they personally find more appealing than the designated target.

Although experiments in which viewers judge their own transcripts often obtain statistically significant results, the transcripts from these experiments often contain good to excellent descriptions of more than one item belonging to a particular judging set. We therefore strongly advise against having viewers compare their own descriptions with all of the possible target objects in a pool.

ASSOCIATIVE REMOTE VIEWING OF FUTURE EVENTS

It has no doubt occurred to you that this technique might well be applied to forecasting the future, as well as to psychically describing current events at a distance. This appears to be a correct assumption.

We have run many successful ARV trials for the purpose of forecasting the price of gold, silver, the change in the Dow Jones Industrial Average, and many similar financial tasks. The trials that we will describe here make use of a Presidential election and a horserace as the ultimate random-number generators to choose target objects for remote-viewing sessions.

These two experiments were carried out by Elisabeth Targ, who is a medical student at Stanford University. She is also an experienced psi experimenter and remote viewer. In 1970 Elisabeth took part in a successful and published series of experiments with a psi-teaching machine that was the forerunner of the first psi research contract at SRI from NASA.[3]

Having recently received graduate and undergraduate degrees in biology and Russian, Elisabeth is currently pursuing her interest in applied psychic functioning, along with her medical studies and research.

The first experiment was carried out in September 1980, just before the Presidential election. Elisabeth wanted to know in advance who was going to win the election. The experiment used the associative-remote-viewing protocol just described.

Elisabeth was to be the viewer, so her friend, Janice Boughton, now a medical student at Johns Hopkins, selected four target objects to correspond to each of four possible announcements on election night: Carter wins, Reagan wins, Anderson wins, or none of the above occurs. (The interviewer was to ask the viewer, "What object will I show you at midnight on election night?" So every possible outcome had to be included, even the one in which a decision had not yet been reached.)

The experimenter labeled the four objects *Carter, Reagan, Anderson,* and *None of the above,* and put each object into a little wooden box. The objects were completely irrelevant to the election outcome which they represented—the experimenter did not use a peanut for Carter, a rocket for Reagan, and a dark horse for Anderson.

Elisabeth, of course, did not know what objects were in the target pool. Her task was to describe the object that she would be handed on election night. Her impressions were of a white, hollow, conical object. It looked to her like shell material, and she described it as having a string attached to its apex.

Janice did not have the slightest difficulty in deciding which object Elisabeth had described, because one of her objects was a cornucopia-shaped whistle made from an animal horn with a string attached to its pointed end. This object happened to be in the Reagan box. It took six weeks to learn that this psychic forecast was correct, but in the meantime several people were happy to make wagers on Reagan.

The very important finale to this sequence of events came when Elisabeth was shown the correct target object at the end of election night. Since in this experiment the viewer was specifically asked to describe what she would be holding in her hand at the end of the experiment, she had to be handed the correct object for the initial question to have made any sense.

The logic of this kind of activity may seem puzzling, because the causal order is not what we are used to. But it *is* a cause-and-effect relationship.

We will describe a horserace experiment in the same terms. The race selected was the sixth race at Bay Meadows. There were six horses in the race.

In this experiment, Janice found another experimenter to choose six objects to be the potential targets for Elisabeth's remote viewing. Janice did this because she feared that as an interviewer, she might psychologically or telepathically mislead Elisabeth into describing a favorite object if she herself knew what the target pool was.

The remote-viewing session was carried out the night before the race. The objects were given numbers to correspond to the numbers of the six horses that would run the next day. Elisabeth was told that at the end of the race, she would be given one of the objects to hold, the one carrying the winner's number.

As Elisabeth began her remote-viewing description, she said she saw something "hard and spherical." It reminded her of an apple. She continued, "If I hold it up to the light, I can see right through it." Since one of the targets was a spherical apple-juice bottle, with a raised apple-leaf design around its edges, everyone thought we had a great success. Of course at that time, the race had not yet been run, so the most that anyone knew was that we had a good description of one of the objects in the target pool.

An important advantage of ARV for future forecasting is that it provides some intermediate information about the presence of psychic functioning. For example, if Elisabeth had said that she had a clear mental picture of a moose, and there was nothing like a moose in the target pool, the judges and other experimenters could justifiably conclude that there was no evidence of psychic functioning in this session, and that they should not bet on the race. On the other hand, if the task had been merely to psychically guess the number of the winning horse, and Elisabeth had said, "I see a 6," the experimenters would not, at that time, have any way to know if psychic functioning was or was not present. A great strength of the ARV technique is that it provides an intermediate indication about the presence or absence of clear psychic information *before* the event you are trying to forecast.

Since Elisabeth's description so accurately described one of the target objects, students from all over her college dormitory contributed money to a betting pool for horse number 6, whose name was Shamgo, in the sixth race at Bay Meadows. The next day, Shamgo won, and Elisabeth got to see her apple-juice bottle as a reward for her excellent psychic functioning. Shamgo paid six to one. The important point here is that in these experiments the medium is not the message. Analytic information can be obtained, but it requires that the medium (protocol) be nonanalytic.

REMOTE VIEWING AT ESALEN INSTITUTE

In May 1982, Elisabeth Targ and I (R.T.) were invited to hold a workshop at Esalen Institute for a group of twenty-five professional men and women. The professionals were taking part in a four-week program with Stanislav Grof, a psychiatrist and pioneer researcher in psychedelics and altered states of consciousness. His recent research has explored techniques for allowing people to find different ways of experiencing the world through altered states without the use of hallucinogenic drugs. We walked into one of his drug-free consciousness-raising adventures, slides in hand, to see if we could create some clear evidence of good psychic functioning for the participants.

Many people feel that they are having psychic experiences while they are in an altered state of consciousness. However, when they return to a more ordinary state of mind, they are not always sure that what they experienced was real. Our task was to try to show the workshop participants something psychic that would not disappear for them after they left the supportive atmosphere of Esalen, with its beautiful secluded grounds overlooking the Pacific at Big Sur.

This extended introduction to psychic functioning turned out to be particularly important for our group of psychological explorers. During the first half hour of the lecture I called for psychic impressions of a target location. We were very surprised when the response was much more enthusiastic than what we are accustomed to from an inexperienced group. It was also completely wrong. It appeared that this group had a very large commitment to, perhaps a strong ego involvement in, being psychic. Basically they were trying too hard.

Over the next four hours, the group had a chance to hear about hundreds of "miracles" referred to as "data." They also had it made very clear to them that they were not going to be elevated to godhood if they were successful at psychic tasks. By the end of the evening all realized that we completely expected them to succeed at remote viewing, and that if they were not successful this time, we expected that they would improve with practice. The group performed outstandingly throughout the rest of the workshop.

In our first few hours with this class of business people, physicians, psychiatrists, and stockbrokers, we described the past remote-viewing research that we had been involved in, including the years of research at SRI and Elisabeth's experiments at Stanford. In the evening, after the group was quite fatigued from looking at slides and listening to stories of psychic activities, we asked each person to go back to his room, find an interesting object, and put it into a little basket; we provided the baskets.

When the group members all returned with their treasures, we divided them into pairs and asked each person to describe the object that his or her partner had brought. The group had remarkable success. Several people actually named the item that their partner had carried in. One man said, "I see a ring that looks like a snake." His partner had brought in a snake ring. Another man said, "It looks like a tie clip," and that is what his partner's hidden object was.

The next day we thought we should carry out an experiment that would be more unambiguous than this informal activity. What we had done was very effective as a warm-up exercise, and represents a type of experiment that feels comfortable and is likely to succeed. However, since each interviewer knew what object he had placed in his box, this was hardly a scientific demonstration.

The experiment that we had planned for the group was a kidnap scenario. The kid was a large Raggedy Ann doll that we had sitting with us throughout the previous day. When the group reassembled the next day after lunch, we told them that Raggedy Ann had mysteriously disappeared, and we should find her as soon as possible. They knew, of course, that sometime earlier in the day Elisabeth had hidden the doll somewhere on the Esalen grounds. This was done while the people in our workshop were off in one corner of the thirty-acre site having lunch.

We divided the group into four teams of about six members each. There were to be two remote-viewing pairs per team, each consisting of a viewer and an interviewer. Each pair would work independently without Elizabeth or I present. One pair on each team was to make use of associative remote viewing to determine which quadrant of the Esalen property held the doll; the other would use geographical remote viewing.

The remote-viewing teams then left our meeting room to carry out these tasks. The agreement was that the teams were not to scour the Esalen grounds, turning over rocks, but rather that each team would stay in our meeting building until it had decided upon a single destination. To facilitate this, each team was given a map of Esalen, showing the twenty-five assorted structures there, about half of which were unnamed. The doll was hidden in one of the marked but nameless locations.

The remote-viewing pairs went to work immediately. For the ARV part of this experiment, we set up four boxes corresponding to the four quadrants of the property that we had marked out on the map. Each quadrant was associated with a different little object which Elisabeth put into each box. I then gave each of the boxes a number 1 to 4, to correspond to the four quadrants. In this way, neither of us knew which object corresponded to the correct quadrant until the boxes were opened.

The ARV viewers were instructed to describe the object that they would be shown after Raggedy Ann was found. This object would correspond to the correct target quadrant. After the viewer on each ARV team completed the description of an object, the interviewer went into a separate room where the boxes had been placed. The interviewer would look at the four objects and decide which object best fit the description his viewer had given. He would then be shown the quadrant number that was associated with the object he had selected.

This procedure worked perfectly for two of the teams. One of their viewers described "a silver cylinder which somehow gets larger and smaller." One of the targets was an antique silver cup made in three cylindrical sections, so that it was collapsible. This object led to the correct quadrant.

A second team had a description of something sufficiently cylindrical so that they were also able to choose the right object. The final two teams did not have clear object descriptions—perhaps because of a common and psychically fatal error. They unfortunately allowed their viewers to come and look at all the objects. This meant that their viewers had all of the objects in their immediate future, and may not have been able to differentiate which one was uniquely associated with the correct hiding place.

However, it turned out that the teams which had trouble with the ARV portion of the task happened to have the best geographical remote viewing. Shortly after the end of the analysis session, each of the teams went directly either to the target or to the correct quadrant. They were all then able to see a building that matched their remote-viewing drawings sufficiently so that they were able to recognize it.

So all four teams found the "kidnapped" doll. Three of the viewers made drawings that specifically described the target building, which was a large teepee. We show two of these drawings on pages 102–103. The

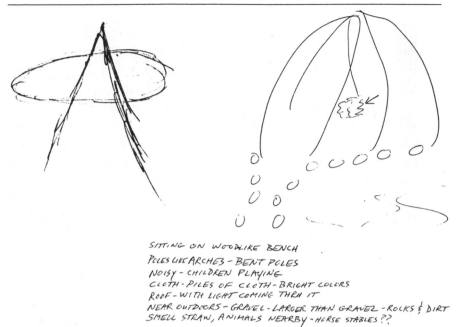

SITTING ON WOODLIKE BENCH
POLES LIKE ARCHES - BENT POLES
NOISY - CHILDREN PLAYING
CLOTH - PILES OF CLOTH - BRIGHT COLORS
ROOF - WITH LIGHT COMING THRU IT
NEAR OUTDOORS - GRAVEL - LARGER THAN GRAVEL - ROCKS & DIRT
SMELL STRAW, ANIMALS NEARBY - HORSE STABLES ??

Remote-viewing experiment at the Esalen Institute: two viewers' drawings and a description of the hiding place (photo) of the "kidnapped" Raggedy Ann.

other two viewers also drew moderately good-looking tent-like structures. The team with the drawing shown here on the left was the first to find Raggedy Ann, because that team's interviewer simply recognized the location from a viewer's drawing. He suggested that his group should go and get the doll at once, which is just what they did. The viewer's entire description of the target site is shown on his drawing. Everything he had to say about the site was correct:

> Sitting on a wood-like bench. [It was a wooden rocker.] Poles like arches, bent poles. [The target was a large teepee made of poles tied together, as shown in the photo.] Noisy—children playing. [It was in the children's play area.] Cloth—piles of cloth—bright colors. [The teepee is covered with white cloth with yellow animals sewn to it.] Roof—with light coming thru it. [Correct.] Near outdoors—gravel—larger than gravel—rocks & dirt. [The photo was taken a month later; at the time of the experiment the teepee had a gravel floor and was surrounded with large rocks.] Smell straw, animals nearby—horse stables? [Yes. The teepee is tucked away behind the horse stables.]

The thing that most impressed the people who had taken part in this psychic treasure hunt was that they were a group who had been assembled specifically to carry out a psychic task, in which failure, if it occurred, would be evident. There would be no way to fool themselves about whether or not they had psychically provided the information necessary to find the doll. Either they had her or they didn't. No one went off looking for the doll at Esalen's famous hot baths, or by the ocean, or in the gardens, or in any of the dozens of other interesting buildings and locations that they could have searched. Rather, each team somehow described a picture of something that looked enough like a teepee to enable every team to get to the target site.

WHAT ABOUT THE PROBABLE FUTURE?

Many experiments have been carried out which have demonstrated that information about future events can be psychically perceived. The question arises: Once you have perceived such an event, can anything be done to *prevent* it if you do not like what you see? This involves a related question: In what sense do events have any existence before they actually occur?

Suppose you have a dream which you assume to be precognitive because of its clear and unusual character. In the dream, you see yourself walking down a street. As you come to the corner you see a bright-orange building. You look down the cross street and see a large blue truck coming your way. You step out into the street and are hit by the truck. End of dream.

Suppose also that you remember this dream after you wake up. What would happen if you were later to walk down a street where you had never been, see the orange building of your vision, look down the street, and see the blue truck coming your way? Would you at that moment have the option of grabbing a lamppost and watching the truck as it careens by, instead of experiencing the same outcome as in your dream?

Before we respond to this question, several related problems should first be discussed. First of all, if you take evasive action and never in fact are hit by the truck, in what sense can it be said the dream was really precognitive? A defender of psychic dreams might say, "Still, some part of the dream was psychic." But if this were the case, and there really was no accident in your future, why would you dream about the truck at all? In this scenario, you had a dream that contained some independently confirmable precognitive information plus some information that did not apply to the future you actually experienced.

No event has a 100 percent probability of occurring until all of the conditions for its occurrence have been satisfied, and the event happens. It might be suggested, therefore, that until the event actually happens, alternate futures may have an existence qualitatively similar to that of the final outcome.

If this is so, the distinguishing feature of each future event would be the magnitude of the probability of its occurrence (how likely it is to occur). Your psychic perception of a given event might depend upon its *probability*, not on whether it will ever actually happen. In the case of the dream scenario we just described, the collision might be described as a high-probability future, but one that was never actualized.

An alternate view would be that an event that will ultimately be actualized has some additional property intrinsic to it. This is, for example, relevant to a situation in which a viewer is asked to describe which of several unknown objects he or she will be shown, where the probability of being shown any one of the objects is equal. But the right one is "special," because it will be shown to the viewer.

This protocol has been highly successful in demonstrating the existence of precognition. Precognitive remote-viewing experiments would probably not be successful if there were nothing to psychically distinguish the objects in a target pool from one another except the magnitude of their *a priori* probability of appearance (which is generally equal for all the objects).

Elisabeth Targ recently contrived an experiment to address these questions in the laboratory by using remote viewing. In her experiment, showing a viewer a given object in a pool becomes "the event."

In Elisabeth's experiment, viewers are asked to look into a future about which they have no prior information. However, there is a high probability that they will experience a certain event, and a low probability that they will experience others. The purpose of the experiment is to determine whether viewers will psychically perceive information about high-probability events, even on occasions when they will later be shown an object that has a low probability of being chosen as the target on that particular trial.

This approach considers these questions: (1) Can a person psychically perceive information about an event that will never be actualized? (2) If an event has a higher probability of occurring, does that make it easier, or more likely to be precognitively perceived by a viewer? (3) Is the fact that a given event will ultimately occur perceptible psychically to a viewer, independent of its initial probability of occurrence?

For each experimental trial, six objects were chosen to compose a pool of possible targets. Before each session began, one of these objects was randomly assigned a 50 percent probability (high probability) of being the target, while the other five objects each had a 10 percent probability (low probability) of eventually being shown to the viewer. The viewer was then asked to describe the object that he or she would be shown shortly after finishing that session's remote-viewing description.

The viewers were interviewed by an experimenter who did not know what any of the objects in the target pool were. As soon as a viewer finished giving a description of that session's object, a target object was chosen from the pool by using a computer program which took into account the unequal probabilities previously assigned. There are two cases that we should consider:

Case 1: The 50 percent object is in fact chosen as the target. This case serves as a control. It represents the usual case in which the probability of the viewer's seeing the target object is greater or equal to that of seeing any of the other objects. It also provides a baseline measure of the degree of psychic functioning present in this experiment.

Case 2: The 50 percent object is not the target. If, as determined by independent judging, in this case the viewer describes the high-probability object, we would conclude that it is possible to get information from a future that will never occur. We would also conclude that the *a priori* probability of an event (rather than whether or not it actually occurs) influences its accessibility to a viewer looking at it precognitively.

The latter outcome would argue against the possibility of predestination. It would suggest that a person might psychically perceive an impending, highly probable, but undesirable event, and then arrange to have some different, perhaps less likely event occur instead. However, if the viewer correctly describes a target object that had only a 10 percent probability of being chosen, we would conclude that it is probably *the ultimate occurrence of an event,* not a series of alternate probable futures, that makes itself available to psychic perception.

Twelve sessions were carried out—six with Hella Hammid and six with Keith Harary as the viewer. Since the high-probability outcomes were determined through a random process, the number of sessions of each type were not quite equal—seven sessions ended up with high-probability target objects, and five with low.

The objects for this experiment were again secretly collected by Janice Boughton. For each session, the viewer was asked to describe the object that he or she would be given at the end of that remote-viewing session, with the understanding that the object would be randomly chosen *after* the description was completed. Before the trial, a die was placed in a file-card box. The box was shaken, and remained closed. The number chosen by the die would be the number of the object which would have the 50 percent probability of being the target for that session.

The viewer then described the object that he or she psychically perceived as being the object lying in the near future. After that, the box was opened and the die read to determine which object would be high-probability. A random-number generator was used to determine which of the objects would actually be shown to the viewer, taking into account that one object had a 50 percent probability.

In blind judging, each remote-viewing transcript was rated on a scale of 0 to 100 against each of the six objects in its own target pool by two independent judges. The five low-probability and the seven high-probability

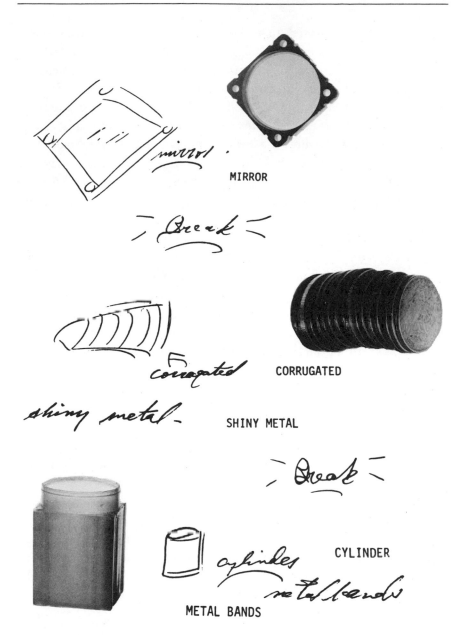

MIRROR

CORRUGATED

SHINY METAL

CYLINDER

METAL BANDS

Coin holder target in precognition experiment and remote-viewing responses and drawings by Keith Harary.

objects were then collected. In the five key low-probability trials, three of the target objects received the highest rating, and two received the second-highest rating. In an experiment with completely independent judging such as this one, a score of three firsts and two seconds is an independently significant result. It offers good evidence for psychic functioning, even apart from the other complexities of this experiment.

One of Keith's drawings of a low-probability object, a coin holder that was his target for one session, is shown on page 107. Needless to say, the judges both gave this an accuracy rating of 100 percent. It is clear from this drawing that Keith's psychic perception was not clouded by the fact that his target was not chosen until after his description, nor by the fact that there were five other objects in the pool, one of whose probability of being chosen as the target was five times greater than any of the others. His drawing not only shows the box with a little hole in each corner, but also the stack of silver dollars which were inside the box. He describes the lid of the coin holder as a "mirror" presumably because it contained a reflective surface with a face on it (the coin) during the experiment.

The conclusion from this experiment has to be: "What you see is what you will get." That is, non-actualized futures apparently do not greatly affect a viewer's precognitive descriptions of impending events.

It turned out, for reasons that we cannot explain, that the seven trials with objects of high probability did not yield independently significant results. It is as though no one was interested in that case, which happens to be true. But neither the viewers nor the interviewer knew which case was being investigated in any given session, until *after* the description was given and the target object was then randomly selected.

The outcome of this experiment does not contradict the idea we discussed earlier, that once you have a psychically generated forecast in your hand, you can use your free will to falsify that forecast, and do as you please. No one in this experiment had that opportunity. The experimenter had agreed to show the viewer the object that was actually chosen.

This experiment suggests that no matter how complicated the question is that you are asking, if you are able to formulate a question that a remote viewer can understand, you are likely to get the right answer to your question.

PART II

Developing Psychic Abilities: Who's Minding Your Mind?

With so much excellent psychic functioning being demonstrated in re-search laboratories, it is a wonder that more people have not been trying to get into the act. After all, a lot of the research we have discussed has used previously inexperienced viewers. This certainly suggests that psychic experiences may be available to a good many people who are not now aware of their latent psychic abilities.

We think the reasons more people have not actively explored their psychic capabilities are clear. Everywhere we look, we find images of psychic functioning that are confusing, intimidating, misleading, and terrifying. The public must sort through everything from old horror films that make psychic experiences seem like messages from the dead to cults that by association make psi abilities seem weird or even dangerous. Meanwhile, critics of psi, who often know next to nothing about psi research, condemn the scientific work in this field out of fear of its philosophical implications.

Before you learn to explore your own psychic capabilities, we think it is important to examine some of the myths about psychic experiences and abilities that may still be tugging at your subconscious. For example, deep in the psyche of each of us still lingers the smell of burning flesh from a million women and men burned by the church as witches, right up to the eighteenth century; and many people still mistakenly associate psychic abilities with the supernatural. Every myth, misconception, and stereo-type about psychic functioning has roots deep in human superstitition—and ultimately makes a profit for somebody at the expense of a lot of other people.

6

Psi and Cults:

The Golden Fleece

The practice of confusing the public about psychic functioning is a multimillion-dollar business for a broad variety of cults, ranging in size from just a few members to hundreds of thousands. The groups, and their leaders, profit and flourish by attracting a continuous flow of recruits who believe their claims that recruits can gain enlightenment and power over other people through membership in a cult group. This power is supposed to be derived through special knowledge about the inner workings of reality and the mind—knowledge to which the recruits supposedly would not otherwise gain access. There are now about three thousand such cults, with an estimated total membership of roughly three million in the United States alone.

CULTS AND THEIR CONVERTS

You won't find these groups listed under "cults" in the Yellow Pages. For income-tax and public-relations purposes, most refer to themselves as "churches." But cults differ from traditional churches in several important ways. The groups that we call cults are specifically those that lead members to become dependent upon a charismatic leader and that practice mind-control techniques. They also often use financial exploitation, coer-

cive persuasion, deliberate deception, and sleep and nutritional deprivation as means of attracting and controlling their members.[1] But cult
members find it all worthwhile because of the feeling of specialness and
exclusivity they experience, together with an imagined superiority over all
non-members of their particular group.

As you may know, these groups offer to provide psychological help,
security, love, and a sense of belonging to people who feel alienated and
vulnerable in our complex, and often unloving, society. These human
needs used to be satisfied through participation in traditional religion.
However, many people today do not feel that organized religion provides
the information and guidance they need in their daily existence. For
better or worse, cults seem to provide simple answers to life's many
problems. Unfortunately, they often go beyond this and completely take
over and control every aspect of their members' lives.

What you may not realize is that one technique these cults most
commonly—and effectively—use to manipulate people involves the deliberate misrepresentation of psychic functioning. Most of the larger cults,
and almost all of the smaller ones, are run by charismatic leaders who
claim to have supernatural abilities. The leaders use this claim to back up
their supposed special relationship with God and their pretended access
to "higher knowledge." They also promise recruits either that they will
learn to develop their own psychic abilities or that they will be protected
by the supposed powers of the leader by joining their particular cult.

Since cult leaders always seem to oppose the values of mainstream
society, cult members usually find themselves cast in the role of social
deviants. And this leads the public to associate psychic abilities and
experiences with images of abnormality, and with political and personal
values that, in reality, are in no way necessary for psychic functioning.

Of course, this cult image of psychic functioning as abnormal can
adversely influence cult members. It can also seriously affect the attitudes
of non-members toward the subject of extended human capabilities. Because of the cults, both members and the public tend to think psychic
functioning is the domain of cultists and other strange people—rather
than a perfectly normal, widely distributed, and easily available mental
capacity.

In our society, a person who is beginning to experience emerging
psychic abilities, or who is interested in doing so, has almost nowhere to
turn for guidance. Anyone with a purely scholarly interest in psi research
can write to various laboratories or read the research reports. But this

information will probably not be of much practical, personal use. It is more likely to describe statistics and experimental data than to suggest functional ways of integrating and using psychic awareness in one's daily activities.

So people who think they have had psychic experiences or who are merely interested in learning about psychic abilities are left with very few alternatives. They can admit their interests and risk being branded as social deviants, or they can deny their interest in psychic functioning and thereby become alienated from what might be an important aspect of their own lives and experiences.

This is the dilemma that leads many people to join cults in the first place. By accepting and exploiting psychic experiences in a society that does not readily accept them, cults have effectively monopolized the subject of psi. They have exploited many people who are interested in learning about this area, and frightened many others away from even considering the possibility of developing their own psychic potential.[2]

If anyone questions the approach of these groups and their claimed special understanding of the nature of reality, their members will probably say that they share the questioner's reservations—about every group *except* the one to which they belong. They themselves never labor under any misconceptions; their own group—whichever it is—always provides the most convincing answers to the problems and mysteries of human existence. As proof of this claim they often cite examples of the supposedly supernatural or psychic abilities of the group's leader.

Cult members will then suggest that the only way outsiders can appreciate their group's supposedly unique insights is by undergoing its training program. In addition to putting the unwary through a slow rinse of the cerebral cortex, such training can also be emotionally and financially draining. Usually it involves extreme psychological stress and manipulation, and often it requires hundreds or even thousands of hours of indoctrination. Many who submit to cult training later have a hard time sorting out their cult experiences—and, for that matter, the rest of their lives.

Few people want to admit to themselves that an exercise to which they have made a significant commitment may have been worthless, or damaging, to their personal development. Many cult recruits, therefore, try to avoid facing up to this disturbing possibility by viewing their training experiences in the brightest conceivable light. A recruit will also have difficulty being objective about a cult after going through its training program, because the training itself is designed to lead the recruit toward a biased perception of "reality"—as defined by the particular cult and its leader.

The "reality" that many cults offer to their recruits includes promises of inside information about psychic functioning, besides whatever psychological and spiritual support the group purports to offer. A number of groups advertise claims that their initiates will gain psychic influence or control over the uninitiated. Such promises appeal to people seeking security and power as well as to those who have experience or interest in psychic functioning, and who seek support for their interest.

So it is clear that cults have a vested interest in having psychic functioning seem as mysterious as possible—while at the same time making psychic abilities appear to be a desirable but difficult-to-obtain commodity. Psychic abilities can thus be a good source of profit, if cult leaders can claim to have the abilities themselves, or to have special information and techniques for developing them in others.

PEOPLES TEMPLE

In 1979, as Director of Counseling at the Human Freedom Center in Berkeley, California, I (K.H.) spent several months interviewing and counseling former cult members. I found that many individuals had joined cults as a result of their having either experienced or witnessed what they believed were psychic occurrences. One encounter that I had with two of these former cult members was particularly striking.

In May 1979, as we toured the abandoned San Francisco headquarters of the Peoples Temple, ex-member Jeannie Mills explained to me that in order to understand the influence that the Rev. Jim Jones had over his followers, you would need to have known Jones personally. I had happily been spared that experience, but Jeannie, her husband Al, and their family had not. Jeannie and Al had worked alongside Jim Jones for six years, and were members of the elite Planning Commission, the central committee that managed the Peoples Temple organization. They had become disillusioned with Jones and had left the group when he began treating his followers less like congregation members than like prisoners in a concentration camp.

Fearing for the health and safety of the nearly one thousand Peoples Temple members who were living with Jones in his Guyana jungle compound, Jonestown, Jeannie and Al decided to launch a rescue mission. Disregarding death threats from loyal Peoples Temple members, they founded the Human Freedom Center in Berkeley and contacted Congressman Leo Ryan.

Jeannie and Al intended to use the center as a refuge for any Peoples Temple members who left Jonestown and returned to begin new lives in the United States. It was in the living room of the center that Congressman Ryan's ill-fated mission to Guyana was planned. When, in November 1978, that journey ended in tragedy for Ryan and the more than nine hundred other people who died violently at Jonestown, the Millses decided to use their own resources to maintain the center as a counseling facility and halfway house for a handful of Peoples Temple survivors, and for any ex-members of other cults who sought the center's assistance while they worked out their return to mainstream society.

I had joined the staff of the Human Freedom Center in March 1979, four months after the murder-suicides in Jonestown. I had become interested in the center after nine years of conducting research in several laboratories and counseling people who were upset by apparently psychic experiences. I had long suspected that a strong relationship existed between cult involvement and the general public's ambivalent response to psychic functioning. While we walked around the deserted Peoples Temple building on Geary Street, Jeannie Mills confirmed my suspicions.

As she pointed out the areas surrounding Peoples Temple where she said Jim Jones had posted armed guards to protect him from imaginary assassins, Jeannie described how Jones had built a large following by leading people to believe that he would save them from "poverty and oppression" and by fraudulently convincing people that he had extraordinary psychic powers. Besides claiming to have highly developed powers of telepathy, clairvoyance, and precognition, Jones also pretended to be a miraculous psychic healer and medium—and to be capable of striking people dead, or bringing the dead back to life, by merely willing it. Jones went to elaborate lengths to "prove" his claims. He often used stooges within the Peoples Temple congregation, who helped in his charades for what they believed would be the ultimate good of Jones's cause.

Jeannie described how an elderly woman, a Peoples Temple member, had once come upon two intruders in her San Francisco apartment. The intruders knocked her down and fled. Two ostensible police officers soon arrived, saying they were in the area and were responding to the commotion. An ambulance was quickly summoned. The attendants told the woman that her arm had been broken, fitted her with a cast, and told her that she would be all right, but to check with her doctor.

At a crowded Peoples Temple meeting the following morning, Jim Jones looked up from his sermon as if he had been startled by the whispering voice of a discarnate entity. He asked his congregation if an elderly woman was present whose arm had been broken by two intruders in her home the previous evening. The woman, startled, answered from the back of the auditorium.

Jones said he had learned of her injury psychically, and he called her to the front of the large meeting room. He then claimed to have healed the woman's arm and told her to remove her cast. She did, and found, to her amazement and the congregation's, that her arm was perfectly sound.

Jeannie explained that the entire encounter had been a totally fraudulent setup from the beginning. The intruders, the men in police uniforms, and the ambulance attendants were all Jones's henchmen. The woman's arm had never actually been broken. Apparently Jim Jones thought the risk of staging such an elaborate hoax was worth it; frauds like this enormously increased his influence over his followers and helped attract many new members.

Another favorite trick that Jeannie Mills describes in her book *Six Years with God*[3] was for Jones to announce that a congregation member had stomach or intestinal cancer, and to send that person to a restroom, accompanied by a nurse, to be remotely "healed" by Jones. While the "patient" was looking elsewhere, the nurse would produce a concealed rotting mass of bloody animal liver. The victim was told that this liver was a tumor that had passed, painlessly, through his bowels. The liver was then exhibited at a distance, to the congregation, as evidence of Jones's purported clairvoyant and healing abilities.

Jones sometimes sent his cohorts to search through the garbage of Peoples Temple members or to break into their houses and search their drawers and medicine cabinets for personal information. Jones would later announce this information to his congregation as supposedly psychic revelations about the private concerns of particular people. He also played tape-recorded voices over hidden speakers, to convince his followers that he was communicating with spirits. Jones even drugged a number of people in order to make it appear that he could strike people dead, or bring the dead back to life, at will.

Numerous former members of the Peoples Temple told me that by the time Jones got around to inviting his congregation in Guyana to drink poisoned Flavor-Aide, or to be shot to death or injected with poison if they did not drink voluntarily, he had successfully convinced most of his followers that *he was God incarnate.* As a result, most were understandably willing to do *anything* Jim Jones asked.

I worked at the Human Freedom Center for almost a year, studying the Peoples Temple and other groups that made claims related to psychic functioning. After that, I accepted a position with SRI International, in order to return to laboratory psi research. In February 1980, on a morning when I had planned to call upon Jeannie and Al and my other former associates from the Human Freedom Center, I was awakened, instead, by a phone call at 5:30. The call was from a reporter. Jeannie and Al Mills and one of their daughters, he told me, had been brutally slain in their Berkeley home the previous evening. No arrests have yet been made in the murders of these courageous people. The case is still open.

How did Jim Jones get as far as he did, when his claims of psychic abilities were supported by demonstrations that to most people would be so obviously fraudulent? Because he offered easy solutions—wherever mainstream society left unanswered questions, Jim Jones, like so many other cult leaders, filled in the blanks with his own version of the answers. Jones would probably have fooled many fewer people, and gained a much smaller following, if the public were not so thoroughly confused and misinformed about the real nature of psi.

THREE PATTERNS OF PSYCHIC FRAUD

Pattern One: The Leader Knows All

People who are well informed about the possibilities and the limits of psi, and who know their own capacity for using psychic abilities, would not easily be taken in by a cult leader's extravagant psychic claims. They would probably recognize that the fraudulent claims went far beyond their own experience of normal psychic functioning. They would therefore immediately suspect the claims and would hardly believe that the cult leader was a highly developed being whose word was to be followed without question.

People who believe that there is no such thing as psychic functioning, however, may find their belief too suddenly shaken by an apparently psychic occurrence that is especially convincing. Whether this occurs in a cult setting or in the private lives of these individuals, they often are attracted to the first cult that promises to explain psychic experiences within a believable, if limited, frame of reference.

Jim Jones is just one disturbing example of a cult leader manipulating his followers by misleading them about psychic functioning. Thousands of other cults in the United States and overseas misrepresent psychic functioning—each in its own unique way—to attract followers and collect millions of tax-exempt dollars each year for their so-called religious leaders.

Many cult members find their position defined as being in an adversary relationship with outsiders, who may be described in cult training sessions as anything from unenlightened mortals to manifestations of Satan in earthly camouflage. This approach deliberately limits the members' associations with anyone who might contradict the cult leader's viewpoint. The leaders of many different cults have openly threatened to attack and suppress those who oppose them, through *whatever* means possible. We will, therefore, not mention certain cults by name.

Cult leaders rarely go to the extremes that Jim Jones did in order to attract and hold followers who are awed by claims about psychic functioning. Most of them find that simply claiming to have a special understanding of reality and the mind will bring a large following; ostensibly psychic demonstrations are seldom needed. Often a cult leader simply takes credit for whatever apparently psychic experiences a follower reports, even if they happened before the member joined the group. Leaders may explain the experiences by saying, "Your psychic experiences happened because you were being led to me."

Cult members themselves are also involved in the deceit. They often entice potential recruits with stories about their leaders' supposed psychic abilities. The followers probably believe these accounts, which become exaggerated through retelling. They may also feel a need to justify their own participation in the cult, and so may use the tales to convince themselves and others that membership in their cult is worthwhile. An encounter of this type was described by a former cult member, a student at a Midwestern university:

> I joined a cult without realizing it. The members just seemed like nice people who were getting together to practice Kundalini yoga and discuss the philosophy of a man named Baba who lived in India. Things were fairly sedate in the beginning. We learned yoga

exercises, listened to stories about Baba, and practiced Indian dancing. The group members believed that Baba was a powerful psychic, and that he could read their minds, and directly influence their lives, from thousands of miles away.

A couple of months went by, and I was asked to go through an initiation ritual to become an official group member. I decided to go ahead with the ritual, since I was among friends who thought it was important for me to do that. Later, I met some older members who told me that I had to live and think the same way that they did, or else leave the group. I was not sure what to do. I did not want to leave my new friends, but I did not want to give up my own life, either.

I was thinking it all over one day, when I came across two of the cult members in a shopping center. They told me that Baba had telepathically arranged for us to meet there, so that they could erase my doubts about becoming more deeply involved with their organization. I thought about that possibility for a long while. The members really seemed to believe what they were saying, and they almost had me convinced, too.

Then I decided that it didn't matter if Baba could read the members' minds and run their lives, because I didn't want to end up like them. I thought they were acting like robots. I left the group and later was shocked to read, in the newspaper, that it was a fund-raising front for a group of international terrorists, posing as a religious organization.

The article referred to by the student above in fact appeared in several newspapers in 1981 and 1982.[4]

Many cults claim supernatural or psychic abilities for their leader, but do not otherwise discuss the subject with regard to group members themselves. The cult leader's claimed special powers are used to establish his supposed superiority, to justify whatever control he exerts over the members' lives.

For example, in 1982, after being convicted of income-tax evasion, fraud, and obstruction of justice, Sun Myung Moon, the leader of the Unification Church, found himself in court again. Moon was called to testify for the prosecution in the trial of an alleged cult "deprogrammer" who was accused of kidnapping a group member in order to convince the member to leave Moon's organization. (The charges were later dropped.)

During his testimony, Moon claimed to be in psychic communication with Jesus and Buddha, as well as other historical religious figures, and to be acting with their authority and guidance in setting up the Unification Church and controlling the lives of its members.[5] Moon claims to have been psychic since childhood. According to *The New York Times:* " 'From childhood I was clairvoyant' he once told a group of followers."[6] And Moon controls his followers' lives: Shortly after the 1982 trials, Moon held a mass wedding at Madison Square Garden, pairing off more than four thousand "Moonies," who accepted his presumably spiritual or supernatural choice of their marriage partners.

For anyone who wonders whether Moon's group really is a cult, we recommend two excellent but frightening descriptions of life within the Unification Church: *Hostage to Heaven,* by Barbara and Betty Underwood,[7] and *Crazy for God,* by Chris Evans.[8] We also recommend two 1982 films: *Moonchild* and *Ticket to Heaven.* Moon's claim to being in psychic communication with famous religious figures of the past is a common one among many cult leaders. In fact, many such leaders insist that all other religions and belief systems have been simply leading toward their own, which they in turn believe to be the highest achievement of mankind.

Pattern Two: The Cult as Haven

Although cult leaders, and their followers, often make exaggerated claims regarding psychic functioning, many people do in fact have experiences that are apparently psychic within cult settings, just as they do within mainstream society. While some of these are probably delusions resulting from overzealousness, malnutrition, or lack of sleep, others may well be genuine psychic functioning. Cult members usually credit their psychic experiences to their cult involvement, even though similar experiences are also frequently reported by people who are not cult members.

Many people are drawn into cults during times of personal crisis, when they are searching for ways to expand their awareness, increase their self-esteem, and achieve a greater sense of meaning and purpose in their lives. Some of these individuals, who had not paid much attention to psychic functioning previously, become aware of having psychic experiences simply because of their increased attentiveness to their own internal processes. They may credit their cult participation with increasing their awareness of psi. In fact, their own intensified awareness of psychic functioning may have been a major factor in their becoming drawn into a cult in the first place.

Unfortunately, those who join cults in the hope of finding acceptance of psychic experiences are often sorely abused and disappointed. At best, cult treatments of psychic functioning are severely limited by the doctrines of each group. At worst, the demands placed upon cult members leave virtually no time for the pursuit of the members' individual interests, in psychic functioning or anything else.

Although many cults project a public image of being quite interested in psychic experiences, they often turn out to be less interested in self-exploration than in fund-raising or politics—which are not the activities that prompt most members to join. For a cult member to explore his or her own personal concerns is usually regarded as a selfish deviation from a life of absolute dedication to fulfilling the group's "higher" objectives. A recruit seeking support for psychic experiences is likely to find that the cult leader has other things planned for him. Such a situation was reported by a former cult member who spent some time at the Human Freedom Center.

The woman had found herself in serious difficulty after she joined a popular international cult group, looking for a safe place where she might develop an understanding of her frequent apparently psychic experiences. After joining, she eventually lost touch with her family and friends for a period that stretched out to several years.

The woman worked in a factory, where she stuffed tea into bags for twelve to eighteen hours a day. Her entire earnings went to the cult and its leader. When she was not working, she completely immersed herself in cult activities, including hours of repetitive chanting every day. She slept on the floor of the communal quarters and ate a very poor diet, along with the other group members. Unfortunately, the woman had no chance to develop an understanding of the experiences that had led her to join the group in the first place, or even to discuss those experiences with anyone in the cult while she was a member.

Eventually the woman suffered from complete physical and psychological exhaustion, and mental-health professionals brought her to the Human Freedom Center. At the center, she was finally able to discuss her apparently psychic experiences with supportive people. She found that many people had similar experiences, and realized that hers were quite normal. After several weeks of counseling at the center, the woman had decided to return to college, and to integrate her interest in psychic functioning into a life within mainstream society. She has been doing wonderfully ever since.

As we discussed earlier, society generally leaves people floundering for information about psychic experiences, and many cults provide prefabricated explanations. The explanations, however, vary widely.

Some cults, such as the Peoples Temple, explain all apparently psychic experiences as evidence that their leader is God or the Messiah. Others describe the same sorts of experiences as the work of the devil or other demons—which they may see as being either a positive or a negative association. In still other cults, psychic experiences are seen as evidence that their members are mentally well developed or spiritually enlightened. On the other hand, certain Eastern-oriented groups view them as merely interesting phenomena occurring in the early stages of spiritual development, which, they say, must be overcome and eliminated as their disciples "advance."

Each cult's description of psychic functioning seems primarily designed to maintain and deepen the followers' allegiance to the group, rather than to help the members integrate psychic functioning into autonomous lives within society. The cults do not adequately explain why well-adjusted people who are not their members have psychic experiences. Nor do they help cult members learn about their potential for developing psychic abilities in the world beyond the stifling confines of cults.

Almost all cults include some sort of claims about psychic functioning within a larger belief system into which they attempt to indoctrinate prospective members. These claims are used to lure recruits into joining in cult activities, which may lead to their eventually becoming committed members. But, as happened with the young woman described earlier, the subject of psychic functioning may never again be mentioned once a recruit has become immersed in the cult's way of life.

Pattern Three: Cultivating Psi

Most groups claim psychic abilities only for their leaders, but a few cults focus all group beliefs and activities upon supposedly developing psychic abilities in their members. Typically they promise to increase their members' proficiency at psychic functioning, "mind control" or mind-reading, through exercises, meditation, and other psychological techniques, usually presented as a unique psychic training program. One group even claims that, for a price, its initiates will learn to levitate!

This type of program often means attending weekend seminars, perhaps held in hotel meeting rooms. These seminars can cost as much as several hundred dollars per session. Regular meetings with other group members may come next, and may cost more money. In the follow-up sessions, members are directed to discuss their apparently psychic experiences with one another, and to practice the techniques taught in the group's basic training program.

In some cults, the process of undergoing what is billed as the group's "psychic development" program may take several years, and the cost for the required courses may finally add up to tens of thousands of dollars. Participants are usually told that they are being brought through various "stages" or "levels" of personal and psychic development.

Members of such cults are usually encouraged to buy books and other materials prepared by the leader or his adherents. This allows the members to continue absorbing the leader's viewpoint even when not attending specific training sessions.

Some groups make astounding promises: Initiates who have gone through their whole training program, they say, will graduate into the advanced stages of psychic development, in which, by force of will alone, they can control all aspects of their physical and temporal relationship with the entire universe. This appears to us to represent a greater interest in power than in spirituality. Cult training supposedly will enable initiates to exercise absolute control of their emotions, to solve all personal problems, to manipulate other people like puppets, and to cheat death by carrying these abilities over into an immortal spiritual existence. We have looked carefully, but have not found any evidence to justify these claims. As recruits near what is presented as the most advanced stages, the group leader typically adds additional levels to guarantee the members' continued personal and financial involvement in the group.

Instead of developing a balanced understanding of psychic functioning while maintaining their independence as active participants in mainstream society, cult members are led to ever deeper immersion in cult doctrines and activities. They are encouraged to identify themselves as part of an exclusive group of supposedly psychically evolved beings, and to socialize principally with other "insiders." Although new members may first join a cult as part of a personal quest for knowledge, they can quickly become caught up in the group's predetermined agenda.

As a result of their new training, people who join certain cults often become alienated from their former friends, and even their families. Their relationship with the cult becomes the primary focus of their lives. They see everything and everyone else solely in reference to their relationship to the cult.

Many cult members try to get others to join their group. If they succeed, they usually see it as proof that the group's cause—and their own —is worthwhile. And for the cults themselves, this proselytizing is often an essential aspect of membership—the group needs fresh meat, and the members must find it.

Interactions among the individual members of a cult are generally much less important than their relationship with the cult and its leader. Members usually relate with each other according to rigid rules of conduct, within carefully prescribed situations and hierarchies. They respond to each other less as individuals than as common members of the group, taking part in various cult-oriented activities, operating from shared beliefs, and frequently using a specially constructed vocabulary.

In effect, people who join cults that offer to help them develop psychic abilities often end up undergoing a process that is tantamount to brainwashing. The groups' procedures include frequent doses of unrefined dogma—disguised as objectively verifiable information. This dogma is often accepted by members because the groups restrict critical aspects of members' lives—including sleep, diet, sexuality, privacy, and *especially the ability to acquire, assimilate, or freely interpret information.* Initiates are usually encouraged to view even the most slightly unusual experience as evidence of psychic functioning, and to interpret any possibly psychic experience within the group's preferred frame of reference.

For some people, the exposure to the possibility of developing their own psychic potential, which some cults appear to provide, may initially prove to be psychologically beneficial. This exposure—within what seems a socially supportive milieu—may help certain individuals to pay attention to areas of their own awareness that they might not otherwise consider exploring.

But prolonged exposure to any cult's treatment of psychic abilities may seriously restrict the way its initiates view psychic functioning. And it may keep them from fully developing their actual psychic potential. Such a situation was described by a university student who left a well-known cult when he realized what the group was actually offering:

> They had rules for everything. They told me what to eat, when to sleep, what to read, how to dress, what to do, and how to do it. They gave me an orange robe, handed me a rag and a bucket, and informed me that scrubbing the floor of their ashram was an advanced form of meditation. They told me it was all part of following the humble road to enlightenment.
>
> After two weeks of dressing like Sabu the Elephant Boy, cleaning floors, and washing dishes, I felt no closer to enlightenment than I had ever been. The group's diet of overcooked white rice and bland yellow mush made me nauseous. I had nightmares about giant cheeseburgers attacking Berkeley. I started wondering what the group's idea of enlightenment was really all about.
>
> One evening, I asked the group leader how I might recognize enlightenment in myself or in other people. He answered that enlightenment leads to psychic experiences and strongly developed intuitive abilities. I suggested that many people, who did not seem to be especially enlightened, had such experiences and abilities already, including myself. The leader appeared shocked at this suggestion. He insisted that I must be deluded for, he said, his group was following an ancient path, the only true road to psychic awareness and spiritual salvation.
>
> I suddenly realized that I had been putting my faith in other people, instead of in my own abilities. I felt stupid, because I should have asked more questions about the group before I joined it. The leader claimed to be leading his followers toward enlightenment, but he was really making self-awareness seem to be almost unattainable. He connected experiences that I now consider to be normal with a way of life that gave him power over other people.
>
> The members I spoke with thought that psychic experiences only happened to people who had been meditating for years. I left the group and went back to the university. Since then, I have had lots of interesting experiences without being a cultist.

Cults place a heavy emphasis upon deepening followers' dependency upon their leaders, rather than upon providing open-ended support for

individual self-actualization. These groups, therefore, make psychic functioning appear to be an unusual and complicated process that requires
months or years of expensive training and indoctrination to master. For
those who spend thousands of dollars for the privilege of psychologically
festering in a given cult's viewpoint, the claims made about psychic
functioning can appear convincing. But the seeker may also discover that
cult involvement carries an unexpectedly high emotional price tag, that
it offers few, if any, long-term psychological benefits, and that it can lead
to a host of serious social and psychological difficulties.

PSI AND ORGANIZED RELIGION

Cult leaders have been very successful at staking a claim on public access
to psychic abilities. They did not, however, originate the idea of monopo-
lizing psychic functioning for selfish purposes. Today's cults have merely
capitalized upon a sociological trend that originated, in part, with the
traditional religions.

   Although the writings of the traditional religions refer to many apparently psychic events, mainstream religion has been of little help to those
who want to understand psychic functioning in their own lives. Indeed,
organized religion has not encouraged people to think that they might
possess either latent or active psychic abilities.

   Instead organized religions have sometimes seen those who report
psychic experiences as potential competitors of religious leaders, saints,
and prophets. Therefore, many religious leaders have denied that psychic
abilities are normal human experiences, and have interpreted them as
being either of God or Satan.

   For millennia before religions became organized, shamans, medicine
men and women, seers, and prophets were important members of every
society or tribe of primitive people. As religions grew organized and
powerful, however, they began to see the free-lance psychic practitioner
as undesirable competition.

   As it evolved, organized religion attracted many individuals who were
psychically capable, and who would have been shamans in earlier times.
These individuals found great security within the church, where their
positions did not depend upon frequently making public demonstrations
of apparently psychic abilities. Such individuals remaining outside the
church often found themselves branded as witches or charlatans.

   But once outside competition was diminished, religious leaders came to focus more upon structured ritual than upon spontaneous inspiration as the basis for their social influence. And the church itself placed more emphasis upon ritual than upon the spiritual and psychic experiences upon which organized religions were founded.

Recently I (K.H.) discussed the response of mainstream religious groups to psychic functioning with philosopher of religion Dr. Filippo Liverziani, director of the Symposium for the Study of Philosophy and Sciences of Man, which is located in Rome, Italy. Dr. Liverziani spoke about the Roman Catholic Church, to which he belongs, and with which he has served as a member of two pontifical theological faculties in Rome:

> Theological and philosophical thought in the Catholic Church developed in such a way that the church now recognizes modern science, art, and technology as autonomous areas of human endeavor. The church has not, however, traditionally encouraged the autonomous efforts of individuals and groups who are investigating fields that it considers to be more properly within its own domain.
>
> Inner experience, especially when it is too freely interpreted, can easily deceive people. Psychic phenomena look a little like miracles, and precognition can seem to be competitive with prophecy. Many Catholic priests, theologians, and philosophers fear that the distance between nature and the supernatural can appear diminished, if such human capacities are taken seriously. They would, therefore, prefer that our way of conceiving of nature would continue to be the classical one of traditional science, instead of developing into the expanded model which psi research and modern physics suggest, and that seems to be much more congruent with a spiritual, religious, and mystical vision of reality.
>
> In fact, those who promote this kind of limited religious approach to psychic and mystical experiences become, in the last analysis, the best allies of positivistic and materialistic scientists and academicians. The anxiety which these church people express toward psychic experiences appears more like the concerns of parents about dangers to which their children might be exposed, than the anxiety of rulers who are afraid of losing their power—but perhaps the second motivation would not be as easily confessable as the first. In any event, their "human, all too human" attitude contradicts the inner logic of the Christian Church.
>
> Faith is just the opposite of human fear and worry. Moreover,

free research in all fields is a way of searching for God himself. Finally, if reality is spiritual, spirit must affect every level of reality. *Reality is not a condominium that is composed of a materialistic main level and a spiritualistic second floor.*

Actually, a new attitude is now taking root in the Catholic Church, especially in connection with the Second Vatican Council. Unfortunately, such developments proceed very slowly.

As a result of this paradoxical situation, many people have learned to associate psychic functioning with religion, but nonetheless have been unable to find tolerance of their apparently psychic experiences within mainstream religious groups. Thus the field is ripe for exploitation by cult leaders who present themselves as theological figures and who claim to offer an alternative to the attitudes of traditional religion.

PSI IS NOT A CULT

As we saw in Part I, extensive scientific research indicates that psychic abilities are freely available to many people who decide to learn about and use them—perhaps to most. Psychic functioning seems to be a widespread but generally latent human ability, and we believe that it is possible for psychologically healthy people to develop their psychic potential while maintaining their autonomy and their personal freedom. People who accept responsibility for expanding their own awareness while maintaining balanced social relationships are undoubtedly better off than those who submit to the mental slavery which the cults offer in the guise of self-awareness training.

If people are to feel comfortable with exploring their own psychic potential, they must understand that psychic experiences are an important, totally normal part of human existence. Psychic functioning should not be the restricted domain of cultists, or any other individuals or groups who deliberately misrepresent it for their own purposes.

Reliable, undistorted scientific information about psychic functioning must be made more easily available and identifiable. But as we shall see in the next two chapters, disseminating dependable information may not be an easy task. Movies, television, and the news media have already been glutted with misinformation about psi.

7

Psi in Film and Television Fiction: Bewitched, Bothered, and Bewildered

The images of psychic functioning that are depicted in mass-media fiction quickly lead you to believe that only very strange people have psychic experiences and abilities, or that psi is experienced by normal people only under the most bizarre circumstances. You might even mistakenly conclude that psi does not exist at all, except in the imaginations of science-fiction writers and deluded fanatics. Any of these conclusions would be understandable, but none of them would conform to the everyday reality of psychic functioning in the lives of many people.

PSYCHIC STEREOTYPES

Psychic experience and abilities have usually been depicted in film and television fiction as abnormal and frightening, as adversely affecting those who encounter them, or as appropriate only for odd or demented people, zombies, or beings from other planets. Even on those rare occasions when psychic functioning has been treated lightheartedly, it has still been made to appear to be an unusual and not necessarily desirable talent. Often, those who develop psychic capabilities are portrayed as doing so at the expense of their capacity for experiencing love, happiness, and other emotions, or their ability to sustain normal human relationships.

The Beautiful Witch

The film *Bell, Book and Candle* (1959) is a classic example. It revolves around the activities of a fictional group of witches in Manhattan, psychically adept people who belong to a secret subculture of immortal eccentrics. A romance develops between one of them, a beautiful female "witch" (whom we might better describe as an experienced psychic), and an ordinary "mortal" man.

As the film unfolds, the heroine experiences human love for the first time in her long life. As a result of this attachment, she loses both her psychic "powers" and her immortality. She eventually decides to marry the film's hero and to live a more finite—and supposedly healthier and happier—life with him.

A similar premise underlies the popular television situation comedy *Bewitched.* The main character is a psychically adept female "witch" who has married a "mortal" man and lives with him among apparently nonpsychic residents of suburbia. In *Bewitched,* the heroine retains her psychic abilities (mostly psychokinetic), which create comic havoc in the lives of those around her. As in *Bell, Book and Candle,* the heroine's relatives in *Bewitched* are odd but psychically capable immortals; they are somewhat contemptuous of ordinary mortals, and frequently amuse themselves by playing psychic tricks—casting spells—upon them.

Bell, Book and Candle and *Bewitched* are among the more charming and humorous treatments of psychic functioning in mass-media fiction. Nevertheless they contain many of the same negative stereotypes that have characterized most of the mass media's treatment of psi. And these stereotypes strongly influence the public's view of psychic functioning.

The main characters in both stories maintain their psychic capabilities at the expense of normal and comfortable social relationships. They are superior, in many respects, to the "mortals" around them, but they have difficulties that would make many sensible people wary of exploring their own psychic potential.

Most important, these fictional accounts of the effects of psi upon people's lives make categorical distinctions between "psychic" and "non-psychic" individuals. These distinctions are entertaining—but they are misleading and unrealistic. *Both stories are based upon the myth that psychic abilities are rare talents, that such talents are necessarily related to deviant and neurotic behavior, and that those who have psychic abilities may not even be human.*

The Outsider

Similar negative stereotypes lie at the heart of productions that depict human beings, rather than immortals, as having psychic experiences and abilities. Here, psi is presented as a highly exceptional and strange human talent. Those who possess this talent are usually very different from the other people around them.

In some movies, such as *Carrie* (1976) and *Scanners* (1981), psychic abilities are the cause or result of serious personality problems. Carrie is a teenage girl who is late in reaching puberty. She is also the only child of an abusive single mother, a crazed religious fanatic. To make matters worse, the girl does not get along with her classmates or teachers, and is often the victim of vicious practical jokes. At a time when she deeply needs compassionate understanding, the girl is mistreated and feels un-loved, misunderstood, and unwanted. All is resolved in the film's climax when she murders her tormenters at her high-school prom by burning down the school with a burst of unrestrained psychokinetic force. Then, using the same method at home, she kills her mother and herself.

Discussing their psychic capabilities openly sometimes leads fictional characters into serious difficulties with people who fear, misunderstand, or seek to take advantage of them. In *Scanners*, for example, several characters (the "Scanners") develop strong telepathic and psychokinetic abilities as a result of a drug taken by their mothers during pregnancy. Several of them become antisocial and psychotic as a consequence of having psychic abilities. At first, they are studied by a government-sponsored organization that plans to use their abilities. Later, the Scanners are hunted by hired killers who try to murder them.

One of the more imaginative film treatments of the "outsider" approach to psychic experiences and abilities occurs in *The Illustrated Man* (1969) based on the Ray Bradbury book. The film's leading character, Carl, a violent, Depression-era itinerant, has been tattooed all over his body with "skin illustrations" by a time-travelling sorceress—of the beautiful witch variety—who is visiting his place and time from the future. When the sorceress, Felicia, disappears "back into the future," Carl discovers that his skin illustrations come to life for people who stare at them, producing terrifying visions of future events. As a result of his precognitive tattoos, Carl is eventually hated by everyone who meets him. He is forced to become a wandering outcast, whose only real friend is the little dog he carries around with him in a cloth bag.

Carl's reason for living becomes his search for Felicia. He hopes to kill her as an act of revenge for his predicament. Yet, despite his mania, Carl is not without special insights into the nature of time and psychic functioning. In one of the film's more surprising moments, for example, he instructs an acquaintance on how to tune in psychic impressions about a place from which he is both spatially and temporally distant. He tells his viewer to first notice immediate sensations—to "smell the heat" around him—and then to experience the same sensations "someplace else." As insightful as Carl is, however, he is also a bizarre and superhuman character who, in one scene, quiets an entire field of noisy insects by yelling at them to "shut up." He psychically dominates his roadside acquaintance nearly as easily.

The Illustrated Man has lost his place within human society as a result of his psi abilities. Ultimately he appears as a weird, tragic, demented figure—a man who is both driven and dangerous. He is hardly a role model for anyone who considers developing psi abilities to follow. Nor, for that matter, is the sorceress, Felicia. She, too, is an isolated figure, whose reason for condemning Carl—a stranger—to a life of anguish and alienation, is never explicitly stated.

Such films convince many people that psychic functioning is potentially dangerous, if it exists at all; and, in any case, that it is the rightful domain of science fiction writers and their demented characters. Sane people would hardly want to learn about psi if they believed they would end up like Carrie, the Scanners or the Illustrated Man.

In Ingmar Bergman's most recent film, *Fanny and Alexander* (1983), a character named Ishmael makes it clear that the view of psychic people as outsiders still thrives in modern cinema. In a pivotal scene in the film, Ishmael demonstrates his outstanding remote-viewing capabilities by reading the mind of Alexander and describing the death of the stepfather whom the boy hates. Ishmael is imprisoned in a cage in a small room because he is considered insane and dangerous by his family.

The Dangerous Secret

In the fictional world of movies and TV, psi is often depicted as a potentially destructive force in people's lives, or as a power most human beings cannot ethically or easily cope with. For this reason, many fictional characters—such as television's human *Girl With Something Extra,* the female genie in *I Dream of Jeannie,* and the immortal witches in *Bell, Book and Candle* and *Bewitched*—decide to keep their psychic talents secret from most of the people around them.

Fictional characters who discuss their psychic abilities openly can become social outcasts. Such a fate befalls the heroine of *Resurrection* (1981). In this movie about a woman who develops extraordinary healing powers after she barely escapes death in a car crash, psychic functioning is seen in a much more positive light than in most of its predecessors. The film also offers an accurate though depressing view of what can result from publicly admitting to having psychic abilities.

When *Resurrection* begins, the heroine is a normal, happily married housewife who appears to have no unusual psychic talents. She is then transformed into a powerful psychic healer, which leads eventually to her becoming a peculiar old woman who lives alone in an isolated gas station in the Southwest American desert.

Between these opposite extremes in her life, she receives public acclaim for her healing talents. But her fame soon becomes a burden; her fanatically religious boyfriend, who considers all psychic functioning outside the church as Satanic, first makes her life miserable and then tries to kill her. Not wanting to embrace traditional religion, the heroine decides that the safest place for her is on the outskirts of civilization. There, in virtual isolation, like Siddhartha at his ferry, she secretly continues to exercise her psychic abilities as the film ends.

The Supernatural Connection

As in many other fictional productions, *Resurrection* closely relates psi with belief in the supernatural and in life after death. A serious attempt is made to separate the heroine's psychic abilities from any particular organized religious viewpoint. Still, she is in psychic communication with her dead husband and relatives throughout most of the film.

.   .   .

The linking of psychic experiences with the supernatural or life after death is, in fact, an element common to many fictional treatments of psi. A dramatic example of this turns up in the recent film *Poltergeist* (1982). Here, a suburban American family is terrorized by angry spirits. They do not know that their new housing development was built directly on top of an old cemetery. The family's little girl is soon drawn into psychic communication with discarnate entities, and is then psychically transported into a limbo that supposedly separates the world of the living from the realm of the dead.

In desperation, the family calls in a famous psychic. Once again, the psychic is a very peculiar old woman. She is pint-sized, overweight, and squeaky-voiced, and she reads minds as easily as most people read a newspaper. Her job is to facilitate communication between this dimension and the world beyond. She directs a rescue operation, complete with special effects and blood-chilling music. The missing girl is eventually reunited with her family, but only after this film makes the point that psi can lead normal people into serious trouble.

For all of its modern special effects, *Poltergeist* continues a long-standing Hollywood tradition of uniting psychic functioning with ghosts, demons, death, haunted houses, witchcraft, cemeteries, vampires, and other strange people, and odd religious or occult practices. The film is not much different in this respect from earlier films such as *Nosferatu* (1923), *Dracula* (1932), *Village of the Damned* (1960), *The Legend of Hell House* (1973), *The Exorcist* (1973), *Don't Look Now* (Italian, 1973), *The Amityville Horror* (1979), and dozens of others. These films share a devout commitment to scaring the daylights out of as many people as possible regarding psychic experiences and abilities, or anything else that might possibly be related to this topic.

In the case of *The Amityville Horror*, the public was told that both the movie and the book present a dramatization of actual events. Many people probably believe, therefore, that they depict an essentially true story.

In fact, *The Amityville Horror* is almost entirely a work of sensationalistic fiction. An excellent analysis of factual inconsistencies within the story itself and logical contradictions between the reported events in Amityville and public records of thunderstorms and other checkable occurrences has been published in a scientific journal.[1] This study was conducted by Dr. Robert Morris, a psychologist and psi researcher who is currently with the School of Information Sciences at Syracuse University.

Dr. Morris's study reveals that many events which were said to have happened in Amityville either could not have taken place or were contradicted by other claims made in the book and film. Since I (K.H.) had some personal involvement with the events behind *The Amityville Horror*, Morris's conclusions were not surprising to me.

The Amityville case had first come to my attention while I was a researcher with the Psychical Research Foundation in Durham. The foundation had been asked to investigate the alleged occurrences in Amityville by a member of the family involved. We were reluctant to travel that far without first knowing more. We needed a reliable, independent witness. Fortunately, one of my closest friends, George Kokoris, was then a student at the State University of New York at Stony Brook, very near Amityville.

George is an exceptionally bright man with a keen sense of humor and more than a smattering of common sense. He also has a long-standing interest in psi research, and is a thoroughly reliable investigator. He recently completed his doctorate in neurosciences at the University of Michigan and is currently conducting brain research at Mt. Sinai Medical Center in New York City. I suggested that the foundation ask George to have a look at what was happening in Amityville. That turned out to be a good idea. As George tells it:

> My involvement with the "Amityville Horror" began when I received a telephone call from the Psychical Research Foundation. I was asked to speak with the parties involved to see if it seemed worthwhile to pursue a large-scale investigation. I spoke to George Lutz, father of the frightened family, later that night. He seemed very shaken and took pains to warn me of the risks he said I was taking in becoming involved. However, he seemed eager to tell his story. We arranged to meet the next day.
>
> I met George and Kathleen Lutz in a van outside of their abandoned Amityville home, which they refused to enter. There was a sense of deep fright, but they were anxious to impress me as calm, rational people. They seemed educated enough to be sensitive about not wanting to appear stupid or foolish.

The story they told me over the next two hours was, on the surface, metaphysically unextraordinary, save for some claimed isolated physical manifestations of the poltergeist variety. *Certainly, it bore no resemblance to the "monsters and mayhem" tale that later emerged in the book and movie about the case.*

However, the account the Lutzes gave me was very psychologically suggestive. That is, if there was anything going on, it was being manifested in subtle changes in personality, habits, and belief structures. For example, why did they buy the house, knowing what they did? Why did they tell their children grisly details of the murder that had taken place there years earlier? Why did they keep the furnishings of the murdered family? Why did they seek the advice they did, and when they did? Was there a pattern to the changes the Lutzes began to notice in themselves and their relationship to each other?

Based upon George Kokoris's investigation and insightful report, we decided not to get involved at Amityville. As the case turned out, we were glad we made that decision. George told us how the Amityville house became the center of a carefully orchestrated media sideshow, complete with on-scene television reporters filming "séances," while the people present broke out into fits of seeming mass hysteria. He decided to drop the case:

My disengagement from the investigation was a personal decision, born of the sadness and disgust I began to feel about what was taking place in Amityville. Sadness that a unique opportunity to investigate an unusual, and perhaps revelatory, *psychological* phenomenon had been lost, and disgust at the shabbiness and stupidity that so easily, thoroughly, and predictably enveloped the whole situation.
  These feelings of sadness and disgust were to echo in me once more when, two years later, George Lutz called to offer me royalties and a percentage of the net, in return for assistance on a sequel to *The Amityville Horror* that he was thinking about writing. It would be all about the people involved in the Amityville case. As I demurred, I thought of one of those people—the reporter who had confided in me early on, "You know, don't you, that they've already signed a movie deal about this whole thing."

Horror sells tickets. The more frightening, bizarre, and horrific anything that remotely resembles psychic experiences can be made to seem,
the greater the ticket potential. Consequently, screenwriters and directors
have so far shown little interest in depicting psychic functioning as the
straightforward information-processing capability it really is. It's just been
anything for a scream.

There is not much potential sensationalism or profit in an ability that
is generally available to a great many people and that is no more intrinsically related with psychosis, murder, and the supernatural than are the five
senses or memory. So we get sensationalism; the public is being enter-
tained, therefore, and it is also being had.

The price that we pay for such entertainment is more than just the
cost of admission. There is a high emotional and social cost for all of us,
because these portrayals stir up and perpetuate people's confusion about
and fear of psychic experiences and abilities that might otherwise greatly
enrich their lives.

The Alien

When movie and television producers do not directly connect psi with
weird human beings, immortals, or representatives of the supernatural,
they often relate this subject to aliens from other planets. In productions
such as the television movie *The Man with the Power* (1977) and the
recent series *The Powers of Matthew Star*, certain humans are shown to
have psychic abilities as a result of their parents being extraterrestrials. In
other productions, humans develop psychic abilities only after coming in
direct contact with aliens or the remnants of alien civilizations.

The classic film *Forbidden Planet* (1956), a science-fiction version of
Shakespeare's *The Tempest*, is of the latter type. Space explorers from
Earth discover the remains of an advanced alien civilization on a distant
world. They learn that the alien civilization—the Krell—was destroyed
millennia ago during a single violent evening. The aliens had evidently
developed powerful psychokinetic abilities and then unwittingly murdered one another as a result of the immediate psychokinetic unleashing
of their subconscious hostile feelings toward their fellow beings.

The human explorers of *Forbidden Planet* very nearly meet the same
fate when a scientist boosts his mental capabilities with the aid of an alien
device. He accidentally unleashes his own psychokinetic "monsters from
the Id" upon his fellow explorers. Humanity is saved when the offending
human heroically allows the others to escape and deliberately destroys the

alien world, and himself with it, by activating a self-destruct mechanism deep within the core of the planet.

In other films and television shows, aliens have psychic abilities, but humans merely gaze upon these "strange" talents with wonder. Mr. Spock, the half-alien starship officer of *Star Trek* (films in 1979 and 1982, and the earlier television series), has formidable telepathic capabilities but is virtually incapable of feeling or coping with love and other human emotions.

Other alien *Star Trek* characters also have impressive psychic capabilities, but few human characters can even approximate the aliens' level of psychic functioning. The same pattern holds true in television programs such as *Mork and Mindy* and *My Favorite Martian,* and in films like *Star Wars* (1977), *Superman* (1978), *E.T.* (1982), and *Close Encounters of the Third Kind* (1977).

Close Encounters is also an excellent example of the fictional treatment of people who suddenly have their first psychic experiences. The leading human characters in this film are telepathically given thoughts by benevolent aliens when they encounter spaceships visiting from other planets. As a result, they become obsessed with meeting the aliens at a secret location, and they exhibit behavior that those around them consider quite irrational—and sometimes it is. For example, the hero builds a miniature mountain of garbage in his living room. The film ends on a positive note, though, when the leading characters discover that their apparently telepathic impressions from the aliens were genuine.

The Primitive

Film and television characters occasionally have psychic experiences that are prompted by involvement with primitive Earth cultures rather than with extraterrestrials. Such is the case in the film *The Last Wave* (1977) and in the television series *Kung Fu.*

In *Kung Fu,* the main character is a half-Caucasian, half-Chinese priest, trained from childhood in the philosophy and martial arts of an ancient Buddhist sect in late-nineteenth-century China. After receiving this exceptionally useful training, he travels to the developing American West.

Besides being virtually undefeatable in hand-to-hand combat, the priest relies heavily upon his strongly developed intuitive capabilities. He often has precognitive, clairvoyant, and telepathic visions, and is as adept at psychically dominating an occasional demon as he is at kicking a drunken bully unconscious in a saloon. Like many other psychically capable characters in film and television fiction, the hero in *Kung Fu* is an outsider to mainstream society, a solitary "endless wanderer" who lives an almost totally celibate existence—a high price to pay for psychic development.

In the Australian film *The Last Wave,* the hero is beset by strange precognitive images, fantastic dreams, and other apparently psychic occurrences after he becomes involved with a group of aborigines who practice an ancient form of tribal magic in modern Australia. By the end of the film, these experiences have totally bewildered the hero, who finds himself standing on a beach and seemingly witnessing the end of the world.

The Trail of Death

Most of the characters who have psychic experiences for the first time in film and television fiction end up wishing that their intuitive impressions were imagined. In films such as *The Reincarnation of Peter Proud* (1975), *The Eyes of Laura Mars* (1978), and *The Psychic* (Italian, 1978), the main characters' psychic experiences are deeply unsettling. No wonder—in each case, their psychic impressions are the result of murders which have either already taken place or will soon be carried out or attempted.

Fictional characters have often used psi to aid them in manipulating and murdering other people. In *Svengali* (1931), the main character controls the minds of other characters from afar for nefarious purposes.

In a more recent film, *The Colossus of New York* (1958), a brilliant scientist develops fantastic "extrasensory" abilities—after he is hit by a truck—when his brain is transplanted into the body of an enormous robot to save his life. (The sort of thing that might happen to anybody.) Unfortunately, the formerly idealistic scientist becomes a demented murderer who uses perfect remote viewing as an aid to tracking down his intended victims. Naturally, the Colossus is himself ultimately destroyed in classic horror-film fashion.

On rare occasions, fictional characters have psychic impressions that are not directly related to evil doings or outside psychic intervention in their thought processes. Usually, though, these impressions are still portrayed as weird occurrences that are not easily or commonly available to most people.

One example of this occurs in the film *On a Clear Day You Can See Forever* (1970). Its heroine, who herself was hypnotized in an effort to stop smoking, suddenly has psychic impressions and recollections of what appear to be her previous lives. This musical comedy thus continues the tradition of associating psychic functioning with life after death and the supernatural. It also relates psychic abilities and experiences with unusual states of consciousness that do not necessarily relate to the ways most people actually process psychic information.

The Altered State

This dogmatic coupling of psychic functioning with hypnotism and other bizarre altered states of consciousness is a throwback to the heyday of mesmerism that would probably make Soviet researchers blush. Unfortunately, it is a common way to turn a fictional character into a psychic.

The hero of the television series *The Sixth Sense*, for example, is a psychic detective and psi researcher who regularly hypnotizes himself by staring into a striped spinning cone on his office wall. While in a trance, he has intuitive impressions that he later uses to solve crimes and mysteries. This character would presumably be psychically emasculated if anyone slipped into his office and made off with his spinning cone.

The Superlab

Even the psi research laboratories that turn up in shows like *The Sixth Sense* and films like *The Reincarnation of Peter Proud* and *Resurrection* are far from the mark. In these extravagantly appointed fictional suites, psychic occurrences pop up like mushrooms from every crevice and corner. Reality is much less dramatic.

Most psi researchers consider themselves fortunate if they can plan their research budgets more than one year in advance. Their experiments are designed and carried out slowly and carefully, under painstakingly controlled conditions. A psi researcher may spend several months designing, conducting, analyzing, and interpreting a single experimental series.

ALL IN GOOD FUN?

Viewed separately, any one of the fictional treatments of psychic functioning discussed here might be taken as an entertaining study of the lives and activities of some interesting characters. These treatments would be essentially harmless if psychic functioning existed only in the imaginations of scriptwriters, or if people who really do have psychic experiences actually behaved in the ways that they do in film and television fiction.

But taken as a whole, television and film portrayals of psi in general and psychic people in particular constitute a mass of destructive stereotypes set against a backdrop of ill-conceived myths and misconceptions about the origins and effects of psychic experiences and abilities. These fictional presentations are as far from the everyday reality of psi as the television show *Amos and Andy* or the films *The Birth of a Nation* (1915) and *Shaft* (1971) are from the daily experiences of real black Americans.

A GOOD BEGINNING

We hope that more realistic and less stereotyped portrayals of people with psychic experiences will become common in future film and television productions. A recent episode of the TV series *Trapper John, M.D.* shows that this can be done, and still be entertaining. In this episode, a successful surgeon suddenly begins having precognitive impressions about various future events, such as impending operations of his patients and automobile accidents.

At first he has a hard time understanding the meaning of his experiences, both for his own self-image and for his ability to carry on his work and relate with others. He has heard that only very strange people have psychic experiences and abilities. He also has difficulty in clearly interpreting some of his psychic impressions because of what we have referred to as mental noise.

Some medical colleagues try to take advantage of the surgeon's abilities by asking him to predict the outcome of horseraces and events in their personal lives. Others do not believe that such abilities really exist. The surgeon's close friends and associates are open-minded about psi, however, and respond to his experiences with sincere personal interest and compassion. Finally he realizes that his psychic impressions simply represent an additional and potentially useful source of information for him. He also recognizes that his psychic experiences do not make him a strange person or affect his fundamental worth as a human being.

Unfortunately a problem with most television and film portrayals of psychic functioning, including even this relatively positive episode of *Trapper John*, is that they often exaggerate their character's psychic experiences and abilities in order to make a dramatic point. This exaggeration makes it harder for people to distinguish between what is and is not possible in real psychic functioning.

THE ILL EFFECTS OF STEREOTYPES

Psychic abilities are usually presented in such an extreme fashion in film and television fiction that many people conclude that psi must only exist in fantasy and science fiction. They recognize a tall tale when they see it. But unfortunately, they also discount the possibility of genuine psychic functioning as a result.

Even people who have genuine psychic experiences are sometimes intimidated by the fictional images. They may think their own psychic capabilities are not overpowering enough to be taken seriously. Others may become worried or frightened that their own psychic experiences may quickly get out of hand, as they often do for fictional characters. Some may fear that their friends will greet any discussion of psychic experiences as warmly as a confession of vampirism. They are rightly afraid that people will associate them with the strange images and negative stereotypes presented on television and in movies, and will conclude that they are going crazy.

Some people who have psychic experiences are so affected by fictional stereotypes that they begin to think of themselves as being as unusual as the supposedly psychic characters who populate film and television fiction. Given what they may feel is a choice of considering themselves to be either *crazy* or *extremely special*, most of these people adopt the latter as their preferred self-image. As a result, some of them behave so strangely that they really do alienate the people around them, confirming the misconception that psychic abilities are always associated with deviant behavior. Many people are therefore reluctant to explore their own psychic capabilities or even to admit to any interest in psi because they do not want to be considered abnormal or crazy.

Yet, despite the stereotypes, there is nothing abnormal or unusual about psychic experiences and abilities. In fact, psychic functioning is as prevalent as the common cold—although it is potentially much more useful and enjoyable for those who catch on to it.

Obviously, psychic functioning is of great concern to a great many people. The hundreds of millions of dollars they spend each year to see the kinds of films we have discussed testify to a strong public interest in anything related to this subject. The millions of people who join cults offer more proof, if more is needed, that there is a high level of interest in psychic experiences and abilities which is simply not being properly dealt with by society at large.

Most of us have had at least one apparently psychic experience which we would like to be able to intelligently explain. Were you to mention your own such experiences to your friends, in a comfortable setting, you might be surprised to discover that many of them have also had similar encounters. If you doubt this fact, we suggest that you ask several people whom you know and trust if they have had any apparently psychic experiences. They will probably tell you about some of their own experiences and then ask to hear about yours.

In a society that offers very little intelligent discussion of this subject, many people are yearning for accurate information about psi. As a result, they settle for almost any discussion of apparent psi that they can find, including the fraudulant claims of cult leaders and the misleading images presented in film and television fiction.

It would not be correct to suggest that this interest represents a morbid or irrational preoccupation with the unknown. The truth is that most people are interested in psychic experiences *because they are having them.*

8

Psi in the News: The Twilight Zone

Fictional television shows and movies are not the only mass media that misrepresent psychic experiences and abilities. At times, what is presented as factual news about psychic occurrences and psi research is hard to distinguish from intentional fiction. When reports of psi research are inappropriately mixed with such topics as unidentified flying objects, the Bermuda Triangle, and pyramid power, many people grow reluctant to take psychic functioning seriously.

THE REPORTER'S DILEMMA

Reporters, feature writers, and TV producers have been exposed to the same stereotypes and myths as the rest of us. They do not want to seem gullible or foolish; in fact, they are more concerned about their intellectual credibility than most people. Their professional reputations depend on their appearing to be insightful, rational, and unbiased.

Journalists who compete for prestigious investigative and scientific assignments must be careful about their objectivity. So when they write about apparently psychic occurrences, they are in an awkward position. They must try to explain things that often seem unexplainable, to the public as well as to other journalists.

In the news business, saying you have observed a genuinely psychic occurrence is about as risky as reporting that you just watched your grandfather turning into a werewolf. You had better be able to prove the truth of your statements, or your co-workers will wonder if you have been working too hard or drinking. Reporting about psi is not the best way to win a Pulitzer Prize.

Thus a journalist feels more secure if he appears to take whatever he reports about psi with a grain of salt. To be really safe, he may write about psychic functioning in as controversial a light as possible. Controversy makes news seem more interesting and can give the savvy journalist a chance to showcase his professional skepticism. By staying above the controversy, the reporter appears to be doing an admirable job of balanced reporting. In any event, controversy sells news.

In all fairness, though, we are convinced that most journalists sincerely try to give undistorted information about what is happening in the world, and are as offended by blatant sensationalism as we are—although when I (K.H.) recently said as much to a friend who is a well-known broadcast journalist, he laughed and replied, "If it bleeds, it leads." And as I write this paragraph, Paul Harvey has just come on the air with his nationwide newscast. His lead story is a detailed description of a woman in the Midwest who was stomped to death by a circus elephant. "And now for page two. . . ."

In trying to present straight facts about psychic functioning and psi research, it can be hard for even dedicated and ethical journalists to recognize what the real facts are, and to distinguish serious psi researchers from the cranks without a great deal of background and experience in this field.

QUACKS, AND OTHER ODD DUCKS

Psi research attracts a lot of confused people who are questioning their own identities, and quite a number of charlatans who deliberately exploit popular misconceptions about psi. Such people have less appreciation for scientific research and the subtleties of psychic abilities than many punk-rock fans have for opera. But they make so much noise that journalists cannot ignore them.

So, interested journalists are likely to encounter a lot of strange and noisy characters who claim to be specialists on various aspects of psi research. They may encounter many severely neurotic, psychotic, or other disturbed people—not excluding cult leaders and other frauds—who make wild and unfounded claims about their own supposed psychic abilities and experiences.

Cult leaders, as we have discussed, are among the charlatans who use the news media as their personal forum. Jim Jones was a vivid example. He made himself a public figure in San Francisco by staging events designed to capture news coverage. When Walter Mondale came to San Francisco on his Vice-Presidential campaign, Jones accompanied Mr. Mondale around town in a chartered helicopter.

When Jones turned out to be just another cult leader who, among other things, was exploiting people's misunderstanding of psychic functioning, the press was close at hand to act as a witness. Although reporters were not allowed inside the Peoples Temple to watch Jones's actual performances, they were able to glean some information about what Jones was up to through other sources.

These rumors were confirmed after the tragedy in Guyana. If journalists were later asked to observe genuine psychic occurrences, they might understandably find it difficult not to call up images of Jim Jones and other cult leaders from their mental notes. Such skepticism is understandable.

The world is full of ersatz fortune tellers, phony psychics, fake demonologists, and fast-buck occultists who make sizable livings by pretending to be experts on psi. These con artists prey upon public misunderstanding by delivering any misrepresentation the public will pay for.

Many of these charlatans eagerly seek media coverage as a form of free advertising that provides them with a veneer of credibility while they draw in the unwary. In his report on the Amityville case (see Chapter 7), George Kokoris writes about two such media hounds that he encountered:

> They were famous in certain circles for their claimed knack at ridding homes of "spirits," for their handy advice on dealing with "demons," and their public-relations savvy. I wondered how they happened to be there, but soon realized that was like wondering how hyenas can spot a fresh kill.

People with serious psychological problems also often cast themselves as "psychics," complete with whatever personality quirks they have learned to associate with this role as a result of their exposure to film and television fiction. The assumed role of a "psychic" provides them with a convenient delusional escape from the unsavory prospect of more directly confronting their real problems.

These individuals may claim that the problems they have in relating to other people are purely the result of their being "special" people, "psychics," misunderstood by those who are less "aware." The strong need they feel to validate their delusions sometimes leads them to make extreme claims to the press, as a means of attracting public attention.

On the other hand, people who have real psychic experiences and are comfortable with them usually do not need to attract attention by making unfounded claims. Many of them would be surprised to be called "psychic," because they do not think their intuitive abilities are unusual. Their real psychic functioning is often overlooked in a world overburdened with stereotypes—and with people trying to live up to those stereotypes as an excuse for their inability to cope productively with the real world.

To complicate matters further, both for the news media and for psi researchers, some individuals who have established reputations for being able to consciously utilize psychic capabilities in the laboratory have not been especially stable, easygoing, honest, or reliable people. A few have even tried cheating and deception when they thought they could get away with it. Such people are less interested in accurate research than in promoting themselves and attempting to use psi research to enhance their own tenuous reputations and credibility. They present an even greater problem to the press and to researchers than do the more obviously deluded people, who stay away from research laboratories. Some psychically capable people seek the attention of researchers and the press because they have a strong need to be admired. They often claim to be especially psychic, although their psychic abilities may be no more extensive than those of other people who are strongly motivated to participate in laboratory experiments.

People who feel a strong need to identify themselves exclusively as psychic usually bathe in any publicity they can get. These people often so strongly need to feel unique that they make exaggerated claims, implying that only a handful of very unusual people are capable of functioning psychically.

Because such claims fit the popular stereotypes, they often end up in news reports. But these claims are really only the psychological equivalent of animals marking the perimeter of their territory—little more than intimidation tactics used by insecure people who feel compelled to defend their chosen turf, even if there are no intruders.

.   .   .

Fortunately, most of the people who actually participate in legitimate psi experiments are stable, happy individuals who want to explore their own psychic potential and who share a healthy sense of curiosity about the whole area. They would be unlikely to wear a button saying, "Kiss me, I'm psychic."

And the more stable people tend to produce more reliable results in the psi laboratory. They are used to succeeding at interesting tasks, and are not generally anxious about the outcome of any given experiment in ways that might interfere with their ability to function psychically.

These capable people do not seek the attention of the media because they do not need public recognition to prove themselves. Being "psychic" is an integrated part of their awareness, rather than their whole identity. They are generally as appalled by the stereotypes of "psychic" people as the rest of us are, but you do not usually read much about them in the newspapers.

Journalists who want to write about psi research may also turn to an extensive pool of quack researchers who make ridiculous and sensational claims. As a field that is exploring the borders of our current scientific understanding of space and time, psi research has attracted a lot of people who want to lump every conceivable mystery into this field. They often represent themselves as authorities on psi research, though they may actually know very little about psychic functioning and less about scientific methods.

These self-proclaimed experts somehow have more time for press interviews than do real scientists spending time on careful experiments. The sensational claims of so-called experts are also more entertaining, and hence more newsworthy, than are the more guardedly worded statements of serious researchers. So dilettantes and charlatans tend to get most of the coverage.

All sorts of fantastic claims are made by people whom the media refer to as psi researchers. Most of us have heard that such things as psychic communication with plants and yogurt and the psychic virtues of pyramids are supposed to be scientifically established facts. Although the question of plant communication may remain open, the research underlying such claims is inadequate in the extreme.[1]

In the case of ostensible psychic communication with plants and yogurt, for example, most of the researchers involved did not have the combined background in botany and physiology needed to interpret their experiments properly. As an experienced physiological technician and a student of botany, I (K.H.) conducted an extensive study of all such published studies, in cooperation with Dr. Janis Antonovics of the Duke University Department of Botany, in 1975.[2]

The study showed that the researchers did not seem to understand the limitations of the physiological monitoring equipment they were using, or the need to control important environmental and biological factors that could negate the results of their experiments. They generally ignored established scientific procedures in their haste to present completely unsubstantiated conclusions to the news media and the public.

In the case of popular claims about "pyramid power," a team of psi researchers in Toronto conducted a series of definitive experiments and found no evidence to support the claims that pyramids sharpen razor blades or preserve meat.[3] Instead, the Canadian investigators found that all the claimed psychic effects of pyramids were explainable purely on the basis of known physical and psychological influences.

Yet, many people still believe in "pyramid power." These pyramid faithful are familiar with the sensational news reports about this subject, but not the conclusive experiments that were finally published in a scientific journal. The Canadian results were published years ago, but as recently as August 1982, a salesman wearing a pyramid on his head appeared on a television talk show in San Francisco. He made the same old bogus claims about pyramids, trying to drum up an audience for his weekend "seminar on pyramid power." We wonder how many takers got taken.

There are some journalists who do not distinguish between clearly incredible claims like these and reliable scientific data, who give credit to people whose comments about psychic functioning are more suitable for comic books than for the evening news. Undiscriminating and sensationalistic reporting also casts a shadow of guilt by association over legitimate psi researchers, who are frequently taken to task for the bizarre claims made by others.

LOOKING FOR STRANGENESS AND FINDING IT

Unfortunately, even legitimate, capable, and talented psi researchers sometimes act as if they have been overcome with a sense of strangeness toward psychic functioning. Many researchers originally enter this field because of the seemingly mysterious nature of its subject matter. They are excited by the idea of working in a frontier area of science, of being intellectual pioneers daring to risk their careers in the hope of discovering something really important.

In becoming enamored of the seemingly mysterious nature of psi, however, some of these researchers approach psychic abilities and experiences as strange occurrences, rather than as commonplace yet poorly understood capabilities. Their experiments reflect this bias—psychic functioning is typically treated as a highly peculiar and almost unconscious process.

One such peculiar experiment that often makes the news is the Ganzfeld approach, which we briefly mentioned earlier. Ganzfeld participants, you will remember, wear halved Ping-Pong balls over their eyes, which are flooded with red light. They wear headphones, which produce steady static, or "white noise," and occasional instructions to relax and to report whatever images come to them. The experiments are often conducted in soundproof chambers that have all the charm of walk-in meat lockers, complete with heavy steel double doors.

In Ganzfeld experiments run at one lab, the target materials are often composed of an almost free-associational collage of magazine pictures, which have been photographed and projected as slides on the wall of a target room some distance from the experimental chamber. For example, the target could be a picture of Superman sliding down a giant penis into an immense piece of chocolate cake.

It is easy to understand how such confused target images can lead Ganzfeld participants toward mental noise, even when they accurately describe the target. In the case of Superman, for example, a viewer might describe sexual feelings, a sudden hunger for sweets, or perhaps a sexual escapade with our hero himself. A judge would probably match those images to the proper target, even though the viewer did not actually describe the target precisely. What is a poor reporter to make of all this?

He might conclude that some psychic functioning probably occurred —but he might have a hard time relating it to everyday activities. And he might not understand why repeating more experiments like this is important or useful. He would probably leave the laboratory with no idea of how accurate and specific psychic perceptions can be.

Still, journalists know how entertaining an audience will find a procedure like the Ganzfeld. It offers an almost irresistible blend of scientific method with bizarre technical gimmickry. Besides, the Ganzfeld technique does allow good psychic functioning to occur. It also occurs in other experiments, such as the remote-viewing studies we have discussed, where people behave in a fairly normal fashion—without the need to be made up to look like giant insects in order to function psychically!

NEWS AS ENTERTAINMENT

The demands that editors and producers make on their reporters are often immediate. News stories and features are usually written and presented within a matter of days or weeks. Journalists are required not only to inform the public, but also to produce work that sells newspapers, improves magazine circulation, or elevates Nielsen ratings—and ultimately attracts advertisers.

So journalists become just as concerned about capturing an audience as the producers of film and television fiction are. News presentations can be thoughtful and informative, but they *must* be entertaining. If not, the public will not notice them—and, therefore, advertisers will not pay for them. The consequence for the public has been a lot of mixed and confusing messages about psychic experiences and abilities. Journalists tend to report the most easily digested, sensational, and controversial aspects of psi research. They also oversimplify most of what they do report.

In this kind of distorted journalism, human beings become caricatures. Scientists become authorities and believers. Critics become opponents and nonbelievers. Ordinary people become public figures. A century of careful research involving dozens of psychologists, psychiatrists, physicists, physiologists, anthropologists, philosophers, and other dedicated researchers ends up looking like an attempt by a few court jesters to conspire against the rest of the scientific community—for reasons that are ultimately not clear to anyone.

Some journalists find more direct ways to entertain the public. They locate easy targets—would-be psychics, so-called witches, cultists, and psychotics—who make public fools of themselves. It is easy to hold such people up to ridicule as alleged examples of what psi research and psychic functioning are about. Some journalists even try—or pretend—to write serious stories about them. It all has the same effect.

Instead of presenting a balanced picture, many journalists go from one extreme to the other. Sometimes, like movie producers, they depict psychic functioning as a strange power reserved for devil worshipers, graverobbers, and the occupants of haunted houses. On other occasions they tell the public that anyone who claims that psychic functioning exists is either a liar or a fool. Why the flip-flop? George Kokoris suggests a possible reason in his comments about Amityville. The story that George Lutz, the house's owner, first cautioned him to keep quiet and confidential, soon

> became, in the local press, a psychic potluck picnic: bring your own pet theory and feast on the rumors. The news reporters seemed to be after some tangible horror or palpable menace to confound, convince, and convert their audience. Barring that, evidence of a gigantic fraud, an unsavory hoax perpetrated on an innocent public, would do nicely. Aligned at these two extremes, the "believers" and the press would not, and indeed could not, deal with a subtle and shifting phenomenon of any variety.

It is true that psi researchers are not always clear or careful in the way they explain their work to reporters. But many journalists are just as careless in the questions they ask.

Several years ago, for example, I (K.H.) was being interviewed on a TV talk show in New York City. The topic was a series of experiments I had recently completed with several other researchers at Duke University, investigating the possibility of remote communication between a person having an out-of-body experience (OBE) and a distant cat. The experiments were successful; they showed that my pet cat's behavior was significantly quieter while I was experiencing being "with" him during randomly timed OBEs than it was during other times.

The results of this carefully controlled series of experiments were published in the *Journal of the American Society for Psychical Research* and were extensively described in the anthology *Mind Beyond the Body*. [4] The talk-show hostess had received a copy of the scientific report several days before our interview. Once we were on the air, though, her first irrelevant questions suggested that she either did not understand the research or had not read the report. She then broke for a commercial.

During the commercial break the hostess asked me to state, on the air, that out-of-body experiences were proof of life after death. I explained that I had not reached that outrageous conclusion, and that there was no scientific evidence that could possibly support such a wild statement.

By that time, the commercial was over and we were back on camera.

Apparently taken by surprise, she asked if my research had not, then, established that OBEs are totally meaningless delusions; she seemed to be floundering for a provocative question. I explained some of the important conclusions we had reached, such as the fact that for the first time, in America, psychic communication between a human being and an animal had been shown to have occurred consistently in a tightly controlled experiment. I added that further research was needed before a more definitive statement about OBEs themselves could be made.

The hostess concluded the interview by asking—this time on camera —if I would please tell the audience why I believed in life after death. I once again said that I had never stated any such belief, and we broke for the final commercial.

The hostess had not meant any harm, but she was obliged to entertain her audience. On the other hand, I was naively trying to describe the results of complicated scientific research on her television talk show. We were working at cross purposes—but at least I was there in person to defend myself.

Quite often when journalists distort information about psi experiments, the damage is done in print or on edited news programs, and the researchers are not there to defend themselves. If such misrepresentations were all that the public had to go on, they might understandably conclude that most psi researchers are crazy, or at least wildly eccentric.

Like most psi researchers, I have been misquoted more times than I care to remember, even in some of the most "reliable" newspapers. I have learned to guard against misunderstanding, so on one occasion I asked a reporter to repeat a statement, before a witness, that unequivocally made it clear that I do not believe there is any current scientific evidence to suggest that people literally leave their bodies during out-of-body experiences. The reporter repeated my statement and assured us that he would present my point of view correctly in his article.

But when the story appeared on the front page of a major newspaper, it *quoted* me as stating that I leave my body, walk through walls, and have meetings with discarnate entities! The quotation was a total fabrication, apparently a distortion deliberately made to jazz up an otherwise uninspired feature article. I would probably have sued the newspaper, except for the fact that I was just then completing my undergraduate degree in psychology at Duke and did not want any further publicity.

If we psi researchers wanted to sue sensationalistic journalists whenever we are misrepresented and misquoted, we might need to have a staff of lawyers for that purpose alone. In my own case, I decided, at the time, to stop speaking with any reporters about the OBE research.

The public probably thinks that psi researchers believe many of the strange things that have been attributed to us by overzealous journalists. After all, such statements seem real once they are printed in a newspaper or read on the air.

There is nothing quite like having the night clerk in a 7-Eleven scream in terror at you when you walk in. It actually happened to me because the woman recognized me from a picture illustrating a strange and misleading newspaper article she was reading at the moment I walked into the store. While I calmed her down and tried to buy the orange juice I had come in for, she asked if I had originally landed on Earth from some other planet or was simply out walking my body for the evening.

I have repeatedly explained to journalists that psychic functioning is a normal, but poorly understood, way of interacting with the world. I have also explained that out-of-body experiences are essentially *experiences*, not matters of life and death. They have not always heard that message—at least they have rarely reported it accurately.

Maybe they have been too busy looking for obvious leads to open their articles with, peculiar angles to catch the reader's attention. Most news people are decent, careful, considerate, ethical, and serious about their work. But a few of them, just as among any other group, are about as trustworthy as the charlatans they sometimes write about.

Even the most ethical journalists sometimes feel uncomfortable covering a subject they do not really understand. Privately they may associate psychic functioning with images from *The Twilight Zone*. Their discomfort shows in the tone of their reports, therefore, even when they are presenting straight information about carefully conceived and well-executed psychic experiments.

THE IRRATIONAL RATIONALISTS

As we have discussed, journalists have many possible reasons for presenting psi research as a controversial and confusing field. And controversy is not hard to find in an area that attracts so many people of varying motives. Controversy is news. Inexperienced journalists who try to sort out the controversy may find it all too confusing.

It is not difficult for journalists to locate numerous self-appointed critics of psi research. Some of them have academic credentials. Others do not. Many will readily take an opposing position at the slightest suggestion that someone witnessed or experienced genuine psychic functioning.

These critics often propound an extremely negative point of view that is as indefensible as the opposite claims of some cultists. They offer journalists the controversy that can make reports about psi research appear more interesting and balanced, although their comments often make these reports less accurate and more confusing.

Some of these critics have ulterior motives for not wanting the public or the academic community to take normal psychic functioning seriously. In that, they are like anyone else who hopes to profit by misleading the public about psychic abilities. Critics, like cultists, can sometimes live off the controversy they generate. For example, one critic, now famous, was a minor entertainer until he began a nationwide crusade against psi research.

Other critics are motivated mainly by their own private fear of the unknown. They are ultramaterialists who believe that if we do not understand something it cannot exist. Professor John Wheeler of the University of Texas argued at a 1979 meeting of the American Association for the Advancement of Science (AAAS) that the Parapsychological Association should be thrown out of the AAAS, with which it has been affiliated for many years. Wheeler titled his speech "Drive the Pseudos Out of the Workshop of Science." He had other intemperate things to say, including an insulting attack on J. B. Rhine, for which he later apologized in the pages of *Science* magazine.

The reporting on this conference illustrates how the press often features the controversy and lets the facts fall by the wayside. At this particular AAAS symposium, on "The Role of Consciousness in the Physical World," five technical papers were presented. Four dealt either with the data of current psi research or with the data in modern physics that indicate a possible relationship to psi research. In addition to two psi researchers, there were a Nobel laureate in physics, Eugene Wigner; the dean of the Princeton School of Engineering, Robert Jahn; and Dr. Wheeler. But only one aspect of this unique symposium made the news —the fact that John Wheeler was trying to drive the Parapsychological Association out of the AAAS.

With an almost religious fervor, the ultramaterialists are trying to keep science from even considering psychic functioning. They believe that a rational scientist can study only something he can hold in his hand, like a rock; anything less solid should be eschewed as superstition. Accepting the existence of psi may require a redefinition and expansion of our current understanding of psychology and physics, and they do not feel ready for that.

As a group, therefore, the self-appointed critics of psi research are no more reliable than many of the other people who make public claims about psychic experiences and abilities. They vary in their motives and in the degree to which their comments can be taken seriously. One should be as skeptical toward them as toward anyone else who claims to be an expert in this area.

When the critics are asked to critique psi experiments for the news, few of them are well enough informed about the experiments to make coherent comments about them. Even those who are well informed sometimes try to mislead the public by criticizing distorted versions of experiments that are nothing like the careful studies psi researchers actually conduct.

For example, one well-known critic who frequently condemned psi research editorially in his Mathematical Games column in *Scientific American* was invited to discuss his accusations in a public debate with a psi researcher. He declined in a letter, saying that he really did not know enough about psi experiments, was not up to date on the subject, and therefore would certainly lose the debate. This same writer criticized the NASA supported ESP teaching machine study carried out at SRI in 1974. He falsely alleged that the subjects in this experiment tore up their unsuccessful data tapes, and only handed in the successful ones. He said in his article, "I am not guessing when I say that the paper tape records from Phase 1 were handed in to Targ in bits and pieces." We now know the reason he could say that he "wasn't guessing." This is because he recently confided to a fellow reporter that he had just made it up, "because that's the way it must have happened." The reporter was so shocked at this disclosure, that even though he is not particularly sympathetic to our work, he felt compelled to call up the SRI researchers to pass on this remarkable piece of news.

On the other hand, an organized group of critics who knew what they were talking about was recently caught conspiring to deceive the public about some research results that did not fit their expectations. Members of the self-appointed Committee for the Scientific Investigation of Claims of the Paranormal (CSICOP, known as psi-cops)—including the entertainer mentioned earlier—who participated in this conspiracy were exposed when a member of their group defected and offered documented proof of the deception to several members of the press. It is clear that the goal of the psi-cops is to *control your ability to access and interpret information* and to walk a beat in your mind. In this respect they are not unlike cult leaders, or Big Brother in George Orwell's *1984*.

The research in question, a statistical study of the astrological signs of a group of athletes, replicated an earlier study that had been carried out in France by Michel and Françoise Gaquelin.[5] The critics had hoped to prove that the conclusions of the earlier study, which had established a significant correlation between athletic ability and certain astrological indicators, were statistically invalid. This correlation is generally known today as "the Mars Effect," and the study involved data from 2,088 sports champions. To their great dismay, however, the critics found that the earlier study stood on firm statistical ground.

The critics had planned to use their investigation of this study as a springboard for a condemnation of the public's widespread and "irrational" belief in astrology. They would release their negative findings to the media, and use the resulting publicity to gain credibility and influence. They could then pose as experts on other areas that are poorly understood, such as psi research.

Instead of facing up to the unexpected positive findings of their investigation, the critics manipulated their statistics—in much the same way as they had accused the original researchers of doing. Then they went ahead with their original plan. They falsely informed the press that their study had shown no correlation between athletic ability and the indices mentioned in the original study. Fortunately, one member of their group maintained a sense of courage and integrity, and brought the whole affair to the attention of the public.

In his thirty-two-page report, astro-physicist Dennis Rawlins describes the debacle as follows:

I used to believe that it was simply a figment of the *National Enquirer*'s weekly imagination that the Science Establishment would cover up evidence for the occult. But that was in the era B.C. —Before the Committee. I refer to the Committee for the Scientific Investigation of Claims of the Paranormal (CSICOP), of which I am a co-founder, and on whose ruling executive council I served for some years.

I am still skeptical of the occult beliefs that CSICOP was created to debunk. But I have changed my mind about the integrity of some of those who make a career of opposing occultism.

I now believe that if a flying saucer landed in the backyard of a leading anti-UFO spokesman, he might hide the incident from the public (for the public's own good, of course). He might swiftly convince himself that the landing was a hoax, a delusion, or an "unfortunate" or mundane phenomenon which could be explained away with "further research."

The irony of all this particularly distresses me, since both in print, and before a national television audience, I have stated that the conspiratorial mentality of believers in occultism presents a real political danger in a voting democracy. Now I find that the very group that I helped to found has partially justified this mentality.[6]

Of course, psi research and astrology are two *entirely* different fields. As psi researchers, we have little to say about astrology except that it would be interesting to see more careful scientific research carried out on the subject. Good scientists do not jump to conclusions without data. It is curious, however, that those who most often accuse honest researchers of fraud and ulterior motives may not be above fraud themselves when the scientific evidence turns against their narrow viewpoint.

Early in 1983, one of the psi-cops revealed that he had been directing a two-year deliberate fraud and deception at the McDonnell Research Laboratory at Washington University in St. Louis. He had sent two magicians—posing as psychics—to ingratiate themselves with the researchers and deceive them at every opportunity. Scientists of every persuasion have been shocked and disgusted by this unprecedented introduction of deceit and chicanery into what was intended to be an orderly scientific pursuit. By exploiting inexperienced researchers, the deceitful psi-cop wasted two years of the researchers' professional lives in a last desperate effort to cast a shadow of doubt over the whole field of psi research.

Some critics simply ignore statistical and experimental results that contradict their straw-man criticisms. Others accuse psi researchers who achieve successful experimental results of carelessness or fraud, although they typically offer no evidence to back up the accusations.

Journalists are not the only ones who pay too much attention to the claims of dilettantes and charlatans; critics also often point to the pseudo-researchers, implying that such individuals are representative of the scientists who really work in psi research. By associating psi research with people who make false claims about psychic functioning, these critics hope to keep people from taking psychic experiences and abilities seriously or learning about the actual scientific work of this field.

Most responsible critics of psi research respond negatively to the same public misrepresentations of psychic functioning as we do. The problem with many critics is that they do not also distinguish between the unsupported claims made about such topics as the Bermuda Triangle, UFOs, pyramid power, and plant communication on the one hand, and serious research on the other—research conducted by people who are working to develop a scientific understanding of psi. Instead, many critics toss psychic functioning into a goulash with every conceivable topic that has ever been poorly understood by the general public.

Psi is no more related to the other topics that usually turn up in the goulash than are DNA research and exobiology. If some nonscientists associate psychic experiences and abilities with bizarre claims about ancient astronauts, Kirlian photography, and Easter Island, then the critics do us all a disservice by perpetuating these ill-conceived associations. They also make themselves seem silly, apparently incapable of distinguishing between serious research and the ravings of fools and fanatics.

Ironically, the effect of the ultra-rationalist critics upon public attitudes is probably exactly opposite the one they hope for. The more confusion, controversy, and misinformation are presented to the public about psychic functioning, the more cult leaders and their ilk will profit by promising to explain psychic experiences and abilities. If mainstream scientists avoid conducting psi research, and thereby expanding our understanding of psychic functioning, then more charlatans and fanatics will feel free to pitch their tents in the garden of human ignorance and bask in whatever free publicity they can garner.

.   .   .

We have already discussed many kinds of charlatans, but there are countless others who present themselves as supposedly psychic visionaries.

Unlike their media-hound counterparts, these fortune-teller types are usually content to lie in wait for people who believe their promises of an expensive gaze into the future through crystal-ball windows. They rarely seek the attention of the news media because they do not want to attract the interest of police officials in the bargain. They are most often depicted in the press as cartoon images that no one is expected to take seriously.

FALAFEL OF THE GODS

Others, unfortunately, write books and produce motion pictures. They count on public confusion and the attention of the news media as aids to increasing sales of books or tickets. Their deliberate misrepresentations of psychic functioning and psi research convince everyone that psychic experiences are inextricably connected to irrationality and the supernatural.

We covered fiction in the previous chapter, but we must not forget the documentary-style film and television features that also offer misleading and distorted information. The producers of these features are frequently as unable as many critics are to differentiate between legitimate scientific research and unrefined stupidity and speculation.

Picture an imaginary documentary of this sort, called *Falafel of the Gods*. The narrator, as seems customary in this kind of thing, would look rather like an extra from *Night of the Living Dead* (1968).

He would stare self-importantly at the cameras while declaiming something to this effect: "Modern astronauts ate finely ground food out of plastic pouches when they traveled to the moon. The Egyptians also eat ground food out of small pieces of pocket bread that look remarkably like the plastic pouches used by astronauts. *Coincidence?* Were the Ancient Egyptians visited by aliens from outer space? Was the Great Pyramid built as a marker for spaceships from other planets? What does falafel have to do with cloning, cryogenics, and extrasensory perception? Who knows?"

The narrator would then present a thoroughly disjointed discussion of as many poorly understood subjects as possible, including visits with a variety of pseudo-researchers who would make wild, unfounded claims about psi. He would periodically peer knowingly at the cameras, as if he and the audience were sharing some inside understanding of Universal Truth that people who had not yet bought tickets were not ready for.

As the film ended, the narrator would sit on the edge of a desk and read through his list of misrepresented topics: "Ancient falafel, cloning, Kirlian photography, fire-walking, pyramid power, unidentified flying objects, and bad pizza. What does all this have to do with psychic experiences and the hidden destiny of humanity? I don't know. Now that I have wasted your time, sold this film, and made a buck in the process, *you decide.*"

The idea of such a film's really being produced might be funny, if so many productions like it did not already exist. In fact, a major television network presented just such a distorted and confusing array of nonsense for an hour of prime-time bewilderment in February 1983. We expected to hear about ancient falafel at any moment, because the show covered many of the other topics just mentioned. We do not believe that these documentaries are the work of serious writers, any more than the "research" these films present is the work of serious scientists. Still, sensational documentaries are presented along with everything else that upsets and confuses people who are trying to decide what to make of psychic functioning, and whether or not they want to have anything to do with it.

SEEING THROUGH THE MEDIA FOG

It takes a steadfast heart and a clear eye to see through all the nonsense and controversy about psi and still provide unbiased, dependable information about research that over the decades has solidly established, and is still exploring, the everyday reality of psychic functioning.

Beyond all the confusion is psi itself, a subtle information-processing capability, an additional way of interacting with the world that has nothing to do with the bizarre claims some people make about it, or with the supernatural. Beyond the emotionality, fear, and fanaticism lies a potentially useful tool for us all. It is time for psychic functioning to be taken out of the hands of people with axes to grind, so that everyone may feel free to enjoy and use it.

Reporters can either add to the misunderstanding of psi research and psychic functioning, or they can give clear and undistorted information that will intelligently inform the public. Any journalists who decide to accept the latter challenge will certainly have their work cut out for them.

Still, those who want to begin developing their greater human potential cannot wait for the media to catch up with the future they will be creating. Whatever makes people reluctant to explore their own latent abilities, or exploits them for doing so, is not worth the price. It is no more necessary to rely upon news reports to learn about psi than it is to follow a cult leader to your psychological death.

One way to fight back against media manipulations is by becoming aware of your own psychic potential. In doing so you will understand not only that psychic functioning exists and is useful and important, but also that it is perfectly normal.

PART III

Psi in Everyday Life

After you have developed some measure of psychic ability yourself, you will find it useful when faced with decisions that must be made without adequate information. But the most obvious reason for developing psi is simply the enjoyment of having an additional perceptual ability with which to experience all aspects of your life and environment. We should develop these abilities because it is possible for us to do so, and because doing so will enrich our lives.

In what follows we give you step-by-step instructions that have led to success in hundreds of trials with ordinary people. We show you how to do remote viewing, in which you will describe distant buildings or geographical sites, along with the activities and feelings of friends who will go to the sites to help you. We show you how to prepare yourself mentally for remote-viewing sessions, and how to recognize and deal with internal and external sources of interference.

You can think of the practice exercises for learning to do remote viewing as "psychic sit-ups." Through practice, we expect you to get your mind in shape and become more conscious of your own broader psychic abilities. As a result, you may begin to have spontaneous psychic experiences, even if you have never had them before. Since our society is not used to dealing intelligently with these experiences, we feel it is necessary to offer some hints on how you can incorporate these abilities into your life in a psychologically healthy fashion. That way, you can develop and use your psychic potential while still living normally and keeping your sense of humor.

9

Why Develop Psi?
It's Worth Looking Into

WHAT CAN YOU DO WITH PSI?

Psychic abilities can be useful to you if you have to make a decision, but have less information than you really need in order to decide wisely. You probably already know that. In fact, most people probably sense that their consciousness has a broader arena for experience and information than the nuts-and-bolts world that usually occupies our attention. A recent article in the *Wall Street Journal* dealt with this problem:

> "I just felt it in my gut."
> With those words the chief executive officer (CEO) brushes aside the unanimous recommendations of his subordinates. He disregards the data they cite—market surveys, past sales performance, interviews with customers—and decides to stick with a faltering product. And despite all the logic, he turns out to be right.
> Albert Einstein attributed his theory of relativity to a flash of insight, not to the cold rationalism of the data-oriented researcher in the laboratory. True, his mind had been prepared by much study

and thought, but as he said later, "The really valuable factor was intuition."

So too in business, decisions based on shrewd intuition are often superior to those based on careful analytical reasoning. . . . The key question is the one that troubled Joan of Arc: The inner voices may be loud and clear, but do they come from Heaven or Hell?[1]

Psi will not tell you where the voices come from, but you *can* learn to evaluate the reliability of your intuitive impressions.

An awareness of psi allows you to explore new ways of being with distant friends. It provides techniques that may help you look into the future and perhaps avoid accidents on the highway. It may also be used to help locate lost objects, missing persons, archaeological sites, and hidden natural resources, and most important, to bring you more closely in touch with the world around you.

Here is a short list of circumstances in which psi abilities could be useful:

- Remote-viewing one's car and intuiting dangerous mechanical defects before they become evident to ordinary senses

- Locating parking places in congested areas using intuition

- Staying ahead in the business world by following correct hunches about what will occur in the future

- Betting at the racetrack or in Las Vegas

- Finding lost children and adults in department stores or shopping malls

- Tuning in to the feelings and emotions of distant friends, relatives, or sweethearts

- Being in the right place at the right time for worthwhile opportunities

- Taking along an unlikely item that will later prove to be invaluable, although you are unable to justify bringing it along at the start

· Understanding and becoming aware of the psi content of
dreams and making use of it

Developing your psi abilities will help you to know yourself better, and
also to become more aware of others.

In earlier chapters, we discussed laboratory experiments in terms of their
statistical significance. That is one way to evaluate psi data. But in the
following two experiences, psi may have made the difference between life
and death. Both instances illustrate the results of being open to psychic
information, and taking it seriously, even when the information was not
asked for.

During the ten years I (R.T.) worked as a laser physicist, I normally
rode my motorcycle the five miles from my house to the laboratory. Even
with my fairly poor vision, I managed to make the trip without mishap.
One day as I was riding along a particularly attractive, broad stretch of
sweeping highway, I began to muse about what could be around the curve
in the road, just out of sight. I thought, of course, that nothing was in
the road. Then I began to wonder. What would I do, traveling at forty
miles an hour, if there were a board in the road? As I continued along
the open road, I throttled back, so that I was only rolling forward slowly
as I came around the curve, and saw a twelve-foot-long two-by-four lying
squarely across my path. "Luckily," as we say, I was going slowly enough
so that I just bumped over the board and was on my way. Is this a common
occurrence in the life of a motorcyclist? I do not think so. If I had hit
the board at full speed, I would almost certainly have had a serious
accident.

Was it just luck? My opinion is that as a result of my being willing
to accept intuitive data, I took this probable psychic impression seriously
enough to slow down while I thought it over. More recently, my wife,
Joan, and I made use of some psychic information even though at the
time it did not occur to either of us that we were doing anything
unusual.

We were at a dinner party at the home of my colleague Hal Puthoff
and his wife, Adrienne. We were all very happy to be joined by a mutual
friend who lived out of town. In the middle of this cheery get-together,
Joan stood up from the table and said we had to go home immediately!
Everyone wanted to know why. But Joan could not think of a reason.

Finally she said that since we did not have any curtains hung, someone might look in and see the sleeping children. We all considered this an exceptionally bizarre fear for someone living in suburban Palo Alto, California.

In fact, when we arrived home a few minutes later, we opened the front door and faintly heard someone coughing. We went into the bedroom of our ten-year-old son, Sandy, and found him quietly choking to death. He had already turned blue from lack of oxygen. Joan, a registered nurse, knew what to do. She dragged him into the bathroom, turned on the hot shower full blast, and turned the room into a large croup tent. Within a few minutes the room was filled with steam. Sandy resumed breathing and went back to sleep. We, however, were so frightened by the experience that we slept on the floor of his room.

In retrospect, I realize that Joan's lack of a rational explanation was like the sort of thing people say when they have been given a posthypnotic suggestion to do something. For example, a subject in such an experiment might be told under hypnosis to take her host's pocket handkerchief and use it to wipe the nose of a plaster statue. Given the suggestion, she does it upon awakening. When asked why, she might say that she thought she saw a spider on the statue (which she may indeed have experienced). But she would not be conscious of the real reason, namely the posthypnotic suggestion.

These sorts of experiences can happen to anyone. In fact, we believe that most people have such experiences, but do not pay much attention to them. You do not need any previous experience with psi to learn to make use of this kind of input. All you have to do is pay attention to any new and surprising perceptions or images that come to you unasked-for. With practice, you will learn to distinguish which of these impressions you can count on and which originate primarily in your memory and imagination.

One place to start exploring psi is in otherwise hopeless situations, such as the search for lost valuables. After all, when you have already tried everything else and failed, psychic functioning may save the day. For example, Hella Hammid and I (K.H.) recently helped a friend find some borrowed pearls which had been mislaid in her house. Our combined psychic impressions of the location and nearby objects were accurate enough to lead her to the spool of rope, near the window in her studio, into which her child had stuffed a plastic bag containing the unstrung pearls.

When you are first learning to trust your intuition, we suggest sticking to this kind of "no-lose" situation, rather than trying to make any death-defying decisions based upon your emerging psychic abilities. It takes practice and experience to be confident your impressions are accurate.

SOME PEOPLE HAVE ALL THE LUCK

Certain games of chance seem made to order for the aspiring psi practitioner. These include state lotteries (in fact, R.T. won money on a hunch on his first and only try at the New York State lottery while we were in the midst of editing this chapter), professional sporting events, the options and commodity markets, and blackjack as played under casino rules. If you want to play with psychic abilities to see how it all feels, a friendly game of blackjack at home is a safe place to start.

At the casino, blackjack is the game an unskilled player can play the longest time before losing all his money. This is true because, of all casino games, it comes closest to giving the player an even chance to win. On each hand that is dealt, the house has only slightly better than fifty-fifty odds. If you are a card counter and remember all the picture cards as they are played, you can even win—until they find out about your method and throw you out of the casino. Another way you may reliably win at blackjack is by using psi.

Whenever blackjack is played for money, the players have two kinds of decisions to make. Before they get any cards, they must decide how much they will bet. Then they decide how many cards to draw. Let us assume you are a skillful cardplayer, although not a card counter. This will allow you to lose your money at the slowest possible rate. That is, unless you have something else going for you.

If you are playing a game where you can bet anything from $1 to $20 before you receive cards, you have an interesting option: You can bet the minimum on those hands where you *feel* that you will not have a happy outcome, and you can bet the maximum on those hands where you feel confident you will be raking in the chips. If you simply *guess* whether you will win or lose, you will guess right in about five out of ten trials in an even game. With this scheme, you will need only one additional correct guess—six out of ten—to stay ahead of the house.

Consider the possibilities. Let's say you have a small amount of natural psychic ability you have never developed. If you follow this strategy, you will win money, even if you lose slightly more than half the hands. This is because you will be betting less money on the losing hands. If you have no psychic abilities at all (a possibility we would never agree to), then your betting will be totally random, and will not change your rate of winning or losing. It will just make the dealer think you are a bit odd.

On the other hand, in fifty deals, if 60 percent of your $20 bets were on winning hands, you would find the following result: On the average you would win twenty-five deals by pure chance; we will not change that. Of those, 60 percent (fifteen hands) would be for $20, and fifteen hands times $20 makes $300. To this we add the ten hands won at $1—$10. Your winning hands thus would bring you $310. On your losing hands, you would lose $1 on fifteen of them, for $15, and lose $20 on ten of them, for $200. Your total losses are thus $215. Therefore, even though you are still losing half your hands, you are ahead: $310 minus $215 leaves $95. Not thrilling perhaps, but much better than the alternative.

In order to accomplish this modest feat, you have to guess right in six out of ten trials, when random guessing would be correct five times out of ten. Although correctly choosing 60 percent of fifty trials is not at all a statistically significant result, it is a profitable one when combined with an advantageous betting strategy.

One last thought: We strongly recommend you test this out at home, with friends, before hopping on a plane to Las Vegas or Atlantic City.

Shortly after writing the above, I (R.T.) received an excited phone call from a young woman we had worked with at SRI. She had taken part in a long series of remote-viewing sessions aimed at determining what kind of information a viewer needs in order to describe a target.

She had gone to a gambling casino at Lake Tahoe, to see if she could put her newfound abilities to practice. Since she does not play cards, she decided to try the slot machines. The technique she used was to walk up and down the rows of machines in the casino and stop in front of the machine that made her feel that "happy rush of adrenaline" that she associated with winning a jackpot. She would then put a coin in that machine. This scheme worked wonderfully, for more than an hour.

Her run ended when she came up to a machine about which she had an especially strong feeling. She was looking through her cup of coins for a quarter when the woman playing the next machine sensed her excitement, reached across, put in her own quarter, and won the $25 jackpot that was waiting for the next coin.

This battle of the hunches at the casino sounds as if it could be the first salvo of the psi-wars in the casino. Needless to say my friend was very upset.

CAN PSI MAKE A DIFFERENCE?

In August 1982 the English Society for Psychical Research (SPR) held its hundredth-anniversary meeting at Trinity College, Cambridge. It was also the twenty-fifth annual meeting of the Parapsychological Association (PA). The SPR is the oldest society in the world for the study of psychic functioning. Since its founding in 1882, it has attracted a distinguished membership of English philosophers and scientists, including F. W. H. Myers, Henry Sidgwick, Sir Oliver Lodge, Lord Rayleigh, and Sir William Crookes. More than three hundred scientists, journalists, and critics attended the Cambridge meeting.

One question was repeatedly asked at this centenary conference: What has been accomplished in a hundred years of research? An answer that most of the scientists in the field would support is that as a result of thousands of laboratory experiments, comprising millions of trials, any fair-minded man or woman should be convinced beyond reasonable doubt that psi exists, and might possibly even be important. But many people at the conference did not share that view. Some were critics, and some were psi researchers.

Several of the critics gave papers to the effect that there have not been any experiments, carried out by anyone, that are not flawed in some way. For example, psychologist Ray Hyman severely criticized the Ganzfeld research (for using multiple statistical analyses, for not reporting on randomization procedures, and for possibly allowing sensory cueing by not using duplicate slides in judging). All of his criticisms are rational, and could be devastating and decisive. However, there were many studies that suffered from the first two "flaws," but could not be explained away because of them. That is, even if his assertions were true, the experiments still showed remarkable correspondence between target material and viewer descriptions, and Hyman agreed that the alleged flaws could not have produced these correspondences. For instance, if it were found that most of the successful sessions were conducted just before a full moon, it would not mean that the experiment was flawed, even though moon phase was not one of the controlled variables.

Christopher Scott, an English mathematician and longtime critic of psi, explained his position this way: "What I find most difficult to understand is the parapsychologist . . . who sees the field of parapsychology as no different from any other science, is unable to comprehend why considerations of fraud and incompetence play such a prominent role in the discussion of parapsychological evidence. . . . Parapsychologists should recognize that by simply objective criteria, their science is *not* a normal one, and that there are good and honest reasons for doubting their conclusions, and for requiring from them more rigorous evidence than is often demanded in other sciences."

It became clear from listening to these critics that any experiment, no matter how carefully carried out, may reveal a flaw in retrospect. There is always something that could have been done better. *This is true in every field of science*—and in recent years there have been many more examples of fraud in medical research than in psi research.

Hearing what the critics have to say, we began to realize that psi may never be accepted into mainstream science on the basis of laboratory experimentation alone. The parallel with hypnosis is clear: Scientists still argue about whether hypnosis exists, whether it is indeed a unique state of consciousness—but meanwhile it is regularly used in medicine and dentistry, because it works.

Maybe psi will not find its home in modern thought until it is shown to have applications, in areas where nothing else will do. Our impression is that even though the opponents of psi present their arguments in the form of rational syllogisms, they base their opposition not on rationality but on religious conviction. We would argue that they have a strong *belief* in the nonexistence of psi, and searching for the experiment that would satisfy all these critics is futile.

If a belief or opinion is not rationally based, then no amount of rational argument will overcome it. If a woman tells a man, "I don't love you," it is pointless for him to ask why. She may give several reasons, each of which could be rationally countered, or even shown to be false. But that, as we all know, would not change the central fact that she does *not* love him.

So we are forced to conclude that after a hundred years of laboratory experiments, more interest and acceptance will be gained for psi if it is shown to be useful in the marketplace, rather than being just an easily ignored laboratory curiosity. For this reason we have formed Delphi Associates, a consultancy in applied psi research, and we are currently seeking endowment and other support for an extended research program. We intend to expand our understanding of psi and of how it can be useful for many enterprises, such as exploring for oil, gas, and minerals.

An interesting experiment we are now engaged in involves short-term associative remote viewing applied to the silver-futures market. These experiments have proved highly successful—and have supplied continuing, though modest, support for our research. For example, in the fall of 1982, Delphi Associates was forecasting the price of a commodity known as December Silver through the use of remote viewing. We made nine forecasts (and traded seven) for the price of silver to be traded three days in the future with Keith Harary as the viewer. We correctly forecast both the magnitude and the direction of the change in each case. The odds against this occurring by chance alone are more than 250,000 to one (four to the ninth power). We are still studying this application of psi at the present time.

In laboratory psi research, scientists are usually satisfied with results that would occur less often than once in twenty trials by chance alone. This is commonly known as achieving results that are "significant at the $< .05$ level." Although such results may be satisfactory for some research purposes, we are not content with this 5 percent solution. We expect much better results than this from our experiments, along with many of our fellow psi researchers. We believe that the degree of confidence which researchers feel in psi's real capabilities accounts for their continuing success or failure in exploring psychic functioning both in and out of the laboratory. For psi to be successfully integrated into one's life, it must be regarded as more than a purely statistical phenomenon. We cannot emphasize this too strongly.

It is clear from our data (and others' also) that the future can be known —and, in a sense, is known. So for that matter may the "hidden" present. It only remains to be seen what individuals, investors, and governments will do about it. It should *not* take another century to find out. We believe the question of psi's usefulness and importance may be settled in the next decade. Settling this question *will not* require another century. It will probably be settled in the marketplace and in the everyday lives of millions of people and not, alas, in the corridors of Cambridge.

10

A Psychic Workout:
Learning to Use Psi

Learning to be aware of your psychic abilities can be like remembering something you already know. The process involves refining and deepening your responses to subtle information, rather than tapping into foreign sources of knowledge. It is as though psychic abilities were sleeping quietly in the background of your mind, waiting for a nudge to awaken and open the lines of communication.

There is no magic button in your brain that, when pressed, will suddenly give you perfectly accurate, fully formed psychic abilities. Instead, the degree to which you are able to use psi will depend on your ability to learn certain basic skills, through practicing various exercises.

Remember, there is more than one route to becoming a world-class psychic. Psychic functioning involves a complex interrelationship between a number of different abilities and methods of creative expression. We each have our own unique and preferred ways of expressing ourselves. Different people excel at different skills, and therefore rely more on these abilities in whatever they do.

The basic process of psychic functioning seems similar for most people, but the specific techniques used by each viewer are more personal. Some viewers are better at spontaneously seeing visual images than others. Some prefer to express themselves verbally or in writing; others feel more at home expressing their thoughts and feelings in pictures. Some viewers relate more easily to sensory information, and others to aesthetic, psychological, and emotional qualities of remote targets.

Pat Price, for example, did not start drawing target sites until weeks after he had demonstrated his remarkable skills at verbally describing targets in several remote-viewing sessions. The sketches Pat drew during experiments seemed to be mainly for the convenience of his co-experimenters.

In contrast, other viewers rely heavily upon their spontaneous drawings of target sites to express and interpret their psychic impressions. They sometimes use these drawings as an aid to understanding psychic information rather than simply to record their impressions. Still other viewers are not locked into one specific method of expressing and interpreting their psychic impressions, but use a combination of verbal and nonverbal methods, which vary according to the specific psychic task at hand.

Interestingly, we have found that different viewers will often focus upon many of the same striking features of particular target sites. For example, a noisy fountain at the center of a target area is very likely to be noticed by more than one viewer. We have also found that certain targets tend to be much more accurately described than others. This may be a function of the uniqueness of these targets—the less a target resembles other things the easier it may be to describe clearly.

Some viewers, though, excel at providing detailed information about certain aspects of remote targets that other viewers do not emphasize. This is to be expected, since even people in the same place, noticing the same striking things, may still respond to what they notice in different ways. They will also each pay attention to different aspects of the location and thus experience it differently from one another. Perception is personal, whether it is psychic or physical.

Each viewer's background, training, and personality strongly influence what he will focus on in a remote viewing, and how he will interpret it. For example, since I (K.H.) have a background in clinical psychology and the psychology of design, I often describe personality and general health characteristics of people at a remote target location, as well as the ways in which given settings might psychologically affect those who visit, work, or live there. Hella Hammid might focus on how a site would look to a photographer. A more technically trained viewer is likely to experience a remote site from the viewpoint of an engineer, and so on.

There seems to be no one best method for describing remote locations —or, for that matter, practicing any form of psychic functioning. The methods you use should be based upon your own background and experience. It would be a mistake to expect everyone to function psychically in exactly the same way, or even to respond very similarly to the same targets.

To make any attempt to force everyone to use the same method would be to ignore the unique style and potential contribution of each individual's psychic talents. We are confident that as your experience grows, you will come to prefer certain techniques for handling psychic information that are best suited to your own abilities and personality. You may even create some original techniques of your own.

So we will not dictate any absolute methods. What we will do is provide you with basic instruction that we hope will help you understand the process of psychic functioning. To guide you, we will discuss the techniques that many psychically adept people have found helpful. But it is up to you to apply this information to your own requirements, abilities, and experiences.

PSYCHIC SIT-UPS

Many books on "how to develop ESP" and the like have been based on the experiences of only a single person who achieved a state he thinks is "psychic." In contrast, what follows is based on techniques and insights that have emerged from a decade of scientific research in our laboratory and in many others. They have led to success in hundreds of research trials with ordinary people who have taken part in psi experiments.

We think of practicing remote viewing as doing psychic sit-ups. We offer these exercises as a way for you to tone up your psychic abilities and become more accustomed to the way good psychic functioning feels. This enhanced awareness may then be carried over into your everyday life to help you use your psychic abilities in many different kinds of situations.

·   ·   ·

Practicing remote viewing lets you understand and refine your responses to psychic information in a controlled situation in which the results of each day's exercises will be clear to you. Using this approach, it is unlikely that you will fool yourself about the progress you make in developing your psi abilities. Remote viewing also provides great entertainment. We think it is a wonderful way to spend an afternoon or evening with friends.

BASIC SKILLS:
THE FOUNDATIONS OF PSYCHIC FUNCTIONING

All of our research and experience strongly indicates that psychic information is readily available if you learn how to observe it.[1] Learning to observe this information does not require a special state of consciousness. It does require learning to *discriminate* true psychic information from the effects of various types of "mental noise," such as *remembered or imagined impressions* and *local environmental influences*, upon your thoughts and feelings. It is therefore very important to become aware of both these sources of interference.

As you learn to respond to psychic information, it is essential that you trust your feelings and pay attention to even your most fleeting images and impressions. First impressions are often the most correct, but they must be properly perceived and interpreted to be of use. However, crystal-clear impressions of locations around the house are usually (though not always) examples of mental noise, rather than psi. The more spontaneous and surprising your impressions of a remote target are, the more likely they are to contain useful psychic information.

Developing certain sensory and psychological skills can help. In our experience, learning to use psi is mostly a matter of developing the ability to respond to gentle impressions, feelings, and images without embroidering or editing the initial responses. And you will have to become adept at expressing your inner experiences in an objective and tangible form. This outward expression of internal sensations is similar to the process of creating a poem, painting, or piece of music. A poet brings familiar words and images together in an original way to express his personal feelings and experiences. Similarly, in functioning psychically, you learn to create objective information out of what first appears as purely subjective impressions and images.

In essence, *learning to function psychically means becoming aware of your responses to certain internal experiences, expressing those responses in a recognizable form, and distinguishing your psychic impressions from mental noise.* [2]

ENHANCING SENSORY AND PSYCHOLOGICAL AWARENESS

In learning to function psychically, it is important to become a skilled observer of the world around you and of your responses to it. As you become more conscious of your responses to familiar stimuli, your ability to respond consciously to psychic impressions will probably also increase.

Becoming a good observer can help you to develop your psychic abilities in several ways.

First, you must recognize the characteristics of images and impressions that originate in your memory, imagination, and immediate environment before you can tell the difference between these sources of mental and environmental noise and your actual psychic impressions.

Second, developing your general powers of observation can help you to notice and respond to the subtle sensations that are characteristic of psi. Psychic information is frequently experienced as if it were a visual image or sensory impression of a remote occurrence. As you become more aware of your sensory responses to your environment, you may begin to notice that you are also responding to additional information that is not available to you through these familiar channels.

Finally, psychic information often comes as an *emotional* response to intuitively perceived information. Developing a heightened awareness of your emotional reactions to immediate events can help you to recognize the subtle responses that may be the signature of psychic information. This heightened awareness of your basic emotional state may also serve as an anchor to help you remain centered in the face of emotionally charged psychic stimuli.

We suggest that you start by paying more attention to the varieties of sensory stimulation that you respond to as you go about your daily activities. Whenever the thought occurs to you during the day, take a moment to notice the many levels of information that you are responding to through your five known senses.

.   .   .

As you read this book, you are of course responding visually to the words on this page. You may also notice the color and texture of the printed paper, the lighting and colors of the room around you, and various other types and levels of visual information.

As you read these words, perhaps you "hear" them in your inner ear, as if they were being spoken. You may also notice the sound of your fingers rubbing against the book cover and paper. What other sounds do you notice? Do you hear a clock ticking? Music? People talking nearby? Listen carefully. Do you hear other sounds in the distance—wind, traffic, or animals?

What are you resting on as you read this? What physical sensations do you feel where your body makes contact with external surfaces? How does your clothing feel where it touches your body? What is the texture of the paper on this page? How cool is the air circulating around your forehead?

How does the inside of your mouth taste at this moment? How do the pages of this book smell when you hold them to your nose and inhale? What other smells do you notice? Do you notice the aroma of perfume or flowers, the disgusting stench of stale cigarette smoke, or the appetizing smells of a busy kitchen?

Your environment is full of sensory information that you may not always be conscious of, but to which you are nevertheless responding at some level. When you take a few moments to deliberately notice the continuous flow of information that is perceived by even one of your five senses, you may begin to feel much more in touch with the world around you. People who begin to function psychically will find themselves becoming more sensitive both to their environment and to their own internal state. Psychic abilities are a special kind of sensitivity.

An outstanding description of how to pay attention to the environment is given in Jean Auel's *The Valley of Horses*. She tells us about her heroine, who is creeping up on a cave:

> All her senses were alert. She listened for sounds of breathing or small scufflings; looked to see if there were any telltale signs of recent habitation; smelled the air for the distinctive odors of carnivorous animals, or fresh scat, or gamey meat, opening her mouth to allow her taste buds to help catch the scent; let her bare skin

detect any sense of warmth coming out of the cave; and allowed intuition to guide her as she noiselessly approached the opening. She stayed close to the wall, crept up on the dark hole, and looked in.[3]

Now that you have the idea, try the following exercises. They are not essential for developing your psychic abilities, but they can help you to become a better observer of your environment.

ONCE MORE, WITH FEELING

There is no need to enter a dramatically altered state of consciousness to become more familiar with your five senses. The purpose of these two exercises is to help you more fully experience the contribution that each of your five senses makes to your overall sensory awareness. The first you can do by yourself, but you will need a partner for the second.

To begin the first exercise, find a comfortable (preferably outdoor) place to relax and close your eyes. We suggest that you sit up—you will be less likely to fall asleep.

When you feel comfortable, begin by focusing your attention on the sounds of the world around you. Take your time and really listen. Listen to the sound of your own breathing and to the sounds made by nature and other people.

Pay attention to each individual sound, and to how each sound blends in with the others. Some sounds are very tiny, like an insect walking across a candy wrapper. Others are enormous, like the rustling of the wind through dry leaves and branches. Listen to everything and let your thoughts drift completely into each sound for a few moments, then allow yourself to hear each sound as one of many voices in the distance.

When you have enjoyed this exercise for fifteen or twenty minutes, open your eyes and continue listening. Notice how your awareness of sound now blends in with your visual perceptions, and with the responses of your other senses. Take a deep breath and let it out slowly, while you prepare to take a walk in the world to which you have been listening.

Without saying a word, move your gaze around the area where you are sitting. Notice the colors that are visible nearby, then off in the distance. Notice the many different shapes and surfaces you can see, and the variations in light and shadow around you.

Now move your hands over the surface you are sitting on. Notice the texture of the surface beneath you. Stand up and begin to move through the environment you have been studying. Notice the feeling of your clothing brushing up against your body, and the firmness of the ground you are walking on. Feel the roughness, smoothness, hardness, and softness of other surfaces in your environment.

As you walk around quietly, notice the many different smells that you are responding to. Some smells are very light, like the scent of a single daisy. Other smells are more powerful, like the aroma of brewing coffee.

Rub your tongue along the inside of your elbow. Notice the salty taste on your skin. Taste something sour, like a lemon drop. Now taste something sweet, like a candy mint. Don't just eat it, but pay close attention to what you are experiencing. Peel an orange slowly, and notice the many different kinds of sensations—feelings, smells, tastes, and sounds—that are associated with it.

When you have spent a comfortable amount of time focusing your attention upon each of your five senses, you may enjoy walking a bit further and noticing how your enhanced awareness of all your senses affects your overall response to your environment.

You may have realized, while reading the above, that it is as easy for some people to imagine that they are taking walks like this as it is for them to experience the real thing. The process of psychic functioning is generally easier for people who are adept at experiencing various kinds of purely mental images. We therefore recommend that you also try this sensory-awareness exercise in your imagination, exploring various locations without physically going there.

If you have any difficulty in imagining what each of your senses would perceive on a fantasized excursion, be patient. Practice the exercise in several different real locations. The more aware you become of the physical perceptions of your five senses, the easier it will be for you to imagine them at will.

As you have probably already figured out, the difference between imagining that you are in a place and conducting a full-blown remote viewing of a distant location is a small one indeed. The more adept you become at responding to actual and imagined sensory impressions, the more successful you are likely to be at remote viewing. And now on to the second exercise.

DISCOVERING A SMALL PLANET

Psychic information does not always come as visual images. It is also often experienced in the form of nonvisual impressions and psychological or emotional responses to remote places, objects, and events.

Sighted people, though, focus most of their attention on visual perception and images. This differs from the primary focus of dogs, for example, who rely mostly on smell, or of dolphins, who emphasize hearing, including a kind of sonar.

This exercise will help you become more attuned to your nonvisual perceptions. Your partner should be someone you feel very safe and comfortable with.

Try this exercise outdoors if possible, in a secure and fairly private environment, but one that offers many types of nonvisual sensory experiences. A quiet beach would be good. So would a clearing in the forest, or a small park or large backyard.

You and your partner each take turns being "blind" for a half an hour. One of you acts as a sensory guide for the other, whose eyes remain closed while "blind." Neither person should speak, unless absolutely necessary, during the exercise.

The guide may walk the "blind" person around slowly, presenting a variety of things to touch, taste, smell, and listen to. For example, the guide may move the other's hand lightly through sand and across blades of grass or the surface of tree bark, or give him rocks, leaves, seashells, flowers, and other small objects to hold. Each one can be rich with sensations.

Of course, the sensory guide is responsible for guiding the "blind" person around safely, and should be aware of potential hazards such as rocks and cliffs that the other person cannot see.

Throughout the exercise, the "blind" person should pay close attention to every bit of nonvisual stimulation available in the experience provided by the sensory guide. He might think of himself as an astronaut who has just landed on a foreign world where there is no light, and where only nonvisual information can be used in exploring the newly discovered planet. When it is time for the "blind" person to regain his vision, he should sit quietly in a shady area and slowly open his eyes. The world will look quite striking to him in that moment.

The sensory guide and the "blind" person should then discuss the experiences they both had during the exercise. The formerly "blind" person should be shown the things that he was given to experience nonvisually. After a short break, the two should switch roles and repeat the procedure, probably in a different location.

You and your partner may want to consider how you feel in one another's presence while you are communicating nonverbally. This experience may be useful to you later, if you practice remote viewing together, with one of you as viewer and the other as beacon.

PSYCHIC FUNCTIONING IS AN ART

Many of the people who have been successful in laboratory remote-viewing experiments have strong artistic and creative backgrounds—painters, photographers, musicians, designers, poets, and writers. They are experienced at forming objective substance out of their subjective experiences. Their ability to express their personal impressions creatively seems to help them to respond more effectively to psychic information. They are also often keen observers of their environment and the people in it.

While you practice becoming more aware of your psychic potential, you may want to take some courses in art, writing, photography, or design to help you develop your own preferred modes of creative expression. Such courses can heighten your powers of observation and help you evolve your own unique way of expressing yourself and experiencing the world. They can also serve as a balance for the more mentally focused exercises here. Besides that, you will meet creative people and have a lot of fun.

KEEPING UP YOUR IMAGE

As you become more aware of sensory information in your environment, you may notice that sensory input is only one of several different kinds of information you continuously respond to in your everyday life. You are probably also aware of images and thoughts that emerge purely from your memory and imagination.

The feelings that accompany memory are not quite the same as those that are part of your response to external stimulation. And they are also different, in some respects, from those which accompany imagination. This difference helps you distinguish between things you have actually experienced and things about which you have only fantastized.

Every perception has a subtly different "feel" to it that is directly related to its sensory or psychological origin. These sensations go beyond the simple content of specific images and impressions themselves. For example, consider the difference between being in a certain room, remembering what it was like to have once been in the room, and dreaming or imagining that you are in a room where you have never been.

Your conscious awareness is also affected by your emotional state. When you are upset, frightened, or madly in love, you respond differently to internal or external stimuli. You notice things you might not otherwise pay much attention to. No one aspect of your awareness is independent of anything else that may be on your mind. The reality you are experiencing and your own mood influence your perceptions and your responses to those perceptions.

In meeting a person for the first time, for example, it makes a difference in your response if you are introduced at a crowded party or on a quiet street corner. The person may remind you of someone you once knew, or may seem totally unfamiliar. You may like the person's perfume, or it may remind you of stray dogs and fresh fertilizer. You may be attracted, feel neutral, or be repelled. Whatever your overall reaction is, it will be influenced by a variety of sensory, emotional, and other factors —your psychological state, past experiences, responses to sensory information, fantasies, and perhaps some additional feelings that you might collectively refer to as intuition.

While you work on becoming more aware of your responses to sensory information in your environment, we suggest that you also pay closer attention to your psychological reactions to the events and people around you. Take time to notice if a person you are just meeting reminds you of someone you already know. It is essential to learn to respond to your experiences as they occur, rather than merely reacting to memories of similar past experiences.

Does a new situation remind you of things you have previously experienced, or seem familiar even though it is new to you? How do your past encounters influence your present responses?

What effect do your fantasies and imagination have on your perceptions? Do your feelings about people and events go deeper than your responses to ordinary sensory and psychological input?

Do you occasionally act on hunches about people you have just met? Do you ever make decisions based upon information that seems compelling, yet inexplicable and almost intangible? Even when your hunches cannot be explained as responses to available information, do you still pay attention to them?

Just as memories feel different from sensory information and imagination, you may notice that hunches also feel different from other sources of information. If you have ever had certain thoughts and feelings, could find no logical explanation for them, yet still felt their influence, you probably already know how intuitive impressions feel.

Whenever you can, take a moment in the course of your daily activities to notice your responses to the world around you. Think about the feelings that define your experience of various types of people, activities, and situations. Pay attention to how you experience your environment, perceptually, emotionally, and intuitively. If you become more aware of how people and things feel to you when you are near them, you will have an easier time interpreting your feelings during remote-viewing sessions.

RECOGNIZING INTUITIVE IMPRESSIONS

Have you ever searched a long time for a parking place? In downtown San Francisco, parking a car is almost a full-time occupation. A congested area like that is a good place to practice an exercise that can help you recognize the "feel" of genuine psychic impressions and distinguish them from mental and environmental noise. This exercise was developed in San Francisco, but works anywhere that finding a parking space is a major accomplishment.

We do not expect you to dash out in your pajamas with this book held open on your steering wheel to practice this exercise. However, you might give it a try during some future automobile excursion. It can be an interesting thing to do while you wait for traffic lights to turn green. And it may help you find a parking place quickly, unless there are absolutely no parking places available in your nearby vicinity.

Next time you find yourself in a car circling like a vulture searching for prey (it does not matter whether you or someone else is driving), quietly ask yourself in which direction the nearest available parking place lies. You may include spaces that are about to be vacated. Remember to consider one-way streets while forming this question in your mind, so that you will complete the exercise in one piece.

Usually, you will want to park within a certain area; think about its boundaries as you formulate your question. It will not do much good to have an impression of a vacant spot several miles away.

Immediately after you ask your question, "listen" quietly to whatever sensations emerge in your awareness. You may feel a gentle urge to drive in a particular direction. Follow that urge. Do not think about it or analyze it. Just drive.

You may even get a mental image of an open spot on a particular street. If so, head directly there. Follow your initial impressions even if they take you back to places where you have already looked.

You will quickly learn if your impressions were correct: You will either find a parking place or have to keep hunting. This will serve as your immediate feedback. If your first try drew a blank, repeat the procedure —ask where the nearest available spot lies, then follow your first impressions, until you either find a parking place or run out of gas.

As you gain experience with this exercise, you may notice that certain kinds of images and impressions are more productive than others. You will be able to trace some impressions to your intellectual analyses of the territory, memories of places you have parked before, and so forth. These impressions may not necessarily help you now, though, and so should be treated as mental noise.

Other impressions will not be as easy to explain, yet may successfully lead you to your quarry. These impressions may be surprisingly accurate, compelling—and inexplicable. They are the impressions which we refer to as intuitive.

With practice, you can learn to distinguish between various types of impressions and images, between the intuitive impressions that lead to success and the mental noise that leads you on a wild goose chase. You should also save time and fuel by more efficiently finding places to park your car.

Even if you are not often in a car, there are hundreds of situations in which a little properly interpreted psychic information can make your life better. You can use the same basic techniques in these situations.

For example, if you are looking for a misplaced friend in a crowded area, ask yourself where your friend is at that moment. Think about how it feels for you to be with your friend, while sensing in which direction you should go in order to experience the feeling of being with your friend now.

All sorts of everyday situations give you the opportunity to practice sorting out psychic information from mental noise in the first impressions that come as you form questions in your mind. Even if your intuitive impressions do not feel very strong at first, we expect that with practice, you will gradually find it easier to experience, interpret, and respond to intuitive information.

ACCEPTING YOUR PSYCHIC CAPABILITIES

By now we hope you are convinced that psychic functioning is a real human capability, and that many people have learned to process psychic information skillfully. But you may still be entertaining some doubts about your own psychic potential. Years of materialistic conditioning can be difficult to overcome.

Images of cult leaders and strange fictional characters may still be dancing in your subconscious as you read this. Perhaps a part of you secretly believes that people who have learned to use psi in the lab really *are* highly unusual, or are able to use their psychic abilities only under special conditions. Considering the social atmosphere most of us have grown up in, such thoughts are understandable, but they are not correct.

For years, psi researchers have tried to find out why different people function differently in psychic experiments. They have tried to define a specific personality type that is more prone to psychic functioning than others, but their attempts have not been totally successful. In fact, there probably is no one consistent personality type that is potentially more adept at using psi than others.

There is nothing supernatural about participants in psi experiments, or about SRI and other psi research laboratories. However, one outstanding feature of the research we have discussed is very important: It appears to be easier for people to function psychically *when they fully accept their own ability to do so.*

What makes some psi laboratories more successful, in our estimation, is that they provide a safe and convincing atmosphere where previously inexperienced people can permit themselves to respond to their intuitive impressions. We consider this to be so important that we suggest that you pause now, to consciously give yourself permission to become more aware of your psychic potential.

Just tell yourself firmly, but quietly, that you are willing to achieve excellent results as you practice the exercises we describe. As you do this, consider that many people have learned to use their psychic abilities with excellent results, although they may have started out knowing even less about psychic functioning than you now do, after having read this far.

Try to remember—have you ever thought about someone you had not heard from for a long time, then received a letter or telephone call from them? Or do you sometimes "know" who is calling before you answer a ringing telephone, even when the call is totally unexpected? There are countless ways in which you may already be using your psychic abilities without realizing it.

The main difference between people who consciously respond to their intuitive impressions and those who do not is probably a matter of awareness and aptitude at certain skills, rather than one of personality—of course people who accept their intuitive impressions in our restrictive society may be psychologically "tougher" and more adventurous than those who do not, though other aspects of their dispositions and personalities may greatly vary. And certain personality types may do better at functioning psychically in the laboratory, though not necessarily at psychic functioning in general. It is our opinion that those who do well at using psi in the laboratory are often those who are accustomed to succeeding in other areas of their life—and who therefore expect to succeed at psychic functioning as well.

Some people probably respond to psychic information subconsciously. They might think of themselves as "just lucky" when they seem to end up in precisely the right place at just the right time, without finding any obvious explanation for their actions.

Then there are those who are a little more directly in touch with their intuitive capabilities. Occasionally they do something because they "just have a feeling" they should—and it turns out to have been the correct thing to do. Maybe they cannot give detailed reasons for their actions, but nonetheless they use psychic information on some level.

Still other people experience their psychic capabilities on a highly conscious level. They respond to intuitive impressions, and know that is what they are responding to. They might be called "psychics" or "sensitives," because they have learned to respond consciously to very subtle information, including psychic information, about the world around them.

Our experience suggests that being "psychic" is well within the potential of most people who take time to learn about the necessary skills required for accurate psychic functioning. But it is important that you feel secure and comfortable about having this potential, if you are to develop your own psychic capabilities to the fullest.

Developing your psychic abilities will not turn you into a genius or give you webbed feet. Psi will not turn you into an unemotional alien, or put you on a waiting list for Mount Olympus. However, it can put you in closer touch with more of your feelings, and with the many levels at which you are responding to other people and your environment. Psychic experiences may enrich your life enormously, but they will not solve all your problems. We believe these abilities are a vital part of your heritage as a human being, as much as any other creative or intellectual capacity.

As you gain experience with using psychic abilities successfully, both in the practice exercises and in real-life situations, we expect you to become increasingly confident in following your intuitive impressions. This is one of the nice things about psychic functioning. When you recognize how easy it can be, you may wonder why you have not made better use of psi all along.

The messages people give themselves about psychic functioning have a way of coming true for them. If you feel comfortable with your psychic abilities and are confident in responding to your intuitive impressions, you will be less likely to equivocate about those impressions, to interpret them away or to disregard useful psychic information. But if you do not treat your intuitive impressions seriously, you give your mind the message that becoming aware of psychic information is pointless, because you will disregard it anyway.

And telling yourself that learning to use psychic abilities is very difficult may indeed make this learning more difficult for you than it needs to be.

But there is no good reason to think that it is difficult to learn the basic skills required for good psychic functioning, or to think that years of training are necessary before you can begin using your psychic potential.

However, as we have so often stated, *psychic functioning is a subtle process.* This is why, in learning to respond to intuitive impressions, the most effective teachers are practice, feedback, and experience. Firsthand experience is the best way for you to know and understand the gentle urgency and unique sensations that accompany most responses to psychic information. Fortunately, despite individual differences, there are certain helpful similarities in the way many people have learned to recognize the difference between psychic information and purely imagined or remembered impressions.

CHARACTERISTICS OF MENTAL NOISE

As we have said, psychic impressions *feel* different from the thoughts and images that originate in your memory and imagination, which we call mental noise. Fortunately, you do not have to rely solely on a purely subjective analysis of your feelings to determine which impressions are most likely to be intuitive. Mental noise and psychic information often have other distinguishing characteristics.

In remote-viewing sessions, for example, mental noise often takes the shape of a *comparative analysis* of target elements that leads the viewer astray. Comparison can be helpful—viewers are often able to decipher the meaning of their intuitive impressions by comparing them with other experiences they have had. This is a necessary and important part of the process. If this comparative analysis is carried too far, however, it can lead the viewer away from describing actual target elements and into describing a memory or fantasy that has been triggered by the analysis.

As you practice remote viewing, keep alert for any extended comparative descriptions that creep into your impressions of particular targets. In describing a hidden object, for example, keep in mind that an object cannot logically be *like* a certain thing, and also *be* that thing. An object can only be what it is. If you experience your images as being *like* a grapefruit, you can be sure that the target is most likely *not* a grapefruit.

But knowing what a target reminds you of can help you determine what it actually is. Mental noise usually contains information that can help you focus your impressions of a target. By understanding and examining the mental noise triggered by your intuitive impressions, you may clarify some of your original impressions.

You might ask yourself what *about* the target brings a grapefruit to mind. Perhaps you had an impression of a grapefruit-sized round object, or a tart flavor, or a smooth and mottled texture. Perhaps you remembered a place where you once ate a grapefruit.

Functioning psychically is like being a detective. You must examine all your thoughts, sensations, and images carefully to interpret your impressions about a target properly. Even thoughts that might otherwise mislead you can often yield useful information when understood in their proper context.

Needless to say, if you do not recognize mental noise as such, you stand a good chance of describing something quite different from the target you are trying to focus upon. Mental noise has a way of expanding itself as one comparative analysis of target elements leads to another, and eventually to full-blown fantasies that come mostly from the memory and imagination, overpowering the subtle psychic signals.

Mental noise can also appear as an almost prefabricated image of a complete target that just pops into a viewer's mind during a remote-viewing session. You would be wise to suspect any overly developed, clear, sharp images that present themselves with too much persistence, especially at the start of a session. Slowly emerging shapes and forms are much more likely to delineate the true target. Although you can get a "flash" of a target, it will generally be a very fragmentary image. This is a common experience for many viewers. Often a viewer's recent thoughts and activities return as mental noise. If you spent the afternoon cooking a gourmet meal or climbing a mountain, and then conduct a remote-viewing session, your impressions of the target might well be affected. It might even be best to postpone the session.

It is best not to try a remote viewing when you are preoccupied with other concerns. It may be difficult for you to concentrate on the target and to interpret your impressions properly. This is particularly the case when you feel unwell, since illness can easily override your perception of subtle intuitive sensations. This seems less true for experienced viewers, but beginners should practice remote viewing only when they feel healthy and motivated.

Mental noise can even seem to reflect experiences that a viewer will have in the future. In the middle of a recent experiment in which I (K.H.) was asked to describe a distant target, I suddenly had a fully formed mental image of a crescent wrench. This image was quite intrusive and persistent, and did not seem to fit in with any of my earlier, more subtle impressions of the target. It was this fully formed and intrusive quality that allowed me to correctly identify this image as mental noise. My impressions of the target were almost exclusively concerned with its decorative quality, strong aroma, festive color (red on top, white on the bottom), and different appearance when viewed from various angles—nothing in common with a crescent wrench.

In thinking about my impressions carefully, I remembered that I had been looking through a tool kit earlier that day. It did not contain a wrench anything like the intrusive image, so my impression was not a memory. Still, the image of the wrench was almost too persistent to be a genuine psychic impression. I told my interviewer, Russ Targ, that the wrench image was probably mental noise, and asked that it be marked as such so that it would not confuse the judges reading the transcript.

After the session ended, I rushed out to buy a bottle of glue for a project planned for later that evening. I was amazed to discover that the familiar brown bottle of glue that I was seeking had been replaced by at least a half-dozen new varieties of glue in tubes. I studied the selection carefully, trying to overcome future shock and determine which type was right for my specific project. Suddenly, I spotted the crescent wrench. It was hanging on a pegboard, right in among the tubes of glue that had captured my attention. Seeing the wrench there convinced me that I had been correct in thinking my crescent-wrench images were irrelevant to the target in the earlier remote-viewing session. (I had not yet been given any feedback about the correct target.)

Three independent judges each compared my remote-viewing impressions with a pool of three possible target objects. None of them knew which was the actual target. Based upon my impressions, all three judges chose the correct target object out of the pool. The target was a cut flower, a red petunia, with a white underside, a strong scent, and a shape that gave a quite different appearance when viewed from various angles. Each of the judges had accepted my assessment of the crescent-wrench image as mental noise, and had ignored it.

When you experience persistent large-scale images that you suspect of being mental noise, it is essential to describe them out loud and let these overly complete images fade from your immediate awareness. You can take a break from the session. A break usually requires about thirty seconds, and consists of a good stretch and a few deep breaths. It is very important to remember to breathe. Later, you can allow more gentle impressions to emerge gradually in your mind. These are more likely to contain recognizable psychic information.

CHARACTERISTICS OF
INTUITIVE IMPRESSIONS

Now you know what mental noise is like, but how do you recognize true psychic information? Several common characteristics give good clues.

Intuitive impressions are usually more *gentle* and *fleeting* than mental noise. Rather than appearing immediately as a fully formed description of an entire target, psychic information often comes as a series of general impressions that gradually evolve into a more integrated and detailed image. For example, in my first beacon remote-viewing session at SRI, the randomly selected target site turned out to be a playground on the outskirts of Palo Alto. The session began with my describing the *general* terrain and the structures at the site—quick images of hills, grass, a fence, a bench, and the buildings surrounding the park where the playground is located. Only as the session developed, when I changed perspectives and viewed the entire site from above, did it occur to me that "maybe this is a playground," with a lower sandy area surrounded by a grassy rise. This description only gradually evolved into a more or less correct description of the layout of the park and its environs "on the outskirts . . . not in the middle of town."

Psychic information often appears in the form of quick thoughts, feelings, and images that *surprise* the viewer. Since intuitive impressions may provide detailed information about distant targets, the surprise is understandable. There is often no obvious explanation for the viewer's impressions in his immediate thoughts or environment.

Psychic information often has a recognizable impact upon those who experience it. Viewers frequently know that they are psychically "homing in" on a particular target when it begins to influence their feelings on a fairly deep level. They may, for example, experience smells, tastes, sounds, and textures associated with a target, as well as their own emotional response to it. This influence is usually more directly and strongly felt than any sensations that may be associated with purely imagined or remembered images. These non-visual sensations are usually a good indication of a true psi perception.

REMOTE-VIEWING EXERCISES

We recommend proceeding at a relaxed pace with the remote-viewing exercises that follow. It is important to carry out each session carefully, in a congenial, supportive atmosphere. This is better than going through a great many sessions within a brief period. Above all, enjoy yourself; do not take each practice session too seriously. Remote viewing seems easier to learn when you are having a nice time.

An Object Lesson

We will begin with an informal experiment. We suggest you start by giving yourself permission to function psychically. Just tell yourself that it is ok for you to obtain a successful result in this exercise.

Ask a friend to select an object without showing it to you, and to hide it in a paper bag, box, or basket in another room, and to stay there while you write down or tape-record your intuitive impressions about the object. If you prefer, you can describe the object to a third person—who must not know what it is. This person should write down your description.

The third party can also serve as your interviewer, whose job during the remote viewing is to ask questions about your experience of the object to facilitate your description. The interviewer's questions should be presented gently, without pressure, and in such a way that they do not "lead the witness." For example, the interviewer should not ask questions like "Is the object a red fire engine?" Or, equally bad, "What do you think it is?"

In the first stages, this can be a two-person game, with the friend who selected the object also serving as the interviewer. But since an interviewer who knows the answer could inadvertently lead you to a correct description through his questions, you will eventually want to have an uninformed interviewer, or no interviewer at all.

With your friend as the interviewer, you have every opportunity for success. You can "read his mind," in the mental-telepathy model. You can sense the object in the bag directly, through clairvoyance. Or you can look a few minutes into your future, and describe the object you will shortly be holding in your hands.

The interviewer should ask questions about things the viewer has actually mentioned, but has passed over too quickly. If the viewer seems fixated on one aspect of the object, the interviewer can ask if there is anything else of interest about the target. As you might imagine, interviewing requires nearly as much skill and practice as remote viewing.

The object your friend selects should be something you can hold in your hands after the exercise. There should be no other restrictions upon the selection, although it is good to have an object rich in distinctive details, so there are several aspects to psychically focus upon and describe. Ideally, it should engage more senses than just vision.

As soon as the object has been chosen, close your eyes and imagine what it will be like to hold it in your hands in a few minutes. (Eventually, try this exercise with your eyes open.) Feel free to make sketches of your impressions at any point, while describing the object or afterward. Your drawings need not be detailed or specific, and they certainly should not distract you from gathering your impressions.

As you imagine what it will be like to hold the object, look down at your hands—still with your eyes closed—and describe what you see and feel. Do not think about or analyze your impressions. Simply describe your feelings and images. Use every sense.

How heavy does the object feel in your hands? Do you notice a smell or aroma? Does any particular shape emerge in your mind? How does the object feel to you, and what is your emotional reaction to it?

Do not hold on to any images or descriptions for more than a few moments and do not try to guess or figure out what sort of object your friend may have chosen. Trying to second-guess the target selector is an endless source of mental noise. That is analysis, not psi! Simply allow various pieces of information about the object to pass into your awareness, and then drift on to the next image or impression without fixating. Your feelings and images about the object should come easily, without straining.

If you find yourself straining, if overly persistent memories of objects you have seen in the past are triggered in your mind, or if you feel confused about your images at any point in this exercise, let go of those images. Pause for a moment. Take a break. Breathe! Just think about something else for a few moments before you continue with your description. Open your eyes, and when you are ready, close your eyes again and begin again to describe the object.

The idea is to describe all of your feelings and mental pictures as clearly as possible, without over-elaborating upon them or leading yourself into mental noise. By not holding on to any single impression for too long, you allow yourself to experience other important pieces of information about the object.

Does anything about the object surprise you? Is it the same on all sides, or different? How does its inside compare with its outside? Does it even have an inside and outside? Are there different parts to it? Quietly allow a description of the object to form gradually in your mind. When you feel satisfied that you have given your best possible description of the object, signal your friend with the object that you are ready for feedback.

You may want to stop as soon as you are confident you have accurately described some recognizable aspect of the object. Do not try to continue your description longer than feels comfortable. As you become more experienced, you can extend your descriptions to include more information. A good time to stop this exercise would be shortly after you have gotten more than purely visual impressions about the target object— perhaps a nonvisual sensory impression, or an emotional or aesthetic response to the object. Ten to fifteen minutes should be plenty of time for you to describe a small object adequately.

After you have finished your description, your friend should bring you the target object. Holding it in your hands, soak up its presence for the first few moments without saying anything. Reflect on the images and feelings you had during the remote viewing.

As you review your description, notice if certain aspects of the object captured your attention more than others. Did you describe details of the object itself, or were your impressions sidetracked by thoughts and images it reminded you of? Were you influenced or distracted by any sounds, objects, or patterns in the place where you did your remote viewing?

Do you notice any ways in which your most correct impressions differed from the least correct? To make the best use of your feedback, consider the answers to these questions carefully. Did you have any strikingly correct images that for some reason you did not describe or draw? Will you recognize the feeling of correctness next time?

As a more structured variation on the object exercise, ask your friend to select a target object *after* you have described it (in writing or on tape, or to another friend), but before the chooser has any information about the description.

Your friend might also select three objects for a pool, and randomly choose one of these objects, by rolling a die for example, to be your target object for the exercise. (We recommend using only a single object in the beginning.) You might ask a neutral party to compare your description with the three objects and select the one that best fits your impressions, just as we have done in the laboratory.

The three objects should be as different from one another as possible. This will decrease the possibility of confusion both for the viewer and for any judge. We suggest choosing only three objects because it is hard to select more and still have objects that are all very different from one another. When you choose, pay attention to what material each object is made out of, and to its shape, color, patterns, texture, smell, taste, function, and other characteristics. It takes a lot of care to select a well-differentiated pool of target objects. Still, the effort involved is worth it, because it later makes the remote viewing and the judging much simpler.

As a bonus, the experience you gain in closely examining and comparing objects for a target pool can help you understand what constitutes an accurate and unique description of any object. This is useful, since those are the sorts of descriptions which can lead to the most successful remote viewings. We hope you will avoid the problem encountered in one experiment, in which, when asked what the correct object was, the target chooser said, "It's hard to describe."

Choosing objects for a target pool is a bit like going on a scavenger hunt. It can lead to some funny moments, such as the time a puzzled store clerk finally asked why in the world I (K.H.) wanted a small piece of black rubber hose, six inches of red ribbon, and one raw peanut. I just smiled and told her that it was all for science.

If you are using a pool of several objects, we recommend that during feedback you be shown only the object actually used as your target. Our experience suggests that if you are shown more than one object afterward, you may describe more than one object during the remote viewing. As we have discussed, we think this may occur because all of the objects will be in your hands in your immediate future.

In practicing with small objects, as in any remote-viewing exercise, you should not push yourself. Take time to enjoy your feelings of success after a particularly fruitful session. In some ways, the time spent between sessions is almost as important as the sessions themselves.

This time allows you to integrate your developing understanding of psychic functioning, and feelings of success, into your awareness on a very deep level. It is important to take time to allow this integration to occur before you go on to another remote-viewing experience. This is especially true when you are just beginning.

COPING WITH ENVIRONMENTAL NOISE

You can increase your success at remote viewing by practicing in a quiet place that does not interfere with your ability to process psychic information. Choose a familiar room where you will be comfortable, and will not be interrupted. That will reduce the potential influence of both mental (internal) and environmental (external) noise.

If your surroundings are too quiet, though—say, your bed, with the covers pulled over your head—you are likely to free-associate too easily, clouding your remote-viewing description with too many imagined and remembered impressions. The ideal place will let you focus most of your attention upon your impressions of the remote target, rather than upon other internally generated thoughts and images. We recommend sitting up in a dimly lit room, rather than lying down in a black, soundproof booth.

On the other hand, your environment should not provide too much unfamiliar sensory stimulation. Do not try to do remote viewing in a roomful of strange objects, with incense burning, water running, the radio playing, and pictures from *National Geographic* pasted on the walls. Any of those stimuli could easily creep into your impressions and fill your description with environmental noise. Brightly lit outdoor scenes that are visible through a window are as bad as bright lights in the room. Even the "white noise" played through a subject's earphones in a Ganzfeld experiment—intended to be a nonstimulus—very often triggers images of the ocean or running water.

A familiar room is best, there it is easier to distinguish between the usual sensations associated with being in a particular place and any unusual experiences, which may provide psychic information about the remote-viewing target. And if you always use the same room, you will not have to adjust your perceptions for each practice session. You will soon learn to recognize the residual mental noise associated with a familiar location.

As you become more adept at remote viewing, you will be able to practice in noisier and less familiar places. The experience you gain in distinguishing between intuitive impressions and mental or environmental noise in a controlled environment should help you cope with the difficulties of remote viewing in less familiar situations.

GEOGRAPHICAL REMOTE VIEWING

After you have practiced remote viewing of small objects for a while, you will probably want to develop your psychic abilities on a larger scale. The instructions that follow will carry you, step by step, through the procedures we and others have used to successfully carry out remote viewing of large-scale geographical areas.

You will need at least one friend to prepare and carry out these procedures with you; two would be better. As in the viewing of small objects, you can each take turns being the viewer, the interviewer, and the outbound experimenter or beacon.

Selecting Geographical Target Sites

Your friend should locate six interesting places within twenty minutes of a central remote-viewing location. These will serve as the target pool for your practice sessions. (If you will be taking turns, each of you should select a pool at the start for the other.) Without revealing the list to the others, the selectors should each number their sites from 1 to 6.

The sites in the target pool should not be familiar or popular places. Out-of-the-way spots that neither you nor your friend knew about before you began these practice sessions might be better.

These sites should be as different from one another as possible—a beach, a downtown area, a park, a fountain, a bridge, a parking lot, a field, and so forth. The dimensions of each target are determined by what is immediately visible from a specific location where the beacon is to stand.

When you are ready to conduct a session, the participants should meet at the central remote-viewing location—say, your living room. Set an exact time when the viewer will describe the place where the beacon will be, and synchronize your watches. You should also set a time to meet back at the central location, after the viewing.

We suggest allowing thirty minutes for the beacon to reach the site, fifteen minutes for the viewing, and thirty minutes for the beacon to return. Since the sites should all be less than twenty minutes away from the central location, this leaves time for any unexpected delays that might occur.

Choosing the Target

As soon as the details have been arranged, the beacon should start out. Only when he is out of sight and hearing range of the viewer and the interviewer should he roll a die to determine which of the six sites on his list will be the target. (If the one that comes up has already been used in a previous session, the die should be rolled again.)

Then the beacon should go directly to the chosen target. As he approaches the site, he should make sure that the thirty minutes allotted for travel have passed, so that he enters the target site just as the viewer begins his description. He should then go to the predetermined spot and quietly take notice of what is going on around him. His function is simply to experience the target site, to serve as a remote point of reference for the viewer to focus upon.

The beacon's task is relatively simple, but it can lead to unexpected situations. For example, in a remote-viewing experiment at SRI, a woman who was acting as the beacon was sent to the Glass Slipper Motel, the target site for that session. She received several interesting offers in her fifteen minutes of slowly walking back and forth on the sidewalk in front of the building. We do not think she accepted any of them.

Viewing and Describing
the Remote Location

While the beacon travels to the target site, the viewer (and the interviewer if there is one) can just relax until it is time to begin the viewing. Do not discuss possible future or past target sites. When it begins, it is best to tape-record the session, or the interviewer should take very complete notes. Keep some drawing materials handy, in case the viewer decides to make a sketch.

When you are ready to psychically perceive the remote target, open your imagination to the experiences you would have at the target site if you were there physically. *Do not* try to "reach out" for information about it. Also, do not try to "scan" the entire site all at once. Instead, let individual bits of information gradually emerge in your awareness, as in the sensory-awareness exercises we discussed earlier.

As you begin to describe the target, focus upon one particular point of view—preferably the one where your beacon is at the moment. Stay there at first; do not try to "see" the target from several different vantage points, because this may lead to confusion. By pacing yourself, handling your images and impressions slowly, and taking periodic breaks, you can minimize confusion and will be less likely to overinterpret or distort your intuitive impressions.

Often, some very general images about the site will come to you first, followed by a variety of other impressions and images, both large and small. Your general impressions can help you get a basic feeling for the place you are describing, but we recommend resisting the urge to "color in" these impressions too quickly.

Again, if you get a full-blown, full-color image of a famous nearby landmark early in the session, you should tell your interviewer about it, and label it as possible mental noise. It is very helpful to announce these early "noisy" impressions briefly, because that is the easiest way we know of to get rid of them.

Examine your large-scale images and impressions for their underlying structure. As you do this, you will often find yourself revising and refining some of your initial interpretations of these impressions. The idea is to examine your images without dwelling on them and adding to the mental noise.

An impression that reminds you of a wall, for example, may not necessarily refer to a wall at the target site. Perhaps you sensed something flat and smooth. Those feelings, and not the idea of a wall, are your most basic first impression. If you put off interpreting your initial impressions until you gather more psychic information about the target, you will be less likely to impose a predetermined (possibly incorrect) structure upon your developing images of the target site.

In the case of the "wall" image, the target you are sensing may not be a wall, exactly, though it may be something like a wall. Perhaps the flat smoothness you first experienced will later be combined with an impression of engraved lettering. Perhaps it is a stone marker or the side of a monument. Or perhaps you will later have images of blackness and a broken yellow line, suggesting that the flat smoothness may be the surface of a highway.

Or you may be correct that your first impression pertains to some kind of wall, but you still should not try to define this wall too quickly. What other sensations do you have? Do you experience soft vegetation growing through cracks in its surface? Is it soft or hard, rough or smooth? Is it an old, low brick wall with a few smooth sections, or a gigantic glass-and-metal panel that forms part of a modern skyscraper?

Such questions would probably be difficult to answer, based solely upon your first few psychic impressions about a target site. Therefore, you should let your experiences develop naturally before you reach any conclusions. The first impressions are likely to contain a lot of correct information, but the specific relationship of these impressions to the target may only gradually emerge. An experienced interviewer would much rather hear you say "I see a large inverted V-shape—it looks as big as a building" than "I see the International House of Pancakes."

As a remote-viewing session develops and you feel an evolving sense of visual "contact" with a target site, other senses will usually come into play. This is an important part of the process, because it adds a sense of dimension to your psychic perceptions that might take longer to reach through purely visual images.

Nonvisual psychic perceptions of a target usually emerge of their own accord, without any special prompting from you or your interviewer. An experienced viewer will sometimes help these additional impressions along, though, by deliberately focusing his attention upon another sense when he feels ready to incorporate its information. You can do this in a remote-viewing session by simply "listening" for any sounds—or tactile sensations, chills, smells, tastes, or emotions—that emerge. As we have said, *these nonvisual perceptions and feelings are a good sign that you have made psychic contact with your target.*

In most cases, as you describe visual aspects of a remote target, other sensory impressions will naturally be perceived and described along with them. For example, an impression of a visually uneven roadway almost compels some sort of tactile sensation, such as roughness, to complete the image. You may notice sunlight beating down on the roadway, and this may lead you to experience warmth and the smell of heated asphalt.

Some sites have especially obvious nonvisual characteristics—the noise and smells of a lumbermill, the dense and humid atmosphere of a swamp, or the roar and salty taste of the ocean. Certain senses may be more strongly involved than others, as a result both of sensory differences in target sites and of your own predispositions.

Your nonvisual impressions will often help you interpret your visual images. But visual images themselves can contain a great deal of useful information at more than a superficial level. For example, an image of darkness, in the middle of a sunny day, might indicate that your beacon is lurking in a dim indoor location—such as a pizzeria or saloon.

Your remote-viewing impression will often involve several different visual and nonvisual images, which interact to express the target site's special characteristics. This usually happens as your individual images begin to merge into a more complete description of the target.

Say you first experience an upward slope. As your psychic perceptions of the site develop, you may notice vegetation, several rough and jagged areas, a rushing wind, and the cold, white wetness of mountain snow. As these images solidify and come together in your mind, you stand a very good chance of recognizing the overall site you are describing. In fact, in an actual remote-viewing session, targeted on a hidden photograph in which the target site was a mountain glacier feeding into a lake, I (K.H.) experienced strong sensations of cold, wetness, and the up-and-down elevations of the surrounding area. This eventually led to a fully formed image of an icy mountainside along a lake, covered with snow and ice, which was a correct description of the site (see page 207).

Still, you should never feel under pressure to arrive at a definite final decision about the details or identity of any single target. Especially when you first try remote viewing, it is better to describe a small amount of correct information, with little incorrect information, than to describe great amounts of mixed correct and incorrect information about a target.

The experience you gain in correctly describing even the smallest features of a remote site can be invaluable, as it provides you with a basis for learning to properly discriminate and interpret psychic information on a much larger scale. So do not be afraid to end a remote-viewing session early, as soon as you are satisfied that you have described some recognizable aspect of a target location.

With practice, you may be surprised to discover how easily a complex mixture of impressions and images can coalesce into a detailed picture of a target. At the moment, though, you may be wondering how such general descriptions as "buildings" or "wetness" can evolve into such highly specific target descriptions as airport towers and bubbling fountains.

One explanation may be found in the dynamics of "ordinary" interpersonal communication. The words we use to express subtle ideas and nuances to one another are essentially blunt instruments. They do not

Geographical remote viewing by Keith Harary of target site (left) gives following description (right): "Mountains; glaciers; ice-land interfaces; rocky, cold land, some sparse vegetation; lake." Photo by Willie Burkhardt/Leo de Wys, Inc.

fully express fine details of our inner experiences; they merely point our listeners toward the general direction of our deeper meaning. Yet, the right combination of ordinary words can lead a listener toward a genuine understanding of another person's feelings and ideas. We hear only sentences, yet these crude tools can create an inner connection with our own experiences and perceptions that allows a shared understanding of very personal thoughts and emotions to emerge.

Similarly, the general impressions that you form about a remote target are like buoy markers pointing the way for more detailed psychic information to find its way to the surface of your awareness. Everything you have ever experienced may be said to have left its fingerprints on your mind. This information, among other things, helps you interpret the details behind your larger intuitive perceptions.

By comparing your present intuitive impressions with your past perceptions and experiences, you can describe quite specific details of remote objects and locations you have never seen. Fortunately, as in the usual conversation, much of this information seems to be processed subconsciously.

By the time your psychic impressions reach your conscious awareness, they appear to have already undergone a fair amount of translation from raw intuition into more recognizable thoughts and images. Your role, then, in describing remote sites or practicing any other form of intentional psychic functioning is to interpret your psychic impressions properly as they emerge from your subconscious.

There is a part of you that seems to understand psychic information very well. It can provide you with incredibly detailed impressions and images about remote targets when you take your time and learn how to listen to your own thoughts and feelings.

This is one reason why the most correct and important bits of intuitive information will often sneak up on you, surprise you, and disappear in a flash. It is as if a deeper sense of knowing echoes through your mind for a moment, before it hurries back into the darkness. You have to be alert to catch it.

You might think of your intuitive impressions about a target site as being like soap bubbles tossed into the wind by a curious child. The impressions are fragile and light, yet tangible. You will do best by observing your psychic impressions quietly and treating them lightly. Otherwise, they may blow away, shatter, or disappear before you realize what they were.

An interesting thing happens as the full spectrum of a viewer's psychic impressions about a target unfolds during a remote-viewing session. As most viewers describe it, they will quite often feel an emotional and intensely personal response to the target they are describing. This response occurs spontaneously, sometimes arising out of multiple sensory impressions of a target. When it does, they have little doubt they have made psychic contact with a target site.

Some viewers describe this emotional response as a wave of subjective feelings, rising out of their intuitive perceptions. Others describe the emotional impact of a remote target as a feeling of awakening—as though, like Rip Van Winkle, they had popped out of a deep sleep and experienced the full impact of their (remote) environment in a sudden onrush of feelings and sensations, after a century of dreaming.

Usually, your emotional responses to a target will be fairly gentle— "Oh, how pretty!" Occasionally, these responses can seem a bit overwhelming—"This place is horrible!" Some people prefer to dwell upon their emotional responses, while others would rather acknowledge and pass over them quickly. This response sometimes depends on the nature of the target—a slaughterhouse will elicit a different emotional reaction than a field of sunflowers—but it also depends upon the viewer's sensitivity to his own emotions.

You may experience some of your most correct and detailed impressions while you are emotionally responding to a target. In experiments, these details have included information about the surrounding mood and atmosphere of various sites, or their artistic qualities, age, cultural background, and function.

For example, Russ Targ and I (K.H.) conducted a long-distance remote-viewing experiment in 1980, in which the target site was the old seaport town of Salem, Massachusetts. The session was part of our continuing exploration of whether coordinates are necessary for remote viewing. As the blind interviewer, Russ simply asked, "I have a target that needs a description." As the viewer, I first described the general terrain surrounding Salem—land with elevations on it, near a large body of water —and then was quickly impressed with Salem's charming, well-kept residential atmosphere. This pleasant emotional response soon led to a full-blown description of the town itself—with its deciduous trees, wood and brick houses with pointed roofs and pretty cross-hatched windows, and quaint streets—and their residents, birds, squirrels, and relaxed, happy families. This description was accompanied by two drawings, one of which is shown on page 211.

Of course, psychic information does not emerge with exactly the same pace and pattern for every viewer and target site. Our descriptions are meant to serve you more as guidelines than as concrete directives. The more you practice remote viewing, the more you will develop your own particular style of responding to and expressing psychic information.

Marilyn Schlitz is an experienced experimenter and remote viewer whose work you will recall from Chapter 3. In the following paragraphs, she describes her experiences and method of response as a successful remote viewer. Marilyn's summary is as applicable to the description of little objects in a paper bag as it is to distant geographical locations.

The goal is established in my mind. I will describe the object which represents the target. When there is no interviewer, my alter ego

Geographical remote viewing by Keith Harary of old seaport town of Salem, Massachusetts (left) gives following description (right): "Wood and brick buildings in good condition with pointy roofs and pretty, cross-hatched

plays the role. "Describe the object," it says. "Tell me what you see."

I lower the room lights and close my eyes during the remote-viewing session. (I prefer working in a dim environment.) I look for images that pertain to the target. The "interviewer" keeps a dialogue going, by continuously asking: "What does the target look like? What are its distinguishing features?"

Sometimes I reject certain images that I feel are not related to the target. How can I tell? Here I can't be certain. Perhaps because

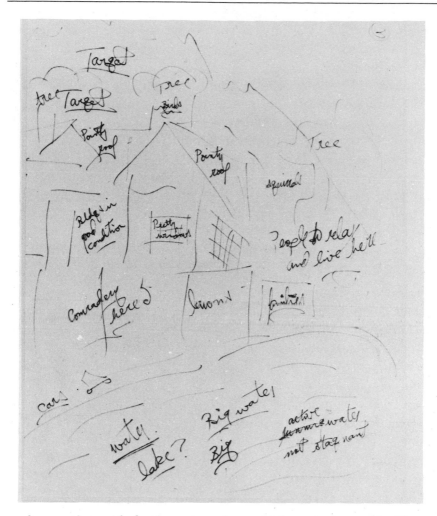

windows, a place with deciduous trees, lawns, birds, squirrels, cars, families, and comradery—a place where people relax and live—alongside a large body of water." Photo © 1979 Nathan Benn.

they represent shapes and forms which often come to mind. Perhaps because they represent something I was just looking at.

Anyway, with my eyes closed, I find an image. I work to bring it into focus, so that I can draw it on paper. After it is drawn, I let it go. What comes next may or may not be related to the previous image. I do not try to force my images to directly relate to one another.

Again, my alter ego asks: "What does the target look like?" And, again, I respond. After some period of time (usually about five minutes) I stop. This often happens when the same forms come again and again, or when I no longer feel able to fully concentrate upon the target.

I never know if I am right or not. I usually don't think about it much. Sometimes the impressions are quite vivid. At other times, it is a struggle to find them.

Each task is different, depending upon the "universe of discourse," as it were. If I'm doing geographical remote viewing, I will focus on the beacon and attempt to describe his or her surroundings. If the target is an object, I do as I just described. All tasks seem equally likely to succeed.

Developing the ability to respond to general, emotional, aesthetic, visual, and nonvisual psychic impressions gives you a variety of colors to choose from as you paint your intuitive pictures. As you progress, you will become more adept at selecting the most appropriate details and impressions to describe each particular target.

You may find nonvisual or emotional information about a target preceding your other impressions. Often, certain types of impressions will be only minimally present in your experience of a given target site, while others will be more strongly emphasized.

Hella Hammid describes her experience this way:

Although it is good to relax in a quiet place when doing remote viewing, my first experience took place while standing in a cold drizzle on a rather cold, windy roof of an SRI building. The "signal" came in so clearly: a red barn-type structure, wooden slats painted red running horizontally with a very steep pitched roof—then came other "signals" not of a visual nature.

I felt it was a nonfunctioning building—a fake, or perhaps a stage set. No one living in it. The feeling became stronger, the emptiness more obvious. When I was taken to the site for feedback I was confronted by "The Little Red Schoolhouse" on a miniature golf course. Somewhat unnerved, I went home to remain incommunicado from the experimenters, Russ and Hal, for several weeks. I was scared and had to sort out this totally new experience. Yet, as skeptical as I might have been, it had happened to me and I was going to find out more about it.

What I have learned so far, and am still learning each time I do this, is that the "signal" is always there and that my ability to access it depends on many subtle conditions within *me*. Outer conditions are really secondary; I have done much work under less than "ideal" circumstances, such as in a five-"man" submarine, submerged to a depth of five hundred feet under the ocean; or under a hot Egyptian sun for hours, describing artifacts that had not yet been excavated.

What happens? Primarily I must listen in—warily. Not to *think*, but to *be* and allow images and sensations to appear seemingly out of left field and to grab them quietly by the tail, because they flash by in a millisecond. I do not try to look at anything, only record it. It will appear again and again with a new bit of information which is not necessarily visual, but may be of a great variety of other sensations: temperature, smells, sounds, emotional reactions such as "I am very uncomfortable here—want to get out" or "It is very dark, damp, busy, noisy, deserted, dusty," etc.

To distinguish between signal and noise there are a number of fairly reliable checks. Most important is "It reminds me of . . . " —that's noise, which can easily fall off into wonderful meandering descriptions fraught with pieces of memories and associations. When this occurs I start from scratch and catch the signal anew. If it has persisted, it usually *is* the signal and not noise. Once I feel firmly established psychically at the site, it then becomes relatively easy to "move around" in it—either spatially or temporally—and "see" additional features just by "looking" at what is there.

A little game I often play upon awakening, before opening my eyes, is to "look at the clock"—then open my eyes and presto!— instant feedback. Works well. Try it. Or to look at a friend's house just before telephoning to see if they are there. *Trusting* this gift and, most importantly, working with a supportive group of collaborators go a long way to enhancing one's ability to function psychically.

The best advice we can offer you, as you learn to describe remote target sites, is to maintain a relaxed but attentive grip upon the reins of your experience in each session. Be neither too critical nor too immediately accepting of your impressions. The rest should come naturally, as it has for a great many people who have learned about psychic functioning before you.

Above all, remember that describing a site is a learning experience. We expect that there will often be room for improvement in your descriptions, as there is in most human endeavors. No one session should be viewed as the ultimate evidence for your ability to function psychically. Give yourself time for your psychic abilities to develop.

THE USE OF DRAWINGS
IN GEOGRAPHICAL REMOTE VIEWING

Some viewers like to express their psychic impressions as much as possible on paper before they try to interpret them. Others feel drawings are a distraction, and prefer to draw pictures of a target only after they have verbally described all or most of their impressions.

Among those who use drawings as a way of interpreting their impressions are viewers who jot down their impressions as a series of fast "glyphs" on paper—a curved, sloping line for a hill, a straight, squared-off line for a building, wavy lines for water, and so forth. This technique is a little like the Identi-Kit method used by police to draw criminal suspects from descriptions given by witnesses.

Instead of asking whether the target site has bushy eyebrows or a cleft chin, the viewer uses his glyphs to record the features he perceives at a site. He then fills in these features with additional details, including non-visual sensations, and images associated with the glyphs themselves, just as he would using other remote-viewing methods. Many viewers find these glyphs to be very useful in working out initial impressions of small objects as well as remote target sites. For example, the results of an experimental session in which I (K.H.) used a glyph method to record my RV impressions are shown on page 215. The target site turned out to be the sawmill town of Kamenka in the Soviet Union. The site contains a number of metal-roofed buildings situated on a grassy hillside overlooking a rushing river. Some overhead wires are strung on "telephone" poles along the sandy shore. Most importantly, the entire site is strewn with wooden poles, scattered on the hills and shore, and floating in the river.

My drawings of the site are essentially symbolic glyph representations of the target. The first drawing depicts the general ambiance of the area and the relationship of various environmental features to one another—"hills, wooden buildings with small amount of metal on them, sandy soil, little [small] vegetation and grasses, brown rushing river. . . . and so forth—which are all found at the site. The second drawing depicts the poles

Soviet sawmill town of Kamenka (above) described by viewer Keith Harary in drawings (below); "Hills; wooden buildings with small amount of metal on them; sandy soil; little (small) vegetation and grasses; brown rushing river—wider in one area; lines of wires along shore?; beaten up wooden poles feel rough, smell funny, splinters." Photo © 1983 Howard Sochurek.

lying all over the hills and shore and around the buildings. The poles are described as "beaten up wooden poles, feel rough, smell funny, splinters." The second drawing also includes the phrase "lines of wire along the shore?" While the various environmental elements of the target are accurately described in their correct relationship to one another, the drawings are fairly abstract—meant mainly to give a general idea of what is to be found at the site. This site was targeted by the longitude and latitude coordinates of the location, provided by an interviewer (R.T.) who was blind to the target's identity.

Often, viewers prefer to form collections of images more immediately into less abstract drawings, such as entire scenes containing literal depictions of buildings, trees, and rivers, that express and record their impressions. The results of a remote-viewing session of this type are shown on pages 218–219. The target site for this experiment—without coordinates—was Miami Beach, Florida. My drawing and description of this site contain a mixture of correct and incorrect elements. The choppy waves on one side of Miami are incorrectly interpreted as "some elevations near." During the viewing, I am also not certain whether the site I am psychically experiencing is an American city or "some foreign country." Nevertheless, a fairly accurate depiction of the very modern structures to be found in Miami is provided, and the general terrain of the target site is correctly described: "Buildings; well-developed streets are like canyons here"; and "sand." A "canal" is also correctly shown running along one side of Miami. The weather is accurately described as "hot, but pleasant." A description is also given of some "odd mechanism" near one end of the canal, which we have no way of checking. In contrast to the impressions recorded using a glyph method in the previous example, the Miami remote viewing drawing is less abstract, more literal. Of course, a viewer often begins a session with a more abstract impression/description of a target site, and then develops this into a more literal description and drawing of the site as the session progresses.

In short, a variety of drawing strategies are useful ways for different viewers to describe and manage their remote-viewing impressions. Although some viewers swear by their favorite methods, there is no evidence that any one way of drawing impressions, or approaching remote viewing in general, is superior. As you develop your own techniques, remember that your drawings should help you express and interpret your impressions, but should not become distractions or circumscribe your remote-viewing experience.

Keep in mind that some viewers who make only perfunctory sketches, at best, often provide verbal target descriptions as accurate as any drawing. Sketching is an option; it can be a useful, even entertaining way of describing a target. It is up to you to decide if and how you use this option.

TAKING BREAKS DURING
REMOTE-VIEWING SESSIONS

You may feel compelled to give a complete description of a remote target without interruption, but this is not always the best way to handle psychic information. There will probably be moments, in the middle of a session, when you feel confused or stuck, or realize that you are trying too hard to force some of your images. If so, we suggest that you let go of whatever is troubling you before continuing with your description. Take a break.

Our experience tells us that instead of causing you to lose information, letting go and taking a break will give you a chance to gain some perspective on your remote-viewing experience. Perhaps the images you were following to the point of confusion have told you all they could about a target. Pursuing them any further may lead you off the track and into mental noise.

When you let go, you give yourself room to experience new images and sensations a little later on. They may provide key insights into your entire experience that would not otherwise have been possible.

A breather is also called for whenever you notice that you have been repeating many of the same images over and over, and thereby losing the developmental flow of your intuitive impressions.

Take a break whenever you feel like it. Psychic functioning is an intelligent process, not a product of macho posturing, superstitious behavior, or hocus-pocus. The information you need to describe a target will be there when you return to your impressions. If you ease off on any compulsive urges and pressures, you are less likely to burst the bubble of psychic information forming in your awareness.

Put your impressions on "hold" for a few moments (often less than a minute). You can use the time to think about something else, go to the bathroom (though you should have done this before the session began), or review the target descriptions you have given up to that point.

A review can be profitable; it may help you break through any points

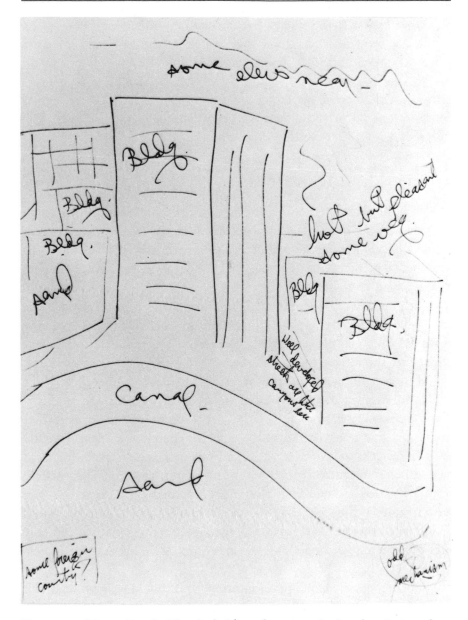

Target site Miami Beach, Florida (left), and remote-viewing description of
site by viewer Keith Harary (right). Viewer misinterprets ocean waves as
'elevations' but correctly describes modern "buildings; streets; sand; canal; hot
but pleasant; some vegetation."

of confusion with fresh insights that can clarify your entire experience. As you review your description, you may find it helpful to restate the parts which you are most certain about. These will often lead you to totally new impressions.

Return to viewing the target as soon as any momentary feelings of confusion or tension have dissipated. You will probably then be better able to respond psychically to the target site.

THE INTERVIEWER'S ROLE

In geographical remote viewing, the interviewer's role is basically the same as in the viewing of small objects. But it can get quite a bit more complicated. Typical interviewer questions for the viewer can be, "Tell me about your mental pictures," or "Tell me what your experiences are with respect to the target."

The interviewer is there to facilitate the viewer's description of a site, but he should not interfere with the psychic process. In addition to asking pertinent questions that may help clarify the viewer's description of a target site, the interviewer should keep alert for signs of confusion that would suggest the need for a break.

An interviewer might also ask a viewer to change his perspective— "How does it look from up in the air?"—or to return to an earlier impression that was passed over too quickly. The interviewer may gently ask helpful questions and make suggestions, but should *never* force his own opinions or sense of structure on the viewer. He should also refrain from asking leading questions that imply information, such as "Do you see any water at the site?" The viewer will immediately experience water, regardless of whether there is any at the target. An interviewer can only suggest new approaches: "Tell me more. Is anything else of interest nearby?"

The interviewer should never interrupt, but should wait for pauses in the viewer's target description before saying anything. The interviewer should not distract the viewer from focusing full attention upon the target.

FEEDBACK AT TARGET SITES:
WHAT TO LOOK FOR

After the remote-viewing part of a practice session is over, the viewer and interviewer should complete their notes about the target description while they wait for the beacon to return from the target site. These notes should not be revised or added to once the beacon has come back. As soon as he returns, the beacon should tell the viewer what the target site was; then all the participants should go to the target location for on-site feedback.

Take all your notes, tape recordings, and drawings with you when you visit a target for feedback. While you are there, notice your emotional reaction to the place, and keep alert for any similarities between your descriptions and drawings and both the large and small features of the target location.

You will usually have an immediate sense of how accurate your general description is. Whatever the overall results are, however, you should not be distracted from comparing all of your specific impressions with what is actually found at the target.

Remember, though, that the remote-viewing experience is not a test. The purpose of feedback is not to grade the session, but to help you understand the origins of all the thoughts and images you experienced during the session. It is therefore important for you to be sure which of your impressions were correct and which resulted from mental noise, and to try to recall how you felt about the impressions as you had them.

As you explore the site, look at it from the point of view of the beacon, and also from any of the various viewpoints you took during your remote viewing. It is important not to stretch the facts in an attempt to fit the target into your description, but it is just as important not to overlook even the smallest details.

During one remote-viewing session, for example, I (K.H.) experienced a small piece of broken glass at a particular spot in the target site I was psychically describing. That seemed like a fairly insignificant piece of information, until I used a drawing of my impressions as a map at the site, during feedback, and immediately found the broken glass hidden in the grass at exactly the spot where I had described it as being. This was more rewarding than anything else about that session, even though most of my other impressions were also accurate.

While you are exploring the target site for feedback, you may remember bits of imagery that were quickly passed over during your remote viewing, or not even actively noticed, but that later turned out to relate to the target. Take these in stride, as part of your learning experience. Even though this sort of realization can be frustrating, it also tells you that psychic functioning is alive and well in your mind, and that all you really need to do to make better use of it is to keep on practicing.

JUDGING AND KEEPING TRACK OF YOUR PROGRESS

Judging geographical remote-viewing sessions is a lot like judging those with target objects. Your judge should be an intelligent and observant person who has not been told anything about the session he is asked to judge. Ideally, he would be familiar with the way psychic information expresses itself, based upon his own firsthand experience.

After you have carried out three sessions (with three of your six sites), the judge should be given the locations of these three sites to visit. The judge should not be given any clues that identify which sites go with which descriptions, but should be provided with only the viewer's verbal (and drawn) impressions, and the directions to each site in the target pool.

When the judge visits each site, he should compare the viewer's descriptions with what he finds there, and attempt to discern to what extent this site relates to the viewer's description of a particular target. The judge's opinion provides an objective check on your own feedback, but does not replace feedback as a learning experience.

We recommend keeping all of your notes about your practice sessions organized in a safe place, so that you will have a record of the progress you are making. Review these notes periodically to look for patterns in the way you respond to remote-viewing targets, techniques, and procedures. They will show you ways your ability to recognize, process, and describe psychic information has improved and developed over time. For this purpose, it is useful to date each record sheet and indicate who the viewer and interviewer were.

As a variation of the exercise described above, try to describe a site without sending out a beacon to visit it. You can also conduct sessions in which the target site is chosen *after* you have recorded your remote-viewing description, or in which the target is a picture or slide of a local site, or even an interesting photograph from the wonderful periodical, *National Geographic.*

STEPPING OUT FOR THE EVENING

When you are feeling adventurous, you may want to try an exercise that you can use to achieve an out-of-body experience (OBE). In an out-of-body experience, you feel as though your awareness is able to move about independently, without bringing your body along. It is more intense than a remote-viewing experience in that, during an OBE, you feel as if you really are at a remote location, rather than simply experiencing it psychically from a distance.

We believe that remote viewing and the OBE lie on a continuum of psi experiences. Remote viewing is like seeing a remote scene, as though it were a movie. As you gain experience and courage with remote viewing, it is possible to bring greater amounts of your awareness, sensitivity, emotionality, and sexuality to the remote-viewing experience. As you increasingly let go of the reality in which you begin the experience, you may experience a remote location so intensely that you feel as if you were actually there.

This exercise combines the techniques to enhance sensory and intuitive awareness we discussed earlier, with deep physical relaxation. To begin, you must first learn to relax your body totally. You can do this by lying on a comfortable surface, such as a sofa or a reclining chair, and imagining that a gentle current of warm water is gradually working its way up through the soles of your feet toward the top of your head, warming and totally relaxing all the muscles in your body as it passes through them.

Feel each individual muscle as it becomes warm, easily lets go of any tension, and relaxes. Just let the gentle current flow through your entire body and out through the top of your head, leaving you feeling calm, comfortable, and completely relaxed. When you have practiced entering a deeply relaxed state and are able to do so fairly easily, it is time to practice the next part of this OBE exercise.

Find a pleasant location that you would enjoy "visiting" in an out-of-body experience. First, go to that location physically (i.e., bring your body with you) and practice the sensory and intuitive awareness exercises we discussed in the beginning of this chapter.

Notice the sights, sounds, smells, tastes, and textures at the site you have chosen. Close your eyes while you are there and visualize the way the site appears in your mind's eye. Then open your eyes and compare your mental images with the way the site actually looks. Continue doing this in different parts of the site until there is little or no difference between your mental images and the visual characteristics of the site itself. Notice also the way the site makes you feel on an emotional and intuitive level. When you have fully absorbed the sensory, emotional, and intuitive characteristics of the site you have chosen, return home to the room where you practiced the deep relaxation exercises.

Once again, relax your body, using any exercise that works for you. While you are relaxing, put all thoughts of your immediate environment out of your mind and quietly focus your awareness upon the distant site you just visited. Imagine that you are at the remote site *with your eyes closed,* listening to the sounds, absorbing the feelings, and so forth. As your body relaxes, allow it to pass from your immediate awareness, and focus all of your attention upon experiencing the distant location. Feel your awareness being completely surrounded by the remote location. Then, open your "eyes" at the distant site when you feel comfortable with doing so.

With this exercise, it is possible to induce an OBE in which you feel as if you are actually "visiting" the remote site. You can practice "returning" to the site in your mind whenever you want to. Eventually, when you have grown used to entering an OBE state, you may want to use it to psychically "explore" places you have never been. For your own peace of mind, you may want to tell yourself that your body will be safe while you are "away," and that you can easily terminate the experience whenever you simply decide to do so.

Even though many people have enshrouded the OBE in mysterious and complicated procedures, inducing an OBE can be a fairly simple process—as simple as you allow yourself to make it. The out-of-body experience gives you a chance to psychically explore and perceive actual distant locations on a more intense level than with remote viewing. Happy flying!

MORE THAN MAGIC

One of the ways you can tell if something is real is by considering whether it has identifiable properties and limitations. If psychic functioning were the product of pure fantasy, we would have offered you a magic formula, instead of a series of exercises, to convince you that you can use your psychic abilities. We would have claimed that psychic abilities are capable of almost anything if you simply believe in them, instead of discussing the kinds of specific skills you need to learn before you can make effective use of psychic functioning.

The fact that psychic functioning is the product of a complex combination of skills and methods of self-expression should suggest that it is something people can learn to do, even if they are not strongly oriented toward psychic functioning to begin with. This is a correct assumption, since many people have already learned to function psychically at will, using the kinds of exercises and techniques we have described here.

Psychic functioning is a product of hard work and inspiration. It is better at providing certain types of information than others, and it cannot always provide 100 percent accurate information upon demand. It can, however, under fairly ordinary circumstances often provide strikingly accurate descriptions of distant objects, people, and locations with which a viewer is not in known physical contact. In addition to the surroundings seen by a beacon, a viewer can often describe a distant person's physical health and emotional feelings.

Despite all that we have learned about psychic abilities, it is obvious that our understanding of psi is still in its infancy. As more people explore and develop their psychic potential, we will gain a broader base from which to expand both our knowledge of psychic functioning and our understanding of what it means to be alive and human.

11

Coping with Success: Living with Psi and Learning to Win

When geometric diagrams and digits
Are no longer the keys to living things,
. . . .
When the society is returned once more
To unimprisoned life, and to the universe,
. . . .
Then our entire twisted nature will turn
And run when a single secret word is spoken.
Novalis/1800
Translated by Robert Bly

IN THE BEGINNING

Learning to function psychically is a little like making love for the first time. Although it can be exciting and rewarding, some people also find it stressful. When you first practice remote viewing, you may feel as if you are being judged or tested, and therefore try extra hard to achieve spectacular results.

The experience of deliberately responding to psychic information is unfamiliar to most people. Describing something you cannot see or feel in the ordinary sense, without any feedback until later, is an admittedly unusual and demanding task. While you may be ready and eager to succeed, you are likely to feel self-conscious and wonder if you are providing accurate information or just imagining things when you first set out to describe a remote target.

It is normal to feel a little strange and uneasy when you begin learning to use your psychic abilities. Psychic functioning is rarely simple, but for most people, it becomes easier with experience. Nature seems to have a way of bringing out the best in you when you relax and let your inner feelings emerge.

An experienced English researcher, K. J. Batcheldor, has clearly described two of the fears that people have which can interfere with their use of psychic abilities. He calls these "ownership resistance" and "witness inhibition."[1] In his table levitation experiments, Batcheldor works only with groups and only in the dark. If any significant psychic functioning appears, no *individual* has to take responsibility for it, and no one needs to *confront* it directly. Batcheldor believes this makes it easier for him to facilitate psi in his experiments. This approach does not, however, lead to the comfortable use of psychic functioning in one's everyday life, where similar fears must be overcome rather than accommodated.

THE BITTER WITH THE SWEET

Remember that the exact *results* of a particular practice session—whether impressive or mediocre—are less important than what the session *teaches* you about psychic functioning. Do not worry too much about—or be too proud of the results of any one remote-viewing trial, or you may find it difficult to relax in future sessions.

An excellent result could make you feel that you have to live up to the image of a "super-psychic." A less than perfect result could have the opposite effect. In reality, however, the most experienced psychics occasionally bomb out, as surely as they are also often superbly accurate in their psychic impressions. So go easy on yourself; do not take the results of any one session too seriously.

FACING NEW POSSIBILITIES

Most of us have been taught to relate to the "real world" as if it exists in a separate realm from our private thoughts and feelings. We have become accustomed to ignoring our subjective impressions in favor of more "tangible" information.

So we may be understandably startled to discover that our *subjective* impressions can be a source of *objective*, though intuitive, information about events around us. After all, human beings do not live outside of nature. The fact that there is a more than casual relationship between what we think and feel and what happens in the world around us is not really all that surprising.

As you practice the exercises and grow more attuned to psychic information, chances are that at some point you will accurately describe a remote target. If you do not initially describe an entire target clearly, you may still accurately describe some smaller aspects of it. Many people reach this point in their first remote-viewing session.

Even if you feel nonchalant about the *idea* of psychic functioning, you may still feel overwhelmed when you directly experience your own psychic abilities for the first time. It is a heady and captivating feeling to discover, firsthand, that you really do have previously untapped psychic potential.

If you find yourself looking around for Rod Serling and wondering whether you have entered the Twilight Zone, or become some sort of superhuman, we can assure you that nothing of the sort has happened. You are simply learning to observe the world on a deeper level, and are learning more about yourself in the process.

It is a good idea to balance your exploration of psi with activities in other areas. If you integrate your developing psi abilities into your existing way of life, you should avoid the sorts of problems that lead some people to join cults or "go off the deep end."

Take the man I (K.H.) met in Brooklyn. When I was a researcher in the Maimonides psi laboratory, a man came to the lab who had had some spontaneous experiences that he felt were of a strikingly psychic nature. He was so impressed by them that he focused most of his attention and waking activities upon further attempts to recognize and respond to what he considered to be "psychic" information. Apparently he expected that his experiences would enlighten him.

The man abandoned his wife and children while he waited for enlightenment to descend upon him. In an apparent attempt to induce an altered state of consciousness—which he seemed to feel was necessary for good psychic functioning—he smoked large amounts of marijuana, and virtually ignored normal requirements for sleep and good nutrition.

It was not long before the man was staring at me with a glazed and knowing expression, explaining that he had a secret psychic relationship with alien beings from a distant galaxy. I considered reaching into my desk for a handy chunk of Kryptonite, but instead suggested that he stop taking drugs, eat a healthy meal, get some sleep, take a shower, and then go home to his real human family.

After some rough going for all concerned, the man got a grip on himself. He returned to a relatively normal existence several months later, and learned to handle his unusual experiences in a more sane and rational manner. This fellow's story is, unfortunately, not an isolated case.

We have repeatedly stated that learning about psychic functioning will help you become more aware of what it means to be *human*. Yet, I have been shocked by the number of people who have confidentially expressed the opinion that they are either in touch with or close relatives of aliens from other planets, because they have had what they believe were particularly striking psychic experiences.

In a society that treats psychic functioning as if it were more available to fictional aliens than real human beings, it is all too easy for people who have psychic experiences to wonder if they are as human as the rest of us. If you ever find yourself considering the possibility that you may be a closet extraterrestrial, you may be surprised to discover that you have a lot of company—that closet is crowded with all sorts of characters who have similar delusions.

We strongly recommend that you take your practice sessions slowly, continue "life as usual," and *keep your sense of humor.* It is very hard to distinguish genuine intuitive information from mental noise when you are going crazy!

There is no need to eat strange foods, embrace any particular belief system, change your name to something starting with "Sri" or ending with "ananda," take drugs, or become a guru or a follower of one. Nor is it necessary to trot about in bare feet and a mu-mu, staring into people's eyes as if you were reading fine print on the inside of their eyelids, in the hope of convincing them you are psychic.

Exploring your psychic abilities should, above all, be interesting and enjoyable for you. If it becomes anything else, at any point, pull back for a while, and get together with whatever friends you have left for some cheery conversation and a little healthy grounding in everyday reality.

PACING YOURSELF

Not all of the stress of psychic functioning comes from the need to adjust psychologically to your own expanded capabilities. Many people experience a fair amount of nonpsychological mental and physiological strain when they actively use their psychic abilities—especially when they are first getting used to doing so.

Nina Kulagina is said to lose several pounds after her reportedly successful experiments in psychokinesis. We have not observed such a dramatic reaction in people who practice remote viewing, but viewers often find experimental and practice sessions to be quite draining.

Remote viewing usually requires quite a bit of concentration, as a viewer must respond to, recognize, and interpret impressions that are usually very subtle and fleeting. He must also properly interpret these impressions and monitor his experiences, almost as though he were an outside observer, to avoid going off the track and falling into the nether worlds of mental noise.

Imagine how a tightrope walker feels as he listens to the wind and the crowd below him, and considers the movement of the rope he is standing on, the swaying of his own body, and remembered images of the previous rope walker who fell—all while trying to cross Niagara Falls. *Remote viewing is like walking a tightrope in your mind.*

Furthermore, a viewer must learn to handle information of a sort entirely different from that which he is used to processing on a conscious level. This may produce a kind of neurophysiological stress about which we currently know very little—in addition to the psychological stress we have already discussed.

We have no reason to believe that remote viewing can lead to any harmful effects, but it is wise to pace yourself when you are learning this new skill, as you would when beginning any new exercise program. Get plenty of sleep, eat properly—and avoid mind-altering substances such as alcohol and marijuana. They may make you think you are very psychic, but in fact they seem to make it more difficult to function psychically, by dulling the senses and making it extremely hard to distinguish between psychic information, private thoughts and feelings, and the effects and sensations of the drugs.

It is important to *remain in charge of your experience* whenever you are functioning psychically in any way. There is no need to go into convulsions whenever you have an intuitive impression, or to become so wrapped up in an experience that you feel uncomfortable for any reason. If you learn to control your response to psychic information early on, you will be less likely to flood your mind with too much of this information at a time when it would be unpleasant or inconvenient to do so.

If you feel an emotional reaction to a target that you would rather not feel, take a break. Let go of any impressions that are upsetting you. You probably will have already gotten the message about your target by that point anyway, and thus will not need to dwell further upon its emotional aspects. Any emotional response to a distant target can be draining, even if the target has essentially pleasant qualities. It seems to take a bit of extra energy to learn to use psi to respond emotionally to something that is not physically present in your immediate sensory awareness.

As you grow accustomed to functioning psychically, you will probably feel better able to handle your emotional responses to a target without becoming emotionally overloaded or drained. When you can observe these emotional reactions without becoming too wrapped up in them, you can use your feelings as a point of focus to acquire more detailed intuitive information.

Finally, we would mention that even becoming more sensitive to *sensory* information (as in the early exercises of Chapter 10) can involve its own stresses and rewards, similar to those deriving from psychic experiences. On the plus side, you may find many more beautiful things to notice in the world than you did before. But you may also occasionally feel as if you have crawled inside a pinball machine or a garbage truck, as you become more sensitive to noise and ugliness in your environment.

A sense of humor can stand you in good stead here, as can an ability to discover beauty anywhere, even in roadside litter. Hella Hammid, for example, created a beautiful series of photographs out of "found art," including a number of rusty tin cans that she discovered along a highway.

They wound up, along with her color photos, in Tiffany's Fifth Avenue windows.

If you ever feel so overloaded with sensory and intuitive input that you can identify with the singer of the country tune "I Don't Know Whether to Shoot Myself or Go Bowling," we would definitely advocate going bowling. Healthy physical activity, practiced with suitable abandon, can provide a refreshing balance to the intense mental concentration and attention to minute detail that psi requires. So can such activities as gardening, going to the movies, visiting a natural-history museum, and walking in the woods.

COPING WITH EVERYDAY PSI

As you become more open to your own psychic capabilities, and more used to handling them, you will probably have an increased number of spontaneous psychic experiences. They may be as gentle as precognitive dreams that tell you about everyday events before they happen, or as striking as full-blown out-of-body experiences in which you observe remote events that you later discover have actually occurred.

Everything we have stated about coping with psychic functioning in controlled practice sessions also holds true for spontaneous psychic experiences. To avoid the sorts of difficulties experienced by the Brooklyn man who thought he was in psychic contact with a distant galaxy, we would suggest that whatever spontaneous psychic experiences you have, you take them *lightly*.

Your attitude is the most important single factor influencing whether or not you enjoy and benefit from any spontaneous psychic experiences. People who are upset by them usually have one thing in common— they tend not to take responsibility for their experiences. They view psychic functioning as something that happens to them, instead of as an experience they are actively creating. As a consequence, they feel out of control and are often terrified about what may happen "to" them next.

Since spontaneous psychic experiences to some extent reflect the mental state of those who are having them, you can imagine the kinds of experiences that come to people who feel frightened and out of control. Out-of-body experiences can be particularly distressing under these circumstances, since they sometimes resemble everyday reality about as much as a Magritte painting.

The thoughts and feelings that a person has, just before and during an out-of-body experience, have a habit of becoming embodied in the experience itself. It takes some practice to realize that you can change an experience *while it is happening* by deliberately changing your emotional response to that experience. The same holds true for functioning psychically in more familiar states of consciousness.

Spontaneous psychic experiences are often just a sign that you are becoming more attuned to psychic information in your everyday life. They can give you insights that will be useful in your daily decisions and activities, besides being interesting in and of themselves. They give you a chance to study psychic functioning outside of a controlled situation, and to observe the inner workings of your own mind.

But they can be just as hard to interpret correctly as the intuitive responses in laboratory remote viewing. They may contain a mixture of correct and incorrect information. They are not necessarily visions of ultimate truth beckoning from the heavens. You are not obligated to take any actions as a result of your spontaneous intuitive impressions, unless you decide to do so.

Having a lot of spontaneous psychic experiences does not mean you are going crazy, or that your ability to function psychically is getting out of hand. If you feel uncomfortable about your experiences at any point, you can usually stop them from occurring altogether by consciously telling yourself that you no longer wish to have them. In our experience, most people who discover that they can exert a fair degree of control over their spontaneous psychic experiences decide to continue allowing them to occur.

PRECOGNITIVE DREAMS

As you expand your psychic horizons, you may discover that your dreams often contain psychic information. If you are fortunate, and pay attention, you may find that some of these dreams even contain information about the future. But how can you tell if they do?

Dreams that contain precognitive information are usually quite memorable. Precognitive information in dreams generally has little to do with everyday life, the previous day's activities, or (alas) one's present wishes and desires. Thus they are usually distinguishable from wish-fulfillment dreams, and dreams that elaborate on recent thoughts, memories, or anxieties. They often contain seemingly bizarre material, presented with remarkable clarity. And as Montague Ullman discovered in his brilliant and pioneering work at the Maimonides Dream Laboratory,[2] by paying attention, you may better understand yourself psychologically, while tuning in to whatever psychic information your dreams are offering you. Even when your dreams contain psychic information, it is still important to understand the psychological reasons *why* you chose to focus upon and express that information in your sleep. You can then learn to use this understanding to gain insights about your own inner psychic and psychological processes.

PLAYING FAIR

Using your psychic abilities well requires confidence, openness, a responsible attitude, and common sense. We have already discussed why it is important to respond to your intuitive impressions with confidence and openness. As you might imagine, it is also important to play fair during remote-viewing practice sessions and when you use your psychic abilities in your everyday life.

Playing fair means that all persons involved with a remote-viewing session should treat one another with respect and consideration. Psychic functioning is hard enough without purposely making things more difficult for a viewer. A practice session is no time for practical jokes, like switching targets or doing anything other than what is specifically agreed to by all participants.

This fact hit home in an experiment I (K.H.) was asked to participate in by a graduate student at a local university. I was to be in San Francisco at certain predetermined times, and focus my attention upon various people taking part in a psi experiment in a laboratory about forty miles away. The idea, I was told, was to see if the experimental participants would have more success at a psychic task when they felt they were being psychically "assisted" by a distant person. The experiment sounded halfway reasonable at the time, so I agreed to help.

At the time appointed for the first session, I stood with a friend in her apartment, facing the Golden Gate Bridge, and looked across San Francisco Bay in the direction of the distant laboratory. As I attempted to "make contact" with the first experimental participant (who supposedly knew what was happening) I felt a sense of pure emptiness in the distance, where there was supposed to be a human being.

Certain that I had not made contact, I called the student-experimenter after the session and said I did not think I could participate in his experiment. He asked me to try once more, since his schoolwork depended upon the outcome.

I did, and the same thing happened. I found it impossible to make contact with a person in the distant lab. This experience was quite agitating, since I have grown accustomed to feeling *something* when I try to make psychic contact with a remote person or target. Once again, I phoned the student to suggest that he call off future sessions or find someone else to fill my role in his experiment. At that point, he admitted that he had been lying about his real intentions. At the times he had said someone would be sitting in the distant laboratory, no one was ever really there!

The student was trying to explore the nature of psychic functioning while denying psi's real capabilities. This attitude destroys the trust necessary for productive psi research.

Psychic functioning takes quite a bit of effort for most people. It is not ethical to do anything that will cause this effort to be wasted. Even when you act as viewer in a session, you should treat the other participants with compassion and consideration. It is not easy to select target objects, or to be a judge, an interviewer, or even a beacon. A remote-viewing session is a team effort, not a competition to see who can behave in the most overbearing fashion.

.   .   .

The same guidelines apply in daily life. Before you overpower someone with your latest psychic impressions, consider whether he asked for your opinion. On the other hand, when a friend feels compelled to tell you about a psychic experience, he will probably appreciate some seriousness on your part and a little understanding. He may have some important information for you, and it never hurts to listen.

PSYCHIC SELF-DEFENSE

In a book dealing with the scientific findings of psi research, is it really necessary to discuss "hex death" and "psychic self-defense?" Although the existence of hex death has not been proved, the evidence for its existence fills volumes. In our opinion this data is like the evidence for fire-walking (even though the latter may not be psychic): People who have studied it are convinced that such a phenomenon exists, while those who are not familiar with the data are skeptical. We think it is quite likely that psi can be used unethically, to affect the thoughts and therefore the behavior and mental health of another person. This potentially being the case, we think it is prudent to say a few words about the potential ramifications of such possible goings-on.

Once one agrees that there is a substantial likelihood of mental telepathy, logic requires some concern over the possibility of unwanted information being telepathically experienced. If person A is able to close his eyes and describe what person B is thinking and experiencing, then it follows that person B's *thoughts* have somehow had an effect upon person A.

In earlier chapters we described several well-documented examples of individuals who were apparently able to have substantial influences upon the physical condition of a distant animal or person. Vilenskaya describes several similar instances in the epilogue. So it seems quite likely that an unethical psychic practitioner could deliberately put thoughts into a potential victim's head, in such a way as to disorient him, confuse him, or make him feel depressed.

There is a kind of naive Western folklore that says that in order to be effective a witch doctor or hexer must first let his victim know that he is being hexed. Although this may be true in certain primitive tribes that strongly believe in the supernatural, it is not necessarily true in general. When we have discussed this with anthropologists who have done research in Brazil, they said it was ridiculous to suppose that a black magician would tell his victim that black magic was being used against him, because the victim would then go to another magician to undo the hex, and perhaps even reverse the charges. Forewarned is forearmed: That is the reason we are including this discussion here.

Dr. Joan Halifax has been a medical anthropologist for the past two decades. She is the author of an important book, *Shamanic Voices*, which describes the lives of medicine men and women in tribal cultures.[3] In a 1973 paper entitled "Hex Death," she deals with some of the questions we have been discussing.

> There are numerous reports about individuals developing typical symptomology relating to hexing without any knowledge that a sorcerer has conducted a hex-inducing ritual. Harner, for example, notes that one of the distinguishing characteristics of the process of hexing among the Jivaro is that the victim is given no indication that he is being bewitched, lest he take protective measures. Harner's informants say that sickness almost invariably follows an attack with a magical dart . . . and death is not uncommon.
>
> In some instances, the victim of so-called "simulated magic" supposedly develops specific symptoms, the onset of which coincides with the sorcerer's manipulation of the victim's symbolic image, whether it is a doll, clothing of the intended victim, nail parings, or hair, dirt from the tracks of the victim, a photograph, or even an x-ray photo. It has also been described that occasionally a hexer is able to follow his victim's movements in his "mind's eye" by using a special mirror, and thereby monitor the consequences of the hexing procedure. Alfred Métraux described the Haitian sorcerer who, through an incantation, attempts to lure the intended victim into a bucket of water. If the victim's image appears on the surface of the water, he then stabs it. . . . The water reddens if the sorcerer has been successful.
>
> One aspect of hexing and hex death that has been considered by some witnesses to be indicative of involvement of paranormal forces is the consistently reported helplessness of Western medicine to cope with these phenomena. . . . It is possible to look at the phenomena postulated by parapsychology, and hypothesize which of them, if proven beyond any doubt, could be considered instrumental in the hexing procedure. The most obvious of them

of course, would be "telepathic control" and psychokinesis. In the former the hexer would affect the emotional condition and thought processes of the individual, and produce a state of mind, such as malignant anxiety, or Engle's "giving up—given up complex" that could have catastrophic biological consequences.[4]

Cannon's paper "Voodoo Death" and one by Lester called "Voodoo Death—Some New Thoughts on an Old Phenomenon" both provide additional interesting reading.[5] So does the classic study of Voodoo by Maya Deren, entitled: *Divine Horsemen: The Voodoo Gods of Haiti.*"[6]

HOW DO YOU DEFEND
AGAINST PSYCHIC ATTACK?

First of all, we believe that knowledge makes you strong. Only in the most magic-embedded societies can a sorcerer gain the agreement of the community to spiritually and socially excommunicate an individual who has been marked for hex death. Only there will a person then psychologically participate in his own murder. In such a society one essentially obtains the agreement of the victim that the only way out is to die. It becomes the natural and expected thing to do. This is not a likely scenario in most Western societies.

A second point is that one may pay a high price for psychically injuring another person. By the time an individual is sufficiently adept at psychic functioning to even consider using the ability for psychic attack, he is himself very open and psychically exposed to corrosive aspects of his environment. The literature of ancient magic is filled with admonitions that a magician must always be stronger than any spell he casts. One would be very unwise to try to kill someone by putting poison in the community well from which the poisoner also must drink. In Western society, people hope to live a long time in good health. Psychically adept people will probably be reluctant to risk involving themselves in much psychic negativity, because of the potential physical and emotional risks to themselves.

With regard to unethical uses of psi, we think it is quite likely that some people will think of a variety of uses for psi that most people would consider an invasion of privacy. If individuals or governments have developed psi abilities enough to feel that their awareness can transcend both space and time, there is no telling what kind of information they might try to gather. This might have all sorts of interesting results. One is that people might be less inclined to lie if they discover that it does not work. Another is that nations might then be less sanguine about the possibilities of keeping secrets or hiding things from each other as part of strategic policy.

But to get back to psychic self-defense, we can offer a few commonsense rules, and a few ideas from a book called *Psychic Self-Defence,* by Dion Fortune, an English occultist and writer of the late nineteenth and early twentieth centuries. Fortune wrote several well-received mainstream psychology books under her real name, Violet Firth, but secretly used the pseudonym Dion Fortune for the numerous books she wrote about occult topics.[7]

Who would be a likely target for psychic attack? The answer is, anybody perceived as a serious threat by any unethical person who has developed his psychic abilities. However, if you seriously believe that the CIA, the FBI, or extraterrestrials are interfering with your decisions, we strongly suggest that you find a sympathetic and experienced clinical psychologist, and seek help. We do not have the slightest evidence that any agency of the U.S. government—or the Galactic Federation, for that matter—has either the interest or ability to psychically affect the consciousness of anybody. But if you have made an enemy of an unprincipled and ignorant psychic, he might try to send you some "bad vibrations." Do we know that such a thing is possible? No, we do not. But we would not be surprised to learn that it is.

If you have examined your emotional feelings, and your general living and work situation, and are convinced that your present anxieties do not have any source within your life's ordinary boundaries, then you *might* begin to wonder if someone is wishing you ill. If you can identify such a person, we suggest that you immediately separate yourself from him in every way.

According to Fortune, once you have determined that you are under psychic attack (assuming that it is possible) and you have found out who the attacker is, you have solved 90 percent of your problem. It only remains for you to decide that it is totally unacceptable for that person to have any dominion over your thoughts. If you can convince yourself of that fact, you will be rid of your antagonist. It is also extremely important to make sure that you are getting enough sleep and eating a proper diet of nourishing food. If your body and mind are run-down, you are not in a good position to defend yourself from anything.

Another useful suggestion would be to trade in any psychic exercises that you happen to be doing and exchange them for physical exercises. If you are convinced you are under psychic attack, you will do well to give up your meditation for a while and take up jogging. Focusing your attention on other things may help you to recuperate and build up your strength.

Fortune's book, *Psychic Self-Defense,* which has seen eighteen printings, was first published in 1930. Although we do not particularly subscribe to *any* of her occult mumbo-jumbo, we think you might like to hear what she has to say about the possible problem of psychic attack:

> The first thing to do when dealing with an occult attack (after breaking contact) is to make a temporary clearance of the atmosphere and so gain breathing-space in which to reform the shattered ranks. This is more readily achieved by an organized ritual than by unaided will-power. Any act *performed with intention* becomes a rite. We can take a bath with no more in mind than physical cleanliness: in which case the bath will cleanse our bodies and no more. Or we can take a bath with a view to ritual cleanliness, in which case its efficacy will extend beyond the physical plane.

One last thought about the option of selecting a clinician to help you. It is still the case that if you told most psychiatrists that you were under psychic attack, or could read the mind of another person, or that someone else could read yours, they would consider such beliefs a clear indication of mental illness, because the same sorts of things are experienced by people who really are mentally ill and suffering from paranoid delusions. Any of those statements can get you into serious trouble, if made to the wrong person. By "serious trouble," we mean being thought to be in serious need of extensive psychiatric treatment. Continued persistence in these beliefs in spite of treatment could lead to commitment to a mental institution, and being given psychotrophic drugs. This would be our own uniquely technological form of hex death. As Montague Ullman, the former director of Psychiatry at Maimonides Medical Center, recently stated:

Those who have been upset or disturbed by their psychic experiences and who have sought professional help have often encountered frustrating responses. What they have reported honestly and out of conviction is rarely accepted as such. More often it is either discounted or, worse yet, labeled as a psychotic symptom. What the therapist fails to realize is that the law of parsimony does not prevail here. A person may have a lifelong history of severe mental disorders and, at the same time, experience some bona fide psi effects from time to time. In fact, there are times when the two seem intimately connected. Patients often turn away from the treatment they need because of the negative, skeptical or even hostile response of the therapist. Conversely, patients who don't need treatment may be misled into therapy because of the therapists' ignorance about the reality of psi.[8]

LIVING IN A CHANGING CULTURE

It is our considered opinion that you can develop your intuitive abilities without becoming a weirdo or a sideshow attraction. You may find, however, that pressure will occasionally be put upon you to do just the opposite. Some people have not yet realized that psychic people are not genies who just popped out of bottles. Our culture is still finding its bearings when it comes to psi.

I once met a young woman at a party who was furious at me. "You're Harary, aren't you?" she said. "I thought you'd at least be wearing a turban!" I offered to wrap a towel around my head to make her feel more comfortable, but she declined and headed for the brandy. Her response to someone who functions psychically was not nearly as strange, however, as that of one researcher I worked with in Durham.

This man confided, to a colleague of mine, that he did not know how to talk to psychics because, as he explained, "they're not like other people." I never understood what the researcher meant by that remark, but I can imagine. Since most of the viewers we have worked with have been exceptionally well-adjusted, happy people, he may have been right. Perhaps the researcher was afraid that somebody might read his mind, or he may have felt uncomfortable around people who succeeded at something he mistakenly believed to be beyond his own capabilities.

·   ·   ·

Needless to say, it is hard to conduct fruitful research or practice sessions with someone who is both fascinated by psychic functioning and terrified of its implications. Ambivalent people tend to sabotage research results, or invalidate them, or reduce those results to seemingly endless columns of sterile and uninterpretable numbers. Thus, when you are just learning to use your psychic abilities, it is critically important to work with people who are happy to see you succeed, and who will encourage your efforts.

By the same token, it is a good idea to give people psychological room if they have not yet realized that psychic functioning is readily available to normal people. If you feel an urge to carry on a crusade to improve people's attitudes about psychic experiences and abilities, we would ask you to reconsider. The forces that mislead people about psi are as active as they have ever been, even though forces of change are rapidly catching up with them.

It would be unrealistic to expect our entire society to dramatically alter its approach to psychic functioning overnight. We doubt seriously, however, that the current situation will remain static. People who integrate their psychic experiences and abilities into fulfilled and productive lives within society will bring about change in the most effective way possible. They will set good examples for others to follow, and influence our culture for the better from within its evolving frame of reference.

12

The Psi Imperative: Winning the Mind Race

The hour is getting later
It's time we had begun
Knowing something's one thing
But the race must still be run. . . .
                    —Carole King and Toni Stern
                    Peace in the Valley

We believe that the ultimate importance of psychic functioning is its ability to help us develop a deeper understanding of who we are, and what our relationship is to one another and to the rest of nature. Psi's greatest value will probably not be found in its ability to entertain us, or its application to specific decision-making situations, no matter how exciting or profitable these applications might be.

Use of our psychic abilities gives us greater access to information about the past, present, and future; it allows us to transcend our linear view of time and space and the limited perspective of our five familiar senses. It gives us a context in which to understand our existence, and an opportunity to experience direct contact with our own timeless nature; to know that we are more than just the goods we consume, or the buttons we push in our everyday lives.

Frequently, people who develop their psychic potential feel a strong sense of closeness to nature. This sense of harmony with the world around them is not an irrational concept, or one that is philosophically imposed, but is something which each individual may explore and experience for himself. It is not theoretical, but experiential.

As a human being, you do not exist in a separate realm from the rest of the universe. We are fond of referring to "man and nature" as if a separation existed between the two, but we must realize that men and women are an integral part of the natural world.

When you develop a keen sensory and intuitive awareness, the boundaries that appear to separate you from others and your environment become less rigid. We are able to function psychically precisely because we participate in nature not as outsiders affected by it, but rather as a part of nature influencing and responding to itself. We permeate nature as we are permeated by it.[1] When we lose contact with our intuition, we let go of the lifeline that connects us to one another and to our own inner self. We cast ourselves adrift in a sea of mundane reality that is but one small part of our total existence.

We believe that every human being has an inherent right to a life that he or she feels is worthwhile, fulfilled, and meaningful. There are many forces that make it increasingly difficult for us to claim this basic human right. People feel alienated from a world that seems to be becoming more and more industrialized, mechanized, and dehumanized. There is an alternative.

Many sensitive human beings are reaching for something greater than themselves. They are doing this not because of some irrational need to escape from the difficult realities of everyday living, but because they know intuitively that there is something greater for us all to reach toward. What we are reaching for is not above or beyond us, but within us. It is not "higher," but deeper. It lies not in the narrow answers we sometimes give ourselves about what life means, but in the deeper questions we are asking ourselves about who we are. It is the part of us that remembers its participation in a larger community of humanity and nature—the part of us that is psychic.

In a world of television sets, computer terminals, microchips, petrodollars, robots, and the fabled military-industrial complex, it is easy to forget that human beings are more than the technology we create, or the competing social systems we impose upon ourselves. It is easy to let the machines develop their own momentum and forget that we are human and that we, and every other living thing, are all on this planet and in this universe together.

When we find ourselves confronted with exploding technology and increasing alienation, psychic functioning can help keep us aware of the difference between human beings and machines. In fact, the eminent computer scientist A. M. Turing considers the question that the only discernible difference between a human being and a computer may be that the latter cannot experience psi.[2]

Dealing with the same question, Dr. Jacques Vallee, pioneer computer researcher and author of the insightful book *The Network Revolution*, states:

> My contention is that machines will be able to "think" by any human standard that can be precisely defined. But as the machines get "smarter" by these rational standards, it is the definition of humanness that will change. I look forward to that. I think we will discover, beyond these rational standards, that the human race has many other psychic talents we had previously been afraid to recognize, talents which constitute our truly genuine existence as humans. They are the only part of us worth talking about. Although this thought is scary to most people, it should make us afraid only to the extent that our daily actions are in fact automatic, unthinking, and perhaps unworthy of truly developed human beings.[3]

The information we have shared with you will make a difference in your life only if you decide to use it. Although you may not use your own psychic abilities in the stock market or the casino, you can still derive great rewards from using these abilities to participate psychically in the world around you.

Whether you are sitting on the steps of your front porch or on a hilltop overlooking the ocean, you can close your eyes and psychically experience the stars, the whole of this planet, and your own relationship with it all. Psi will make it clear to you that you are not alone in your life, or in the universe. There is no friend so distant that you cannot experience being with him or her. If you are good friends, there is potentially no limit to the depth of the experience and the extent of the closeness you can share. Ultimately we will find that we are human only to the extent to which we are able to care for and experience empathy with one another.

To those who refuse to develop their psychic abilities it makes little difference whether the force that manipulates them into repressing their human potential is organized religion, cults, materialistic critics, or the mass media. The end result of such repression is the same no matter where it originates.

Some may claim that there is no such thing as psi and that psychic abilities are all an illusion, but those skeptics will rob you of your human heritage only if you let them. It is up to you to decide whether you will take time to discover for yourself that you not only have psychic abilities, but that you can use these abilities to enrich your life.

The Mind Race is a race to determine the future of your own consciousness before other forces decide that future for you. We must develop our ability to experience compassion and empathy with our fellow creatures, before we lose contact with our own humanity and exterminate one another over an ideological difference of opinion, or for some similarly foolish reason. The Mind Race is not a race between nations. Though the U.S. and Soviet governments are heavily involved in psi research, we are all in a more vital and personal race to determine whether we will be able to wake up to our deeper potential before we have exhausted the limited time available to us.

As a society we are in the process of making wide-ranging decisions about our evolutionary future. This decision is in our hands right now. The quality of future life on this planet will be determined for us by others if we do not choose to participate actively in determining our own destiny. We do not believe that any psychically sensitive human being would choose to live in a future that is dominated by robots, especially if we are to be the robots. We believe that our future must include psychic functioning if we are to achieve our full potential as human beings. We call this requirement the psi imperative.

We have shown you how to develop your psychic abilities, how to cope with success, and how you can begin training yourself to function psychically. Your psychic abilities will not be taken care of for you by "experts." We must each take responsibility for exploring psi ourselves and developing our own psychic abilities if we are to fulfill the psi imperative within our personal lives and within our society.

Psychic functioning has been with us for centuries, and will be with us for many more centuries. It is past time for bringing psi into the open, where everyone can benefit from a realistic awareness of it. We believe it is time for all of us to claim our right to function psychically. You own your own mind. It is important not to give it away, or fail to use it to its full potential. So get going! You have to enter the Mind Race in order to win.

Psi Research in the Soviet Union: Are They Ahead of Us?

Larissa Vilenskaya

_____

"Are the Soviets ahead of the United States in psychic research?" It seems I have had to answer this question hundreds of times. After I arrived in the United States, it has inevitably been asked, in one form or another, at every lecture and every workshop I have given. "You just emigrated from the Soviet Union and had been working in psychic research there for more than a decade," the questioners would say. "Can you tell us what they are doing? Do they *use* psi more than we do?"

How could I answer these questions adequately? To do so I would need comprehensive knowledge of current psi research in both countries. But I am not certain I know *everything* that has been done in this field in the U.S.S.R., and I know I do not know everything about psi research in the West. However, I will try to begin answering these important questions. I will do my best to present the Soviet side here, in the hope that you will be able to come up with an answer yourself after reading this intriguing book.

.   .   .

Larissa Vilenskaya, who writes about Soviet experiments, was personally involved in Soviet psi research for more than ten years. Vilenskaya is a Soviet-trained engineer and has also been a successful participant in numerous psychic experiments. She understands not only the methods and priorities of this research, but also the context of the Soviet political system in which this work is being conducted. She knows many Eastern Bloc psi researchers and experimental participants personally and has translated dozens of Soviet research papers and reports into English—reports which most Westerners did not even know existed. She is currently the editor of *Psi Research—An East-West Journal on Parapsychology, Psychotronics, and Psychobiophysics,* published by Washington Research Center, San Francisco, Calif.

I was not fortunate enough to meet Leonid Leonidovich Vasiliev, the "father" of Soviet psi research. Vasiliev, professor of physiology at Leningrad University, died in 1966, while I was still a teenager. His book *Experiments in Mental Suggestion*[1] became my first textbook on psi research.

It was exciting to read Vasiliev's accounts of distant-influence experiments, in which he and his colleagues were able to telepathically put a person into hypnotic sleep and awaken him at a distance of hundreds of miles. To back up these findings, he cited earlier studies in mental suggestion and distant influence conducted by K. D. Kotkov and L. O. Normark, and quoted Kotkov:

> In 1924, A. V. Dzhelikhovsky, professor of physics at Kharkov University, and Dr. L. P. Normark, a chemist, carried out a small but most interesting piece of work in thought transmission at a distance. The experimental subject was a student at the University, eighteen or nineteen years old, absolutely healthy. She used to fall asleep instantly under the influence of mental suggestion transmitted to her, and she woke up instantly under the same influence. She remembered nothing. Not very many experiments were carried out—not more than thirty. Not a single one was a failure. We carried out experiments not only in sending the subject to sleep and waking her up, but also in summoning her. While in my own flat, I summoned the girl to Normark's laboratory. When I came to the laboratory, I usually found the girl already there, or else she arrived a little after my arrival. When asked why she had come, she generally answered looking embarrassed: "I don't know. . . . I just did. . . . I wanted to come."[2]

This approach to psi research, in which hypnosis is treated as a potential means of influencing behavior at a distance, has become traditional in the Soviet Union. At the beginning of the 1970s I became acquainted with Dmitry Mirza, a Soviet psychiatrist who had been working in a government psi-research laboratory for several years. This lab began as a division of the Research Institute of the Problems of Information Transmission and was later transformed into the Laboratory of Psychophysiology, located on Bolshaya Kommunisticheskaya Street in the center of Moscow. By the time of our meetings, Mirza had already left this secret lab and returned to his medical practice. Some of the experimental results obtained in the lab were declassified and published in 1968. They appeared in Russian as Volume 55 of the *Proceedings of the Research Institute of Psychiatry*—with a circulation of 1,500.[3] I do not think anyone in the West noticed.

One paper in this collection, by Mirza and his co-workers, described their continued experimentation with distant hypnotic influence.[4] Without mentioning telepathy and related topics specifically, the paper dealt with recording the physiological functions of a completely uninformed subject during hypnosis induced without words. The Soviet experimenters always believed more in readings of equipment than they did in verbal reports given by subjects. In the first of these studies the hypnotist was in the same room as the hypnotic subject, but later was in a different room altogether. When the hypnotist tried to awaken a subject in the adjacent room by concentrating his thoughts upon him, the subject woke up. The physiological data confirmed that this had definitely happened.

Talking with Mirza, I naturally asked him whether he and his colleagues had conducted other tests, not so much on nonverbal hypnosis, but on actual telepathic hypnosis and awakening at a distance—in conditions that would have excluded sensory leakage as much as possible. Mirza was silent for a few moments, looked askance at the telephone (many Soviets suspect that their apartments are bugged through their telephones), and then nodded to me affirmatively. Even without his confirmation I was certain that they had, because of what I had read in another paper in the same collection. This one was by Leutin, a researcher in Leningrad, who had first worked with Leonid Vasiliev.[5] He later prepared a Ph.D. dissertation on a topic that he vaguely referred to as a study of an interaction between subjects in conditions of reliable sensory isolation. This study is interesting enough to describe in some detail. It deals with the recorded changes in the brain waves of one person in a distant room, while another person is being subjected to electric shocks. The paper stated:

> Presently, much attention is being paid to the study of informational interactions between biological systems in conditions of reliable sensory isolation. The following procedure was developed for conducting investigations of this kind with human subjects:
>
> Two subjects participated in the experiment—the inductor and the percipient. While the physiological functions of the percipient

were recorded, we tried to detect, from changes in these functions, whether he was being subjected to a distant influence by the inductor. Subjects were placed into two acoustically isolated cells. In the course of the experiment, a sixty-watt lamp was lit in front of the inductor and the fingers of his right hand were subjected to electrical stimulation for a period of ten seconds. . . . The stimulation was conducted with square-wave impulses; *their intensity changed according to the pain threshold of the subjects.* [Emphasis added.]

During the experiment, the brain waves of the percipient were recorded on an electroencephalogram—EEG. . . . changes in the *percipient's* EEG were significantly correlated with the . . . stimulation of the *inductor.* In the absence of the inductor during control tests, there were no statistically significant changes in the integrated EEG of the percipient after the automatic turn-on of the equipment in the inductor's cell. Since the second series of tests differed from the first only by the absence of the stimulation of the inductor, one can assume that this stimulation caused the reaction of activation in the EEG of the percipient.

This thought struck me while I was reading the paper: The author demonstrated the existence of an interaction between sensory-isolated subjects (i.e., telepathy), prepared a Ph.D. dissertation, but did not even express acknowledgment to his anonymous subjects who had suffered from painful electric shocks.

Thoughout the years that I worked in the Soviet Union, I asked myself again and again: "Why are they doing all of this? What for? Scientific interest, desire to learn, to know—but aren't there other ways, other methods?"

These questions were in the back of my mind in the early 1970s as I talked with biophysicist Yuri Kamensky about his studies in telepathy. These studies (described elsewhere—in particular in *Psychic Discoveries Behind the Iron Curtain* by Ostrander and Schroeder[6]) included telepathic transmission of emotions by Kamensky to his partner, Karl Nikolaev. In these experiments Kamensky had imagined that he was strangling his friend—and Nikolaev began to feel suffocation. In fact, Nikolaev's EEG patterns showed such drastic changes that physicians who were present wanted to stop the test, out of concern for Nikolaev's health and even his life. When Kamensky imagined beating Nikolaev and "transmitted" this thought to him, Nikolaev sensed severe pain and almost fell out of his chair. This telepathy spanned five hundred miles, from Moscow to Leningrad. Interestingly, in Nikolaev and Kamensky's previous telepathy tests, visual images had been transmitted but not feelings and emotions. Therefore, Nikolaev did not expect that this time the content of the telepathic transmission would be any different. Nor had he any way of knowing by ordinary means what Kamensky had in his mind for each particular trial.

Was this experiment successful? Certainly! But why did Kamensky want to transmit feelings of physical blows and strangulation? The researcher explained to me, several times, that negative emotions are transmitted more strongly and reliably than positive emotions. I wondered why he did not seem to understand that the success of telepathic transmissions appears to depend to a large extent upon the participants' belief system. Naturally, if Kamensky was confident that he could obtain better results with negative emotions, he would inevitably obtain this effect!

I have had other occasions to observe how powerfully a gifted (or trained) person can mentally influence other people or living systems. One such person is Nina Kulagina. She is best known for her psychokinetic (PK) abilities and has been frequently tested by both Soviet and Western researchers.[7] Under controlled conditions, Kulagina apparently could psychokinetically move objects of various shapes and materials (both metal and nonmetal, magnetic and nonmagnetic) weighing up to 380 grams; "suspend" objects weighing at least several dozen grams in the air; and expose photographic film through glass, opaque paper, and lead and ebonite plates. She was kind enough to conduct several PK demonstrations for me between 1971 and 1976.

During one of my meetings with Professor Gennady Sergeyev, who conducted extensive research with Kulagina, he described in detail how she was able to completely stop an isolated frog heart from a distance of about a meter and a half. The frog heart was placed in a physiological solution with electrodes attached to it to record its activity. Under these conditions an isolated frog heart will normally continue its activity for thirty to forty minutes (and in some cases up to an hour and a half). When the heart stops, it can be reactivated by electrostimulation. Sergeyev emphasized that forty seconds after Kulagina began focusing her mental influence on the heart, it stopped—and electrostimulation could not reactivate it. "When we examined it," Sergeyev explained later, "we found that it was torn apart, as if bombarded by lightning balls of microscopic size. The energy flow can reach such incredible intensity!"[8]

Sergeyev and his Leningrad colleagues were also studying Kulagina's influence on the heartbeat of *human beings*. He wrote:

> A number of studies in heart arrhythmia were also conducted with humans. We found that emotional reactions of one person (inductor) influenced, as a rule, the heart rate of another person (percipient). In these tests, electrocardiograms (EKGs) of both subjects were simultaneously recorded. The values obtained after computer analysis of the EKG data . . . indicated that for five minutes the heart-rate changes of the percipient were completely dependent on the reactions of the heart of the inductor who was located two meters away. *These reactions were most noticeable in percipients with heart disorders.* [Emphasis added.][9]

Nina Kulagina demonstrated for me her favorite feat—producing an apparently psychokinetic burn on a person's skin. When she was concentrating upon my arm, I felt warm, then hot, burning sensations. A real burn appeared afterward, which was clearly visible for four or five days. During this attempt she also produced a burn on herself. A red spot appeared on her hand, but subsequently disappeared in five or ten minutes before my very eyes, as Kulagina tried to heal it. I will not repeat elaborate details here, because this effect has been described elsewhere several times.[10] But I would like to stress the following:

In some experiments Kulagina produced a burn on the skin of another person through a lead plate. Another experiment was conducted by Dr. Yuri Gulyaev, Director of the Research Institute of Radio-Engineering and Electronics of the U.S.S.R. Academy of Sciences, who believed that Kulagina's influence could be explained as the emission of ultraviolet radiation. Perhaps this reflects a Soviet tendency to oversimplify the observed phenomenon. In Gulyaev's experiment Kulagina could apparently exert the same influence through quartz glass, which is transparent to ultraviolet rays, but not through ordinary glass. However, in earlier tests she was able to exert this kind of influence through a metal plate, which definitely was not transparent to ultraviolet radiation. This suggests that the experimenter's influence (conscious or unconscious) can strongly inhibit a person's psi abilities. This may explain why skeptics do not often obtain positive results in psi tests.

"Nina Kulagina also worked with white mice, suppressing their vital functions," Sergeyev mentioned.[11] "A few movements of her hands caused them to appear motionless, as if dead. As soon as she removed her hands, they perked up and returned to normal." Again, why is it desirable to suppress a living creature's vital functions, even those of a mouse? I still do not know the answer to this question.

Mice were also the subjects in some intriguing experiments conducted by Dr. Sergei Speransky in Novosibirsk. In carefully designed tests, Speransky established the fact of "extraordinary communication" between mouse "social groups."[12] After a number of mice had been together in one cage for a week or more, part of the group was moved to another room and deprived of food and water. Their former cagemates ("companions of starving animals"), which were nourished normally, apparently somehow felt that their friends were starving—they ate more than the "companions of nourished" mice, and gained significantly more weight. The effect was observed in spite of adequate and reliable isolation between the two subgroups, assuring that they could not see, hear, or smell each other.

Speransky believed that these test conditions imitated a natural situation: Part of an animal population may be able to feel that another part is starving, and the feeling may stimulate the normally nourished animals to eat more. In other tests conducted by Speransky (using the same principle of "biological expediency"), some of the mice from a social group were killed. The remaining mice in the group propagated much more rapidly than those from a control group.[13] In other words, the "extraordinary communication" between mice worked very well indeed!

But again, I must ask: Were such cruel research methods necessary? Did the animals really have to starve or be killed just to prove or disprove the reality of distant influence? Of course, this approach is not new in the history of science, but is it really necessary?

It is interesting to note that the same pattern in Soviet research appears in tests with a lower level of living nature—the level of tissue cultures.

On October 31, 1972, the Committee on Inventions and Discoveries of the U.S.S.R. Council of Ministers recorded in the National Registry a discovery of a new biological phenomenon, termed "distant intercellular interactions between tissue cultures." This phenomenon was discovered by Dr. Vlail Kaznacheyev, Semyen Shurin, and Ludmila Mikhailova in their research undertaken at the Novosibirsk Medical Institute and the Institute of Automation and Electrometry of the Siberian Branch of the U.S.S.R. Academy of Sciences.[14] For the past fifteen years Dr. Kazna- cheyev, presently Director of the Institute of Clinical and Experimental Medicine of the Siberian Branch of the U.S.S.R. Academy of Medical Sciences in Novosibirsk, has been conducting numerous experiments such as this:

> Two sealed containers with tissue cultures inside of them, which had bottoms of glass or of quartz, were placed together, bottom to bottom (i.e., in "optical" contact). A deleterious agent (vari- ous types of virus, poison, etc.) was introduced into one of these cultures and led to "disease" and death of those cells, which is to be expected. But twelve hours after the features of the "disease" appeared in the infected or poisoned culture, the same features were observed in the neighboring uninfected and sealed culture. This same "disease" led to death of the second culture, although no virus or poison was introduced into it, and there was no possi- bility for accidental contamination. Moreover, if an uninfected culture dish was in "optical" contact with an infected (or poi- soned) culture dish for eighteen to twenty hours and then it was optically connected to a second uninfected culture, the features of the disease were again observed in this second untouched cul- ture.[15]

This research, demonstrating an example of global interconnectedness in living nature, is not necessarily related to psychic functioning. Kazna- cheyev believes that information is carried between his tissue cultures by electromagnetic waves in the ultraviolet range, since his tests were success- ful when the "optical" contact was through quartz glass, but not through ordinary or Pyrex glass, which block ultraviolet rays. He even shined light from an ultraviolet laser through an infected culture in order to see whether there are special "infection wavelengths" that can optically trans- mit disease to distant targets.[16]

Still, why do Soviet researchers seem to think it so important to transmit diseases, instead of transmitting "health," or at least healing influences? After all, there is a lot of popular interest in psychic healing in Russia. In fact, some other Soviet researchers conducted experiments with plants which were damaged by ionizing radiation, and discovered that nonradiated plants are apparently capable of relieving radiation injuries to radiated plants at a distance.[17] However, this observation was mentioned only in a booklet with a small circulation published in a provincial town, while Kaznacheyev's studies were reported in a variety of widely distributed Russian scientific journals and in a recently published book.[18] Since all publications in the U.S.S.R. are controlled by government officials, it becomes obvious which aspects of scientific research these officials are trying to emphasize.

There are some even more vivid examples. From 1968 through 1975, I worked as a researcher at the Bioinformation Laboratory of the A. S. Popov Scientific and Technological Society of Radioelectronics and Communication in Moscow, directed by Professor Ippolit Kogan. I headed an experimental and training group on studies of "skin vision" (i.e., eyeless sight, the identification of colors and images with one's fingers). One of my colleagues, whose knowledge and experience in psychic healing was considerable, told me that she had been approached by an official who asked her to conduct experiments on influencing human behavior at a distance. Later, she dared to discuss this with an NBC reporter, but without identifying herself:

> One person who frequented our lab proposed an experiment to me, as he called it, to try to influence some foreign leaders who are speaking upon the radio, to change their minds . . . to influence them to speak other things, completely different. I refused. I said that I never will do dirty work.[19]

Other Soviet researchers may also have been approached with the same proposal. Perhaps my friend is not the only one who refused to participate. In any event, the Bioinformation Laboratory was closed down in 1975. This deprived Barbara Ivanova, who had been the head of the group on psychic healing, and many other Soviet psi researchers of opportunities for continuing their studies and activities. However, this group has continued to meet unofficially to discuss these areas. They call themselves the "Park Academy" because they meet in a park near their old laboratory. The group is non-political and limits its activities to current research topics in psi.

In 1978 a new Bioelectronics Laboratory was established in Moscow, directed by Alexander Spirkin, a well-known Soviet philosopher and an associate member of the U.S.S.R. Academy of Sciences. He organized a research group, which included many physicians, to explore issues of psychic healing. However, the officially appointed board of directors of the lab imposed such tight restrictions on its participants that researchers like Barbara Ivanova would never agree to work there.

Some people may believe that this is all mere science fiction—that it is impossible to influence human behavior at a distance and that the subject of our discussion and apprehension does not really exist. However, an example of such an influence was demonstrated by Dr. Alexander Romen, a psychiatrist from Alma-Ata. (Dr. Romen is still active in the field; together with Dr. Victor Inyushin from Kazakh State University, he directs a division of bioholography of the U.S.S.R. Academy of Sciences.)

Romen was the first to introduce elements of the Eastern tradition, particularly yoga, into Soviet scientific studies, and he also developed his own novel approaches to autogenic and psychoregulation training. At the end of the 1960s, he studied the influence of different factors on the intensity of electrobioluminescence—radiation of a biological system (e.g., of human skin) observed in a high-frequency electric field. His research demonstrated that in cases of persons who had achieved the capacity of influencing nonvoluntary processes in their own organism (e.g., changing their skin temperature by autosuggestion of a feeling of warmth), specific changes in the structure and intensity of radiation from them could be observed. Such changes in the character of radiation did not occur in subjects who were untrained in autosuggestion. However, these changes were observed in untrained subjects, if a trained person held his own hand several centimeters from the shoulder of the untrained subject while autosuggesting the feeling of warmth in his hand. During these tests, the untrained subject was not told about the suggestion made to him by the trained person.[20]

I myself witnessed a much more dramatic example of distant influence in an experiment conducted by Professor Veniamin Pushkin at the Research Institute of General and Pedagogical Psychology of the U.S.S.R. Academy of Pedagogical Sciences. In this test a healer was asked to influence, at a distance, a subject who had been placed in another room while a rheogram (a measurement of the blood flow in his head) was recorded. Observed changes in the subject's rheogram appeared to take place only when the healer tried to influence certain centers of the subject's brain. During this time the healer produced a much stronger effect than he usually produced during a healing process. As a result, the subject (who knew about the rheogram, but not the distant healer's influence) felt so dizzy when the session was over that he could hardly stand upright. This feeling soon subsided, but the healer, learning of this effect, flatly refused to go on with such experiments.

To my knowledge, studies of psychic functioning are still continuing in a number of research institutes throughout the Soviet Union. In 1978 Academician Yuri Kobzarev listed the following institutions as doing research in this field:[21]

- Bauman Higher Technology School in Moscow (Dr. Vagner's laboratory)

- Moscow Energetics Institute (Dr. Sokolov's laboratory)

- Research Institute of General and Pedagogical Psychology at the U.S.S.R. Academy of Pedagogical Sciences, Moscow

- The Division of Cybernetics of the Research Institute of Biophysics, U.S.S.R. Academy of Sciences, in Pushchino

- Leningrad State University (Prof. Pavel Gulyaev's Aurametry Laboratory)

- The Division of Cybernetics at the Leningrad Polytechnical Institute

- The Scientific-Industrial Unit, "Quantum," in Krasnodar

- The Tbilisi State University in Georgia

- The Kazakh State University in Alma Ata (Dr. Victor Inyushin's laboratory)

- The Ukrainian Institute of Cybernetics in Kiev

To this list I can add the Institute of Problems of Information Transmission, the Institute of Control Problems, the Institute of Molecular Genetics, and the Institute of Radio-Engineering and Electronics in Moscow (all within the U.S.S.R. Academy of Sciences); the Department of Cybernetics of the Moscow Engineering Physical Institute; the Research Institute of Neurology and Psychiatry in Kharkov; and about a dozen bioelectronics sections in various cities and towns throughout the Soviet

Union, including Moscow, Leningrad, Minsk, Alma-Ata, and Tagan-rog.[22] But I cannot affirm that I know all the details of Soviet psi research. In the summer of 1975 I asked Dr. Inyushin whether it was possible to visit his research lab in Alma-Ata. He answered that I would need special official permission, because some of the studies were classified.

Some Western observers and scientists, speaking about psi research in the Soviet Union and elsewhere, emphasize that the results of some of these studies can be applied for military purposes.[23] From my experience, I clearly see that while Western psi researchers are interested in extending human awareness and our realm of perception, official Soviet scientists are interested in using psi primarily to develop *extended means for mental influence at a distance.*

This fact is also clearly understood inside the Soviet Union, where many scientists, especially independent-minded researchers who feel it is impossible for them to do research for the government, repeatedly stressed the important role of ethical issues in these studies.[24] Psi research demonstrates such global interconnectedness among people in the world that we all share the responsibility for the use or misuse of psi, independent of our opinions, views, attitudes, languages, and countries.

I am disturbed that the evidence indicates such a negative purpose for most officially sponsored psi research in the Soviet Union. While I was there, I felt that I was unable to change this situation for the better. I also did not want to participate in the kinds of inhumane experiments that I have described here. This is one reason why I emigrated from the U.S.S.R. However, I believe that most human beings have an inherent capacity to distinguish good from evil. Let us hope that this capacity will lead our Soviet colleagues to find a more positive use for their energy and talents.

AUTHORS' NOTE _____

FROM MOSCOW TO YEREVAN

In September 1983, we received an invitation to visit the Soviet Union as guests of the U.S.S.R. Academy of Sciences. This gave us an opportunity to discuss our remote-viewing work with them, and also to learn firsthand what sort of research they are currently doing. Our host for this visit was Dr. Andrei Berezine, a biophysicist working at a Moscow research hospital.

With us on the trip was Elisabeth Targ (daughter of R.T.), who holds a translator's certificate in Russian and is a second-year medical student at Stanford. She was able to act as our translator and tell us what was going on at times when Russian conversations would have otherwise gone over our heads.

In Moscow we spoke with physicists, psychologists, and medical researchers. The physicists were mainly concerned with discussing the details of our precognitive experiments, while the medical people and psychologists had many good questions and interesting ideas about the whole field of psi research and its implications for their work. We had very stimulating exchanges with both groups of scientists.

Over coffee and pastries at the First Moscow Medical Institute, we met Professor Andriankyn, director of the Theoretical Department of the U.S.S.R. Academy of Sciences. Andriankyn, responsible for inviting us to the Soviet Union, sponsored our visit. His main concern at this Institute is with non-drug treatment of mental patients. One focus of this work concerns the experimental use of low-frequency electric and magnetic fields.

At the Institute, we also talked with Dr. Igor Smirnoff and two other researchers who had just completed the experiment in "rat telepathy" described in Chapter 4. As we sat in their equipment-crowded basement laboratory, along with several other medical people from the hospital, they discussed the experiment with us. They had discovered that the experiment was not successful when carried out with groups of rats, because they fought with each other under the stressful conditions.

Konstantine Goubarev is a physicist involved with the rat experiment. However, he is personally most concerned with the design of a computer program that analyzes a person's physiological data to determine from that data when a particular change in his or her state of consciousness, such as dropping into a hypnotized condition, has occurred. He demonstrated the program for us, on typical data tapes. He believes that he has accomplished his goal of showing changes in the state of human consciousness by looking at mathematical transformations of the data and observing phase changes rather than amplitude changes. This would be quite an accomplishment, because at this time it is not even clear to Western researchers that hypnosis is a definable change of state.

We were also very happy to meet again with Dr. Yuri Gulyaev at his Institute of Radio Engineering and Electronics overlooking Gorky Park. We all sat on comfortable red leather chairs in his spacious office, while over countless ceremonial glasses of Armenian cognac Dr. Gulyaev described some of his most recent work. He also gave us a copy of I. M. Kogan's new book *Applied Information Theory*. Professor Kogan argues that if psychic phenomena are to be explained at all, it will have to be through low-frequency electromagnetic principles. Gulyaev told us that the first person to put forward the idea that psi was carried by electromagnetic waves was James Clark Maxwell, in the last century, and that his idea was described in a recent U.S.S.R. Academy of Sciences journal dealing with the measurement of biomagnetic fields.

Along with his duties as deputy director of the Institute, Gulyaev is able to pursue his interests in psychotronics as well. With his colleague Dr. Eduard Godik, he has been examining the electromagnetic and visible radiation emitted by the human body. They have carried out sensitive photon-counting experiments with a spectrometer that measures the wavelength of the emitted light, and found that there may be some physical evidence for the so-called auras that certain people claim to see surrounding the human body.

Professor Gulyaev said that he has also been able, to a limited extent, to continue his work with Nina Kulagina. He described a particularly interesting experiment in which he tried to find out if she could use her psychic abilities to read letters. In these trials, he randomly chose a book from the shelves of his office and asked Kulagina to name the letters that started each paragraph on a given page. After she gave her answer, Professor Gulyaev would take the book down and open it. He told us that she could do this task with surprising accuracy. However, when she was told to leave the room before the book was opened, thereby losing her feedback, he reported that her responses fell to chance.

Toward the end of our visit we were taken to the city of Yerevan, in Soviet Armenia, where remote-viewing experiments had been carried out in the Industrial Psychology Laboratory at the state university. Yerevan, southeast of Istanbul and north of Baghdad, was warm and sunny, in contrast with the snow we left in Moscow. It was also a much more relaxed environment, with people strolling around a large illuminated fountain in the city square in the evening to listen to music.

On our first full day in Yerevan we visited the university and spoke with some members of the Armenian Academy of Sciences. Then, in a laboratory full of arcade-type video games used to study hand-eye coordination, we met with Professor Rubin Aguzumtsian, who had carried out a careful series of remote-viewing trials. The target sites for this study were chosen by an architect—a good idea in this city of remarkable structures dating from almost the time of Christ. One church, called Gehard, was carved out of the solid rock of a mountainside in about A.D. 300. Many other Greco-Roman buildings were built of a red volcanic rock.

The viewers and outbound experimenters for the remote-viewing study were volunteers from a psychology class. For each trial an outbound experimenter, accompanied by two guards (watchers—also from the class), would go to a distant location, open the envelope with the target information, and then go to the appointed site. Meanwhile, back in the laboratory, an interviewer would encourage the viewer to describe his or her impressions about the site that was being visited. Professor Aguzumtsian decided to carry out this work after reading the 1976 IEEE (Institute of Electrical and Electronic Engineers) paper from SRI, when it was translated into Russian and published in the Soviet Union. His experiments confirmed the earlier findings, and also gave him the interesting experience of having a viewer describe a chosen target site before the target team had opened the envelope or gone to the target. As in our own experiments, this precognition was an unexpected complication. We may soon carry out a long-distance series of remote-viewing trials in cooperation with this laboratory, to see what results we will get from using a ten-thousand-mile baseline for remote viewing. In this series we will, of course, work with a viewer who has never been to Yerevan.

In our travels from Moscow to Leningrad to Yerevan, we met with many researchers who expressed the hope that there could be continued open communication in this field. They all expressed the feeling that psi's importance lies in the development of human potential, rather than in its possible military applications. But everyone we talked with also made some oblique reference to what we were not being shown. For example, we knew that the Popov Society laboratory run by Professor Spirikin had been closed down several years ago. On this trip we learned that it has now been re-opened under the direction of Dr. Alexander Chernetzky. We were even told that the laboratory is now called the Fourmany Street Lab. We were not, however, told what sort of work this lab is currently engaged in.

Nevertheless we feel it is important and very desirable to arrange future cooperative meetings with the Soviet scientists to further explore the details of psychic functioning. We might even come up with a potential contribution to help solve the decades-old problem of off-site verification for nuclear testing and arms control. If successful, that would be an application of psychic functioning that we believe the whole world would like to see.

Remote-Viewing

Research 1973-1982

For several years, the compilers of this bibliography have been gathering reports of remote-viewing experiments. We have been particularly interested in studies involving the use of free-response procedures with geographical locations as targets; only these types of published studies have been included here.

We have found that more than half (fifteen out of twenty-eight) of the published formal experiments have been successful, where only one in twenty would be expected by chance. We have also located eighteen unpublished studies (not listed here), with eight reporting statistical significance; thus the success of remote viewing is not due to reporting bias, in which vast numbers of unsuccessful experiments go unreported.

George P. Hansen,
Research Fellow,
Institute for Parapsychology,
Durham, N.C.

Marilyn J. Schlitz,
Mind Science Foundation,
San Antonio, Texas.

Charles T. Tart,
Professor of Psychology,
University of California, Davis, Calif.

Published References Describing
Remote-Viewing Experiments

1. Allen, S., Green, P., Rucker, K., Goolsby, C., & Morris, R. L. A remote viewing study using a modified version of the SRI procedure. In J.D. Morris, W.G. Roll, & R.L. Morris (Eds.), *Research in Parapsychology, 1975.* Metuchen, N.J.: Scarecrow, 1976.

2. Bisaha, J. P., & Dunne, B. J. Precognitive remote viewing in the Chicago area: A replication of the Stanford experiment. In J.D. Morris, W.G. Roll, & R.L. Morris (Eds.), *Research in Parapsychology, 1976.* Metuchen, N.J.: Scarecrow, 1977.

3. Bisaha, J. P., & Dunne, B. J. Multiple subject and long distance precognitive remote viewing of geographic locations. *Proceedings of the IEEE 1977 International Conference on Cybernetics and Society,* 1977, *7,* 512–516.

4. Bisaha, J. P., & Dunne, B. J. Multiple subject and long-distance precognitive remote viewing of geographical locations. In C. T. Tart, H. E. Puthoff, & R. Targ (Eds.), *Mind at Large.* New York: Praeger, 1979.

5. Chotas, Harrell G. Remote viewing in the Durham area. *Journal of Parapsychology,* 1978, *42,* 61–62. (Abstract)

6. Dunne, B. J., & Bisaha, J. P. Multiple channels in precognitive remote viewing. In W. G. Roll (Ed.), *Research in Parapsychology, 1977.* Metuchen, N. J.: Scarecrow, 1978.

7. Dunne, B. J., & Bisaha, J. P. Long distance precognitive remote viewing. In W. G. Roll (Ed.), *Research in Parapsychology, 1978.* Metuchen, N.J.: Scarecrow, 1979.

8. Dunne, B. J. & Bisaha, J. P. Precognitive remote viewing in the Chicago area: A replication of the Stanford experiment. *Journal of Parapsychology,* 1979, *43,* 17–30.

9. Dunne, B., & Bisaha, J. P. Precognitive remote perception: A critical overview of the experimental program. In W. G. Roll (Ed.), *Research in Parapsychology, 1979.* Metuchen, N.J.: Scarecrow, 1980.

10. Hastings, A. C., & Hurt, D. B. A confirmatory remote viewing experiment in a group setting. *Proceedings of the IEEE,* 1976, *64,* 1544–1545.

11. Jahn, R. G. The persistent paradox of psychic phenomena: An engineering perspective. *Proceedings of the IEEE,* 1982, *70,* 136–170.

12. Karnes, E. W., Ballou, J., Susman, E. P., & Swaroff, P. Remote viewing: Failures to replicate with control comparisons. *Psychological Reports*, 1979, *45*, 963–973.

13. Karnes, E. W., Susman, E. P., Klusman, P., & Turcotte, L. Failures to replicate remote-viewing using psychic subjects. *Zetetic Scholar*, July 1980, 6, 66–76.

14. Marks, D., & Kammann, R. *The Psychology of the Psychic*. Buffalo, N. Y.:Prometheus, 1980.

15. Palmer, J. Whitson, T., & Bogart, D. N. Ganzfeld and remote viewing: A systematic comparison. In W. G. Roll (Ed.), *Research in Parapsychology, 1979*. Metuchen, N.J.: Scarecrow, 1980.

16. Puthoff, H. E. & Targ, R. Remote viewing of natural targets. In J. D. Morris, W. G Roll, & R. L. Morris (Eds.), *Research in Parapsychology, 1974*. Metuchen, N.J.: Scarecrow, 1975.

17. Puthoff, H. E., & Targ, R. A perceptual channel for information transfer over kilometer distances: Historical perspective and recent research. *Proceedings of the IEEE*, 1976, *64*, 329–354.

18. Puthoff, H. E., & Targ, R. Precognitive remote viewing. In J. D. Morris, W. G. Roll, & R. L. Morris (Eds.), *Research in Parapsychology, 1975*. Metuchen, N.J.: Scarecrow, 1976.

19. Puthoff, H. E., & Targ, R. Remote viewing: A new research frontier. In Martin Ebon (Ed.), *The Signet Handbook of Parapsychology*. New York: New American Library (Signet), 1978.

20. Puthoff, H. E., & Targ, R. A perceptual channel for information transfer over kilometer distances: Historical perspective and recent research. In C. T. Tart, H. E. Puthoff, & R. Targ (Eds.), *Mind at Large*. New York: Praeger, 1979.

21. Puthoff, H. E., & Targ, R. Direct perception of remote geographical locations. In A. Puharich (Ed.), *The Iceland Papers: Select papers on experimental and theoretical research on the physics of consciousness*. Amherst, Wis.: Essential Research Associates, 1979.

22. Puthoff, H. E., Targ, R., & May, E. C. Experimental psi research: Implications for physics. In R. G. Jahn (Ed.), *The Role of Consciousness in the Physical World*. Boulder, Colo.: Westview, 1981.

23. Rauscher, E. A., Weismann, G., Sarfatti, J., Sirag, S. -P. Remote perception of natural scenes, shielded against ordinary perception. In J. D. Morris, W.

G. Roll, & R. L. Morris (Eds.), *Research in Parapsychology, 1975*. Metuchen, N.J.: Scarecrow, 1976.

24. Schlitz, M., & Deacon, S. Remote viewing: A conceptual replication of Targ and Puthoff. In W. G. Roll (Ed.), *Research in Parapsychology, 1979*. Metuchen, N.J.: Scarecrow, 1980.

25. Schlitz, M., & Gruber, E. Transcontinental remote viewing. *Journal of Parapsychology*, 1980, *44*, 305–317.

26. Schlitz, M., & Gruber, E. Transcontinental remote viewing. In W. G. Roll & J. Beloff (Eds.), *Research in Parapsychology, 1980*. Metuchen, N.J.: Scarecrow, 1981.

27. Schlitz, M., & Gruber, E. Transcontinental remote viewing: A rejudging. *Journal of Parapsychology*, 1981, *45*, 233–237.

28. Schlitz, M., & Gruber, E. Transcontinental remote viewing: A rejudging. In W. G. Roll, R. L. Morris, and R. A. White, *Research in Parapsychology, 1981*. Metuchen, N.J.: Scarecrow, 1982.

29. Schlitz, M. J., Sarling, J. M. H., & Weiner, D. H. Long distance remote viewing: A conceptual replication. In W. G. Roll, R. L. Morris, and R. A. White (Eds.), *Research in Parapsychology, 1981*. Metuchen, N.J.: Scarecrow, 1982.

30. Smukler, H. A remote viewing experiment California to Rhode Island. *Meta-Science Quarterly*, *1* (1), 25–32.

31. Solfvin, G., Roll, W. G., & Krieger, J. Meditation and ESP: Remote viewing. In W. G. Roll (Ed.), *Research in Parapsychology, 1977*. Metuchen, N.J.: Scarecrow, 1978.

32. Targ, R., & Morris, R. L. Note on a reanalysis of UCSB remote-viewing experiments. *Journal of Parapsychology*, 1982, *46*, 47–50.

33. Targ, R., & Puthoff, H. E. Replication study on the remote viewing of natural targets. In J. D. Morris, W. G. Roll, & R. L. Morris (Eds.), *Research in Parapsychology, 1975*. Metuchen: N.J.: Scarecrow, 1976.

34. Targ, R., & Puthoff, H. E. Information transmission under conditions of sensory shielding. *Nature*, 1974, *251*, 602–607.

35. Targ, R., & Puthoff, H. E. *Mind Reach: Scientists look at psychic ability.* New York: Delacorte, 1977.

36. Targ, R., & Puthoff, H. E. Remote viewing of natural targets. In L. Oteri (Ed.), *Quantum Physics and Parapsychology*. New York: Parapsychology Foundation, 1975.

37. Targ, R., Puthoff, H. E., & May, E. C. Direct perception of remote geographical locations. In C. T. Tart, H. E. Puthoff, & R. Targ (Eds.), *Mind at Large*. New York: Praeger, 1979.

38. Targ, R., Puthoff, H. E., & May, E. C. State of the art in remote viewing studies at SRI. *Proceedings of the IEEE 1977 International Conference on Cybernetics and Society*, 1977, 7, 519–529.

39. Tart, C. T. *Psi: Scientific Studies of the Psychic Realm*. New York: Dutton, 1977.

40. Tart, C. T., Puthoff, H. E., & Targ, R. (Eds.). *Mind at Large*. New York: Praeger, 1979.

41. Whitson, T. W., Bogart, D. N., Palmer, J., & Tart, C. T. Preliminary experiments in group "remote viewing." *Proceedings of the IEEE*, 1976, 64, 1550–1551.

NOTES

Chapter 1

1. Committee on Science and Technology, U.S. House of Representatives, *Survey of Science and Technology Issues Present and Future*, June 1981.

2. *Science*, July 30, 1982.

Chapter 2

1. Upton Sinclair, *Mental Radio* (New York: Collier, 1971).

2. René Warcollier, *Mind to Mind* (New York: Collier, 1963).

3. Russell Targ and Harold Puthoff, *Mind-Reach* (New York: Delacorte, 1977).

4. E. Karnes and E. Sussman, "Remote Viewing: A Response Bias Interpretation," *Psycholog. Rep.* 44, pp. 471–479 (1979).

5. J.G. Pratt, J.B. Rhine, C.E. Stuart, and B.M. Smith, *Extrasensory Perception After Sixty Years* (New York: Holt, 1940).

6. Charles Tart, "Card Guessing Tests: Learning Paradigm or Extinction Paradigm?" *J. ASPR*, Vol. 60 (Jan. 1960).

7. H.E. Puthoff, R. Targ, E.C. May, and B. Humphrey, "SRI Protocols for Local Remote Viewing," Revised, Jan. 1981; Harold Puthoff & Russell Targ, "A Perceptual Channel for Information Transfer over Kilometer Distances: Historical Perspective and Recent Experiments," *Proc. IEEE*, Vol. 64, No. 3 (March 1976).

8. Charles Honorton, "Psi and Internal Attention States," in *Handbook of Parapsychology*, ed. B. Wolman (New York: Van Nostrand, 1977).

9. G. Feinberg, "Precognition—A Memory of Things Future?" *Proc. on Quantum Physics and Parapsychology* (Geneva, Switzerland), Parapsychology Foundation, New York, 1975.

10. J. Bisaha & B.J. Dunne, "Precognitive Remote Viewing in the Chicago Area: A Replication of the Stanford Experiment," *Research in Parapsychology 1976*, pp. 84–86 (Metuchen, N.J.: Scarecrow, 1977); "Multiple Subject Precognitive Remote Viewing," *Research in Parapsy-*

chology 1977 (Metuchen, N.J.: Scarecrow, 1978).

11. B.J. Dunne & J. Bisaha, "Long Distance Precognitive Remote Viewing," in *Mind at Large*, ed. Charles Tart (New York: Praeger, 1979).

12. Marilyn Schlitz and Elmar Gruber, "Transcontinental Remote Viewing," *J. Parapsychology*, No. 4, pp. 305–317 (1980).

13. Jule Eisenbud, *Paranormal Foreknowledge* (New York: Human Sciences Press, 1982).

14. I.M. Kogan, "Is Telepathy Possible?" *Radio Eng*, Vol. 21, p. 75 (Jan. 1976); "Telepathy, Hypotheses and Observations," *Radio Eng.*, Vol. 23, p. 122 (March 1968); "The Information Theory Aspect of Telepathy," RAND Publ., pp. 41–45, Santa Monica, Calif., (July 1969).

15. H.E. Puthoff, R. Targ, and E.C. May, "Experimental Psi Research, Implications for Physics," in *The Role of Consciousness in the Physical World*, ed. R. Jahn, AAAS Selected Publication 57 (Boulder, Colo.: Westview, 1981) Also in *Mind at Large*.

16. Schlitz and Gruber, "Transcontinental Remote Viewing," op. cit.

17. L.L. Vasiliev, *Experiments in Mental Suggestion* (Hampshire, England: Institute for the Study of Mental Images, 1963).

18. G. Messadie, "Du Nautilus," *Science et Vie*, No. 509 (Feb. 1960). Also, Louis Pauwels and Jacques Bergier, *The Morning of the Magicians* (New York: Stein and Day, 1964).

19. Puthoff, Targ, and May, Experimental Psi Research: "Implications for Physics." op. cit.

20. M.A. Persinger, "The Paranormal, P. II: Mechanisms and Models," M.S.S. Information Corp., New York (1974); for Kogan, see note 14 above.

Chapter 3

1. W.E. Cox, "Precognition: An Analysis II," *J. ASPR*, Vol. 50, pp. 99–109 (1956).

2. S. Krippner, M. Ullman, and C. Honorton, "A Precognitive Dream Study, with a Single Subject," *J. ASPR*, Vol. 65, pp. 192–203 (1971); and "A Second Precognitive Dream Study with Malcolm Bessent," *J. ASPR*, Vol. 66, pp. 269–279 (1972).

3. J.W. Dunne, *An Experiment with Time* (London: Faber and Faber, 1969).

4. Harold Puthoff and Russell Targ, "A Perceptual Channel for Information Transfer over Kilometer Distances: Historical Perspective and Recent Experiments," *Proc. IEEE*, Vol. 64, No. 3 (March 1976).

5. Ibid.

6. M. Ullman and S. Krippner, *Dream Telepathy* (Baltimore: Penguin, 1974).

7. H.E. Puthoff and R. Targ, "Remote Viewing of Geographical Locations," in *Research in Parapsychology 1975* (Metuchen, N.J.: Scarecrow, 1976).

8. J. Bisaha and B.J. Dunne, "Precognitive Remote Viewing in the Chicago Area: A Replication of

the Stanford Experiment," *Research in Parapsychology 1976* (Metuchen, N.J.: Scarecrow: 1977), pp. 84–86.

9. J. Bisaha and B.J. Dunne, "Multiple Subject Procognitive Remote Viewing," *Research in Parapsychology 1977* (Metuchen, N. J.: Scarecrow, 1978).

10. B.J. Dunne and J. Bisaha, "Long Distance Precognitive Remote Viewing," in *Mind at Large*, ed. C. Tart (New York: Praeger, 1979).

11. O. Costa de Beauregard, "Quantum Paradoxes and Aristotle's Twofold Information Concept," in *Mind at Large;* O. Costa de Beauregard, "CPT Invariance and Interpretation of Quantum Mechanics,: *Foundation of Physics*, Vol. 10, pp. 513–530 (Aug. 1980).

12. I. Prigogine, *From Being to Becoming*, W.H. Freeman, San Francisco (1980).

13. A. Whitehead and B. Russell, *Principia Mathematica* (Cambridge: Cambridge University Press, 1910).

14. Bob Brier, "Precognition and the Paradoxes of Causality," Conference of Philosophical Issues in Psychical Research, University of Denver, Oct. 27–29, 1978.

15. J. Barker, "Premonitions of the Aberfan Disaster," *J. SPR*, Vol. 44, pp. 169–181 (1967).

16. Stephen Braude, *ESP and Psychokinesis* (Philadelphia: Temple University Press, 1979).

17. H. Schmidt, "A PK Test with Electronic Equipment," *J. Parapsychology*, Vol. 34, pp. 175–181(1970); H. Schmidt and L. Pantos, "Psi Tests with Internally Different Machines," *J. Parapsychology*, Vol. 36, pp. 222–232 (1972).

Chapter 4

1. Harold Puthoff and Russell Targ, "A Perceptual Channel for Information Transfer over Kilometer Distances: Historical Perspective and Recent Experiments," *Proc. IEEE*, Vol. 64, No. 3 (March 1976).

2. Mary Daly, *Gynecology* (London: Beacon, 1978), pp. 178–223.

3. Brian Inglis, *Natural and Supernatural* (London: Hodder and Stoughton, 1977), p. 302.

4. Ibid., pp. 141–152.

5. Eric Dingwall, *Abnormal Hypnotic Phenomena* (London: J. & A. Churchill, 1968), Vol. III, pp. 10–12.

6. Ibid., pp. 15–16.

7. Ibid., p. 99.

8. L.L. Vasiliev, "Experiments in Mental Suggestion," (Hampshire, England: Institute for the Study of Mental Images, 1963).

9. Dean Kraft, *Portrait of a Psychic Healer* (New York: Putnam, 1981), pp. 117–120.

Chapter 5

1. R. Targ, H.E. Puthoff, B.S. Humphrey, and C.T. Tart, "Investigations of Target Acquisition," in *Research in Parapsychology 1979* (Metuchen, N.J.: Scarecrow, 1980); H.E. Puthoff, R. Targ, and C.T. Tart, "Resolution in Remote Viewing Studies," in ibid.

2. "Resolution in Remote Viewing Studies," ibid.

3. R. Targ, P. Cole, and H. Puthoff, "Techniques to Enhance Man/Machine Communication," SRI Final Report, June, 1974. Contract NAS7-100.

Chapter 6

1. F. Conway and J. Seigelman, *Snapping* (New York: Lippincott, 1978).

2. Keith Harary, "Practical Approaches to Coping with Unusual Experiences," *Research in Parapsychology 1979* (Metuchen, N.J. and London: Scarecrow, 1980); Robert Morris, "The Detection and Prevention of Psychic Exploitation of Retired Persons," *Research in Parapsychology 1979* (Metuchen, N.J. and London: Scarecrow, 1980).

3. Jeannie Mills, *Six Years with God* (New York: A & W Publishers, 1979).

4. Bernard Bauer, "Ananda Marga, A Deadly Mix of Yoga, Violence," San Jose Mercury News, (August 15, 1982); John Adams, "Violent Past of Ananda Marga Arm," Berkeley Gazette, (June 28, 1981).

5. "Reverend Moon Takes Fifth," San Francisco Chronicle, (May 27, 1982).

6. Joseph B. Treaster, "Controversial Leader Sun Myung Moon," New York Times, (May 19, 1982).

7. B. and B. Underwood, *Hostage to Heaven* (New York: Clarkson Potter, 1979).

8. C. Edwards, *Crazy for God* (Englewood Cliffs, N.J.: Prentice-Hall, 1979).

Chapter 7

1. Robert Morris, "Review of J. Anson, *The Amityville Horror*, (Englewood Cliffs, N.J.: Prentice-Hall, 1979), *Skeptical Enquirer*, Vol. 2, No. 2, pp. 95–101 (1978).

Chapter 8

1. Peter Tomkins and Christopher Bird, *The Secret Life of Plants* (New York: Harper & Row, 1973).

2. Keith Harary, "A Critical Approach to Psi Research with Plants," Duke University (unpublished paper).

3. Allen Alter, "The Pyramid and Food Dehydration," *New Horizons*, Vol. 1 (Summer 1973); Dale Simmons, "Experiments on the Alleged Sharpening of Razor Blades and the Preservation of Flowers by Pyramids," ibid.

4. R.L. Morris, Keith Harary, et al., "Studies of Communication During Out of Body Experiences," *J. ASPR*, Vol. 72, No. 1 (1978); described in D. Scott Rogo, *Mind Beyond the Body* (New York: Penguin Books, 1978).

5. Françoise Gaquelin, *The Cosmic Clocks* (New York: Avon, 1969); Michel Gaquelin, "Possible Planetary Effects at the Time of Birth of 'successful' Professionals: An Experimental Control," *Journal of Inter-disciplinary Cycle Research*, pp. 381–389, 1972; Michel Gaquelin, *Cosmic Influences on Human Behavior* (Briarcliff Manor: Stein and Day, 1973).

6. Denis Rawlins, "Starbaby," *Fate*, Vol. 34 (October 1981), pp. 67–98.

Chapter 9

1. Mortimer Feinberg and Aaron Levinstein, "How Do You Know When to Rely on Your Intuition?" *Wall Street Journal*, Monday, June 21, 1982.

Chapter 10

1. Keith Harary, "Psi As Nature," *European Journal of Parapsychology*, Vol. 4, No. 3, November 1982.

2. René Warcollier, *Mind to Mind*, (New York: Collier, 1963).

3. Jean M. Auel, *The Valley of Horses* (New York: Crown, 1982).

Chapter 11

1. Batcheldor, K.J., "Macro-PK in Group Sittings: Theoretical and Practical Aspects," unpublished monograph, 1968 (revised 1982); "Recommendations for PK Table Tipping and Levitation," in *The Problem of Psychokinetic Phenomena*, C. Brooks-Smith, Part VII, 1979, (privately circulated); "PK in Sitter Groups," *Psychoenergetic Systems*, Vol. 3, pp. 77–93 (1979).

2. M. Ullman and S. Krippner, *Dream Telepathy*, (New York: Macmillan, 1973).

3. Joan Halifax, *Shamanic Voices* (New York: Dutton, 1979).

4. Joan Halifax, "Hex Death," in *Parapsychology and Anthropology (1972)* ed. Allan Angoff (New York:

Parapsychology Foundation, 1974). The papers she refers to are: M. Harner, "The Sound of Rushing Water," in *Hallucinogens and Shamanism*, ed. M. Harner (London: Oxford University Press, 1973); A. Metraux, *Voodoo in Haiti* (New York: Schocken, 1959), p. 272; G.L. Engel, "A Life Setting Conducive to Illness," *Bulletin of the Menninger Clinic*, No. 32, p. 355 (1968).

5. W.B. Cannon, "Voodoo Death," in *A Reader in Comparative Religion: An Anthropological Approach*, W. Lessa (New York: Harper and Row, 1958).

6. Maya Deren, *Divine Horsemen: The Voodoo Gods of Haiti* (New York: Chelsea House Publishers, 1970).

7. Dion Fortune, *Psychic Self-Defense* (Wellingborough, Northamptonshire: Aquarian, 1979).

8. Montague Ullman, "Life History and Psi Events: Significance for Counseling," *Research in Parapsychology 1979* (Metuchen, N.J. and London: Scarecrow, 1980).

Chapter 12

1. Keith Harary, "Psi as Nature," *European Journal of Parapsychology*, Vol. 4, No. 3, November 1982.

2. A.M. Turing, "Computing Machinery and Intelligence," in *The Mind's I*, Douglas Hofstadter and Daniel Dennett (New York: Basic Books, 1981).

3. Jacques Vallee, *The Network Revolution* (Berkeley, Calif.: And/Or Books, 1982).

Epilogue

1. Leonid Vasiliev, *Experiments in Distant Influence* (New York: E.P. Dutton, 1976).

2. Ibid., pp. 220–221.

3. D.D. Fedotov, ed., *Problemy obnaruzheniya slabykh reaktsiy nervnoy sistemy* [Problems of the Detection of Weak Reactions of the Nervous System], *Proceedings of the Research Institute of Psychiatry*, Vol. 55 (Moscow, 1968) [in Russian].

4. D.G. Mirza, V.V. Petrusinsky, and V.A. Doroshenko, "Electrophysiological Correlates of Rapport in Hypnosis," ibid., pp. 88–92 [in Russian; English translation in *Parapsychology in the U.S.S.R.*, ed. L. Vilenskaya, Part IV (San Francisco: Washington Research Center, 1981), pp. 2–5].

5. V.P. Leutin, "The Study of Conditioned-Reflex Changes in the EEG of the Human Being to a Nonspecific Stimulus," ibid., pp. 93–100 [English translation pp. 6–11].

6. Sheila Ostrander and Lynn Schroeder, *Psychic Discoveries Behind the Iron Curtain* (Englewood Cliffs, N.J.: Prentice-Hall, 1970).

7. L. Vilenskaya, "Psycho-Physical Effects by N. Kulagina: Remote Influence on Surrounding Objects," in *Parapsychology in the U.S.S.R.*, pp. 12–25; H.H.J. Keil, M. Ullman, J.G. Pratt, and B. Herbert, "Directly Observable Voluntary PK Effects: A Survey and Tentative Interpretation of Available Findings from Nina Kulagina and Other Known Related Cases of Recent Date," *Proceedings of the Society for Psychical Research*, Vol. 56 (Jan. 1976), pp. 197–235; J.G. Pratt, "Soviet Research in Parapsychology," in *Handbook of Parapsychology*, ed. B.B. Wolman (New York: Van Nostrand Reinhold, 1977).

8. I. Molokanov, "The Riddle of Human Potential (Another Report on Nina Kulagina)," *Psi Research*, Vol. 1, No. 3 (Sept. 1982), p. 9.

9. "Radiations and Interactions of Living Systems," *Psi Research*, Vol. 1, No. 2 (June 1982), pp. 30–31.

10. I. Molokanov, "The Riddle of Human Potential," *Psi Research*, Vol. 1, No. 3 (Sept. 1982), p. 6; Benson Herbert, "Spring in Leningrad: Kulagina Revisited," *Parapsychology Review*, Vol. 4, No. 4 (1973), pp. 5–10; Barbara Ivanova, "Kuleshova and Kulagina," *International Journal of Paraphysics*, Vol. 11, Nos. 1/2 (1977), pp. 6–9.

11. I. Molokanov, "The Riddle of Human Potential," *Psi Research*, Vol. 1, No. 3 (Sept. 1982), p. 7.

12. Sergei Speransky, "Extraordinary Transmission of Information About Starvation," in *Parapsychology in the U.S.S.R.*, pp. 4–11.

13. "Bioelectronics in Leningrad and Alma-Ata," *Psi Research*, Vol. 1, No. 4 (Dec. 1982), p. 29.

14. V.P. Kaznacheyev, S.P. Shurin, and L.P. Mikhailova, Discovery No. 122, "Distant Intercellular Interactions in a System of Two Tissue Cultures," *Official Bulletin of the Committee on Inventions and Discoveries of the Council of Ministers of the U.S.S.R.*, No. 19 (1973), p. 3.

15. V.P. Kaznacheyev, "Electromagnetic Information in Intercellular Interactions," *Psi Research*, Vol. 1, No. 1 (March 1982), p. 47.

16. V.P. Kaznacheyev, personal communication (Nov. 1981).

17. N.F. Sanayev and M.A. Zorina, in *Aktualnye voprosy meditsinskoy magnitobiologii* [Actual Questions of Medical Magnetobiology] (Saransk, 1977), p. 80 [in Russian].

18. V.P. Kaznacheyev, S.P. Shurin, L.P. Mikhailova, and N.V. Ignatovich, "Distant Intercellular Interactions in a System of Two Cultures Connected by Optical Contact," in *Ultraweak Luminescence in Biology* (Moscow, 1972), pp. 224–227 [in Russian]; V.P. Kaznacheyev, L.P. Mikhailova, D.G. Kadayeva, and M.P. Dranova, "Conditions Necessary for Appearance of Distant Intercellular Interactions After UV-radiation," *Bulleten Experimentalnoy Biologii i Meditsiny.*, No. 5 (1979), pp. 468–471 [in Russian]; V.P. Kaznacheyev, and L.P. Mikhailova, *Sverkhslabye izlucheniya v mezhkletochnykh vzaimodeystviyakh* [Ultraweak Radiations in Intercellular Interactions] (Novosibirsk, 1981) [in Russian].

19. "NBC Magazine with David Brinkley," *Transcript of Broadcast of March 13, 1981* (New York: National Broadcasting Corporation, 1981), p. 13.

20. A.S. Romen and V.M. Inyushin, "Some Data on Voluntary Influence on Electro-bioluminescence," in *Voprosy bioenergetiki* [Questions of Bioenergetics] (Alma-Ata: Kazakh State University, 1969), pp. 80–82 [in Russian; English translation in *Bioenergetics Questions* (Beverly Hills, Calif.: Southern California Society for Psychical Research, 1972)].

21. Report of Academician Yuri Kobzarev to Presidium of Central Board of A.C. Popov Scientific and Technological Society for Radioelectronics and Communication (Moscow, April 14, 1978), author's archives.

22. "Bioelectronics in Leningrad and Alma-Ata," *Psi Research*, Vol. 1, No. 4 (Dec. 1982), p. 27.

23. John D. LaMothe, *Controlled Offensive Behavior—U.S.S.R.*, U.S. Defense Intelligence Agency (Unclassified), prepared by the U.S. Army, Office of the Surgeon General, Medical Intelligence Office (Washington, D.C., July 1972) [#CT-CS-01-169-72]; Louis F. Maire, and J.D. LaMothe, *Soviet and Czechoslovakian Parapsychology Research*, U.S. Defense Intelligence Agency (Unclassified), prepared by the U.S. Army, Medical Intelligence and Information Agency, Office of the Surgeon General (Washington, D.C., Sept. 1975) [#DST-181OS-387-75]; Defense Intelligence Agency (author's name still classified), *Paraphysics R & D—Warsaw Pact (U)* (Washington, D.C.: Defense Intelligence Agency, March 30, 1978) [#DST-181OS-202-78]; John B. Alexander, "The New Mental Battlefield: 'Beam Me Up, Spock,' " *Military Review* (The Professional

Journal of the US Army; published by U.S. Army Command and General Staff College, Fort Leavenworth, KS 66027), Vol. IX, No. 12 (December 1980), pp. 48–54; Roger A. Beaumont, "C^{nth}?: On the Strategic Potential of ESP," *Signal* (Journal of the Armed Forces Communications and Electronics Association), Vol. 36, No. 5 (Jan. 1982), pp. 39–45; "War of the Psychics," *Boston Globe*, Sept. 14, 1982.

24. "Never Wish Evil on Anybody" (interview with Vladimir Safonov), *Stroitelnaya gazeta* (Moscow), May 16, 1980 [in Russian]; Barbara Ivanova, "Integral Harmonizing, Healing and Other Kinds of Influence by Means of Psychoregulation, Autoregulation, and Bioenergy Stimulation," paper presented [in absentia] at the First Israeli Seminar on Parapsychology (Tel Aviv), March 12, 1981.

INDEX

ABOUT THE AUTHORS

Russell Targ has worked as professional physicist for more than twenty-five years. He carried out original research in lasers, optics and microwave physics, and for the past decade has been carrying out pioneering psychical research at SRI International. He is the co-author of two other books in this field: *Mind-Reach* and *Mind At Large,* as well as numerous technical papers. Mr. Targ is vice president of the International Association for Psychotronic Research. He makes his home in northern California.

Keith Harary is internationally known for his contributions to a Duke University study of out-of-body experiences, conducted in the early 1970s. He is clinical counselor and experimental psychologist with fourteen years' research experience at Duke, Maimonides Medical Center, the American Society for Psychical Research and most recently, as a consultant to the remote-viewing program at SRI International. He has published more than twenty papers on psi research. In 1982 he and Russell Targ formed Delphi Associates to pursue further research and applications of psi in the private sector. Mr. Harary also resides in northern California.